Stairway to Heaven

Stairway to Heaven

True Stories of Encounters with God

Mary Batchelor

Hodder & Stoughton
LONDON SYDNEY AUCKLAND

British Library Cataloguing in Publication Data
A record for this book is available from the British Library

ISBN 0 340 69475 0

Typeset by Avon Dataset Ltd, Bidford-on-Avon, Warks

Printed and bound in Great Britain by
The Guernsey Press Co. Ltd, Channel Isles

Hodder & Stoughton Ltd
A Division of Hodder Headline PLC
338 Euston Road
London NW1 3BH

To my family
with heartfelt gratitude for their never-failing
help and support

Contents

Introduction

'Is there anyone out there?' Well, *is* there? Some people claim to have encountered alien spacecraft and seen some version of little green men. Others claim to have made contact with the dead or to find spiritual strength from crystals or sacred stones. How should sensible people like us respond? Insist always on the evidence of our five senses and discard anything that goes beyond them as fantasy and nonsense? A few years ago that might have been what most thoroughly modern men and women did. But today we have grown a bit wiser. We recognise in ourselves a hankering after something more than the things that satisfy our senses. We are searching for a spiritual dimension to life and wonder if that very desire may indicate that a spiritual world beyond our own actually exists. If so, we need to discount what's phoney and discover what is real and important for us to know and explore.

Many millennia ago, a young man set out from home to make his way in the world. He had cheated his old father and his twin brother, and his doting mother had sent him on his way before it all came to blows. Jacob was a home-loving man, not suited to the hard, solitary journey that lay ahead in order to reach the home of his mother's family. When the sun sank on the first night Jacob, feeling very much alone, lay down on the bare ground, finding a stone for a pillow. At last he fell asleep and dreamed. In his dream he saw a wide stairway, one end on the earth and the other stretching up to the heavens. Angels were going up and down ceaselessly, from their world to ours and back. Then God came and stood beside Jacob, promising to be with him wherever he went and eventually to bring him safely home.

When Jacob woke up he called the place Bethel, meaning the

1

House of God; but he could equally well have given that name to any other place on earth. His dream revealed that God's world and our world are not separated. God has penetrated and still does penetrate our world and his messengers go constantly between the two.

This book recounts the stories of many different men and women who have experienced that meeting of the two worlds. They come from different countries and different periods in history and their experiences are widely different. But all have experienced that other world of the Spirit and have had their lives changed by the encounter.

By way of apology

Before I began this book, I planned to group the stories neatly within different categories. It all seemed quite straightforward. I would put together in one section those who had seen a vision or had a dream, keeping them separate from those who had experienced God through nature or music. But once I began in earnest I found that my system kept breaking down. And in the process I discovered two important things. First, God cannot be tied down to tidy compartments or schemes of our making. He kept breaking out of my pre-planned pattern and acting in ways that were unexpected. Over-tidy schemes and self-contained compartments had to go.

I also discovered that when God impinges on a person's life, he does not restrict himself to a single way of doing so. He often bombards a man or woman with glimpses of himself and the spiritual world from various angles – and all within a short time. And, again unexpectedly, it often seems to be God, not men and women, who takes the initiative in the search for spiritual reality.

I decided that I must let God *be* God – never mind order and neat human patterns. I have in fact kept to my original plan of grouping the stories, but, as you will soon discover, they refuse to obey any limitations I may have set and sprawl across the boundaries with typical human contrariness. I'm sorry – but that's how it happened. God is too big to be contained within my parameters and human nature is too varied and creative to respond according to rules.

1

Visions

William Blake – a visionary par excellence – would have agreed
with St Teresa of Avila, whose writings he loved, when she said
about visions: 'There is nothing we can do about them, we cannot
see more or less of them at will, and we can neither call them up
nor banish them by our own efforts.' If that is the case, it poses a
problem for those of us who don't see them. We can't summon
them up nor can we really imagine what the experience is like. Is
the dividing line between our world and the spiritual world less
solid for some people than others? Is that why they can see sights
hidden from the eyes of the rest of us? Are most of us too
spiritually blind to see the other world that lies close to our own
world, whether we have eyes to see it or not?

A story is told in the Old Testament of a prophet whose servant
was terrified one morning when he woke to discover that the
army from a neighbouring tribe was surrounding the town in
which they lived. They were intent, he knew, on taking his
master prisoner. Terrified, he ran to tell his master. For answer,
the prophet prayed: 'Lord, open the young man's eyes.'
Immediately the servant saw, ringing them around in far greater
strength than the enemy soldiers, powerful, angelic, supernatural
forces. The warriors of God had been protecting his prophet all
the while, but the servant was only able to see them when he was
granted temporary, spiritual sight. Whatever the special powers
that visionaries possess, they may be able to bring us news of
another world and of the spiritual forces that impinge upon our
own.

4

William Blake

'I have very little of Mr Blake's company,' his wife once said, 'he is always in Paradise.' It certainly seems as if William Blake moved constantly and easily between the two worlds he inhabited – the everyday world of London town and the unseen world of the spirit.

Blake was a Londoner, through and through; he once described London as a 'human awful wonder of God'. He was born in 1757 and brought up in Broad Street, which was then a new thoroughfare occupied by tradespeople. His own father was a hosier and there were carpenters, engravers and a harpsichord-maker in adjoining premises. Both parents were pious people – Dissenters – and therefore deeply attached to the Bible. But that does not mean they sympathised with young Will's visions. He was only about ten years old when at Peckham Rye he saw a tree crowded with angels, their bright wings shining like stars on every bough. When he told his parents he only escaped a beating from his father through his mother's intervention. But his practical, down-to-earth parents could not banish the visionary world that seemed so real to him. 'A Spirit and a Vision are not,' he once said, 'as the modern philosophy supposes, a cloudy vapour or a nothing: they are organised and minutely articulated beyond all that the mortal and perishing nature can produce.'

His father was aware enough of the boy's 'nervous fear' of beating to decide not to send him to school. Blake was truly thankful and later wrote:

> Thank God I never was sent to school
> To be flog'd into following the style of a fool.

When he was ten or eleven, Blake was sent to a school in the Strand for promising young artists. For the next five years he learned draughtsmanship, copying and study of the art classics. His father was indulgent enough to give him money for prints and bought him classical pictures. Blake's own favourites were Michaelangelo and Dürer – neither of them fashionable at that time. He did not go on to the Royal Academy School – recently set up – perhaps because the premium was too high for his father to afford. Instead his father apprenticed him to an engraver, Basire, for seven years, where he worked twelve hours a day for six days a week. So it was through the medium of engraving that Blake learned to express his creative gifts. Engraving is an exacting and exhausting craft involving water, grinding stone, pumice, charcoal, chalk, candle flame, oilstone, aqua fortis (or nitric acid), varnish and ink. Hogarth said that the greatest virtue an engraver needs is patience and the young Blake learned discipline and precision skills alongside his creative abilities.

When he was still a young lad his master sent him to Westminster Abbey to make drawings of some of the tombs, to be used for book illustrations. There was no crowd of tourists in those days and Will was usually left to work alone in the dim, vast abbey. Sometimes, though, the heavy silence would be broken by sudden shrieks and echoing shouts as boys from Westminster School rushed in. They used the abbey as a playground. They played skittles in the aisles and climbed and romped among the ancient tombs. They loved to tease Blake and would clamber up to be level with him on the scaffold where he perched in order to get a better view of the effigies he was sketching on the tombs below.

One day, the silent, echoing abbey came alive for Blake with its own ancient occupants. He saw a procession of robed figures and heard their chanting as they walked slowly through the church. When Blake referred to this early abbey assignment he said, 'Inspiration and vision was then and now is and I hope will always remain my Element, my Eternal dwelling place.'

When his apprenticeship was finished, Blake set up shop himself in Broad Street, along with his wife Catherine. Opening hours were 6 a.m. to 9 p.m. and during that time he would work at orders for book illustrations, reserving night-time for his own work. He produced books of his poems illustrated with his own engravings, each book slightly different so that every copy was unique.

Will adored his younger brother, Robert, himself a promising artist. When Robert was nineteen he died; Blake had nursed him tirelessly night and day for the last two weeks of his life and continued to be aware of his presence and influence as long as he lived. He kept and used Robert's sketchbook and believed his brother to be the inspiration for his work. When he evolved a new engraving technique, he said simply that Robert had told him how to do it.

Blake was by no means an orthodox Christian. He has been described as 'a heretic among the orthodox; here among infidels he was a saint and staunchly defended Christianity' (the 'infidels' referred to such contemporary philosophers as Thomas Paine). He evolved his own philosophy but his abiding belief was that 'everything that lives is holy'. He cared about people, children and animals and, in an age that tolerated it, he hated cruelty of every kind. When he saw a husband beating up his wife in the street and another time a boy hobbled with a log tied to his leg, he was so angry that he physically attacked their tormentors.

Not many people appreciated his genius as an artist or a poet during his lifetime and many dismissed him as mad. One article dubbed him 'an unfortunate lunatic' who would have been locked up if he were not so inoffensive. Blake himself believed that those who were religious and aware of the spiritual world were likely to be considered mad in the eighteenth-century world of philosophy and reason.

One thing is certain: Blake was able to see the world beyond our own as clearly as he saw the London streets around him. Both worlds existed and flowed together, the world of God and the Spirit informing and illuminating all that he did. He once exclaimed: 'What, it will be Questioned, When the Sun rises do you not see a round Disk of fire somewhat like a Guinea? O no no I see an Innumerable company of the Heavenly host crying Holy Holy Holy is the Lord God Almighty.'

Blake refused to curb or clip his beliefs or his art to fit the fashion of the age. He was not disobedient to his heavenly vision. One young artist said: 'Before Blake began a picture he used to fall on his knees and pray that it would be successful.' Another young artist described him as 'Divine Blake, who had seen God, sir, and had talked with angels'. It is not surprising perhaps that Blake used to say that he could not consider death as 'anything but a removing from one room to another'. And for him, when death came, it seems that was all it was.

Paul James-Griffiths

Paul was born in the early 1960s and lived for a few years in Malaysia where his father was stationed in the RAF. When he came home to England his parents sent him to a church school. Paul's experience there, where harshness and caning were the order of the day, was enough to cure him of any sympathy for the Christian religion. There was a rumour going round among the children that God was a creature – half man and half bull – who breathed fire and punished small children. And that could have been true for all Paul experienced. Instead of love he knew fear. At his next school, where he was a boarder, the children were often beaten and were sexually abused by the visiting French master, until he was caught in the act and hastily dismissed.

By the time he was sent to public school he was in rebellion against all religion. He flatly refused to go to chapel. 'God doesn't bother to turn up, so why should I?' he reasoned. Not surprisingly he was severely punished until he had to give in and conform. But having to go through all the religious formalities only set him against religion even more. He made life a misery for any boys who claimed to be Christians, so much so that one was driven away from the school; another boy he nearly succeeded in suffocating in a trunk. Paul reasoned that they deserved what they got because Christianity was oppressive and controlling. Wasn't it responsible for the Crusades and the Spanish Inquisition?

But at heart Paul had a deep longing for spiritual experience so he began to explore all kinds of other possible avenues. As a child he had avidly read ghost stories and watched *House of Hammer* films; now he began to experiment with ouija boards and astral travel. It wasn't long before he began to experience spiritual presences. He got together a group of teenagers at his school who shared his interests and they used to meet as a secret band of explorers into the spirit world. What at first was meant as no more than good fun and a bit of a laugh soon became more serious. The boys chanted and meditated under red lights, called up spirit beings and used a crystal prism as a focal point of spiritual energy. Sooner or later the staff came to hear of their goings-on and Paul was summoned to report to his housemaster, who ordered him to disband the circle immediately. But Paul's pursuit of the spirit world continued, though he was now experimenting on his own. He used to visit old pagan temples in the school grounds and continued to call up spirits. He had answers in the form of visions and encounters with spirit beings. One of these Paul called 'the Muse' because of the revelations and inspiration he gave. God, the Muse assured him, was the energy present in all things and in order to know him Paul must release the spiritual potential within him through meditation.

When he was about seventeen, Paul began writing a fantasy novel, directed by the Muse, who promised that the book would be used to spread this teaching. One day, when Paul had nearly finished the first draft of the book, a sudden drowsiness came over him. He lay down and closed his eyes and suddenly he seemed to be flying swiftly, passing high over all the cities of the world. The vision seemed to be showing him the whole course of his journey through life. In one swift moment he found himself hurtling down a dark tunnel, which led suddenly to an oak-panelled corridor with doors that opened on either side. In some strange way he was able to see his spirit guide standing in two separate forms outside each of these doors. As he reached a door, his spirit guide would beckon to Paul to go into the room and a strong force seemed to try to propel Paul inside. But at the same time an even stronger force held him back from entering. He looked inside each door and saw that there was no back wall to the rooms, in which strange happenings were taking place. Paul recognised that each room represented a different spiritual dimension. At each door, a strong force held him back from entering, in spite of the guide's invitation.

But when Paul reached a room on the far left, the powerful force that had been holding him back allowed him to go in. Inside the room was a long table and at the table sat his spirit guide, a large leather-bound book in front of him. He smiled and beckoned to Paul to come and sign the book, but before he could do so he was snatched up by that other, stronger power and transported up and up, to a place where he could look down on his Muse far below. He was aware that he was now in a completely new dimension. He was looking down on the now distant earth, which was burning and raging in flames. In complete contrast, all around him was peaceful and serene. He looked up to see a king sitting in majesty on his throne, surrounded by angels and hosts of people in white robes. Then the king opened a gate and revealed a beautiful garden. A crystal-clear river ran sparkling between banks lined with laden fruit trees. All around him was filled with beauty, love, peace and joy.

When the vision ended and Paul came to himself he found that he was trembling – less from fear than with awe and wonder at what he had seen. He believed that he had experienced a vision of God, and that God was warning him to give up his experiments with the occult and his excursions into the spirit world. Paul decided to visit a priest, then went through Christian rituals, yet came no nearer to knowing God for himself.

By now Paul's schooldays were over and before going to university he decided to go to Australia, where he had relatives. He planned to try out his powers of endurance with some survival trips. The first, in the outback, was extremely tough, and without staying there too long he went on to the rainforests in Cape Tribulation, Queensland. He explored alone, and now, when he thinks back or reads the letters he wrote home that his mother still treasures, he wonders at his own courage – or foolhardiness. He narrowly escaped attack from a highly poisonous king brown snake and faced many other dangers. But he also had time to think – long and hard. Some of his Australian relatives had talked to him about finding God through Jesus. Paul had taken a Bible with him and he began to read it. In the rainforests he read from the last book of the Bible – Revelation. To his amazement he found that the author's vision of heaven was almost exactly like the vision he had had of God, which had impressed him so much and held him back from his occult experiments. Along with the visions and strange events described there, he also read some plain words of Jesus, giving an invitation that kept ringing in his thoughts. 'Listen!' the words of Jesus read, 'I stand at the door and knock; if anyone hears my voice and opens the door, I will come in.'

Paul thought long and hard. From the time that he was a schoolboy he had opened up his life to many kinds of spirit forces;

10

he had sampled many of the multifarious ways that New Age had to offer. In his vision, he had almost signed the book that he now believed to be the Book of Death. Now he recognised that the greater Power that had held him back was Jesus, who was waiting to come to him, offering life instead of death, giving him peace and forgiveness. There and then, far from human company in the solitude of the rainforests, Paul prayed, asking Jesus to make him clean, give him his forgiveness and to be master of his life. He says: 'The sense of peace, acceptance and joy that filled me was indescribable. It felt as if a weight had fallen off my shoulders. I knew I had found God at last and he had found me.'

Paul was baptised as a Christian at Alice Springs, then came back to England to begin his university studies. But his 'Muse' and the other spirits he had once dealt with did not leave him in peace. When Paul was in bed one night he woke to the sound of footsteps in the corridor. A few moments later he felt the bed sink beneath someone's weight. Quickly he snapped on the light, but there was no one there. Then he felt unseen hands around his throat, squeezing the air out and strangling him. He knew now that in spite of the spirit's superhuman strength, Jesus was stronger. He breathed the words, 'I belong to Jesus.' Immediately the stranglehold was released and the presence left him. Three nights following the same thing happened, but always the name of Jesus proved greater than the spirit that attacked him.

When I talked to Paul on the phone he told me that when he had ventured into the spirit world he had no thought of doing wrong. He had been told that there was white magic as well as black, two sides to every spirit activity and he had tried to choose the 'good', 'white' side. Later, when he read in the Bible that Satan can sometimes appear as an angel of light, he realised that dark or light, black or white are all manifestations of the spiritual powers that are ranged against the true God and Jesus his Son. 'How thankful I am,' Paul said, 'to have found the truth in Jesus. He promised his followers, "You shall know the truth and the truth shall make you free." '

Norman X

It was not until Norman called attention to it that I realised that the last two fingers of both hands were gone, only stumps remained. But that was only one strange and tragic part of the story he had to tell. Norman is a slight, gentle-looking man of thirty-two, with an appealing, shy expression but a face that looks scarred in several places. When he told me his story it was hard to reconcile the violence and terror it involves with the quiet, almost timid, bearing of the man in the chair opposite to me.

Norman spent his early years some thirty miles outside Belfast, one of six children in a Protestant family. Because he had not been quick to learn he managed to go through junior school without learning to read or write adequately. Then, when he was eleven, his father who was a mechanic left home, leaving his mother to bring up five of the children as best she could with no financial help. Norman started secondary school and quickly got in with the wrong crowd of lads. He began to break into houses and then to break into gas meters to get money to help his mother pay the bills – and for himself too. He used drugs when he could, but more often sniffed glue – or any other chemical or medicine that gives a 'high'. It was easy enough to steal a tube of glue from a shop or a bottle of cough mixture from a chemist. That was what he and his pals regularly did.

One night a gang of them had planned to stay out all night with a bonfire they had lighted. But somehow things went wrong. I wasn't told the details – clearly Norman still found the memory very painful. The police arrived on the scene and in the mêlée that resulted a twelve-year-old lad died, suffocated by smoke. Norman was gutted. He blamed the police but above all he bitterly blamed God for his friend's tragic death and determined from that day on to spite God in every way he could. He decided that he would search out the Devil and welcome all the powers of evil.

At thirteen he ended up in Borstal, where he learned a lot more about crime from the three or four other boys in his dormitory. By the time he came out, schooldays were over. He enrolled in a government training scheme but never completed it because he was soon back in trouble again and this time he was sent to a

young offenders' centre. The strict army-type discipline came as a
shock at first, with its early rising and scrupulous rules for tidying
and cleaning. But the shock wore off and when he emerged after
six months he had no intention of changing his lifestyle. He was
back on glue-sniffing and also continued his experiments with
black magic and the occult. He tried out ouija boards, crystal
balls and tarot cards. One day, in an attempt to flout God, he and
a friend went into a church, found a Bible and set fire to it near
the altar. But when they both experienced a sudden inexplicable
flash of light they took to their heels and ran out of the building.

Soon Norman began to hear voices telling him what to do –
strange, often violent acts – some of them against his own body.
On four different occasions a voice told him to cut off his fingers
and on four different occasions he did so – once with a hatchet.
But he had become violent against others too. In the end his
mother was so terrified of him that she carried a knife to protect
herself. Once, in desperation, she tried to suffocate him with a
pillow, afraid to let him live because of what he might do. He
moved out of home into a flat of his own, where he and his friends
could meet to sniff glue together or use any other easily come-by
substance that would give them a buzz. But Norman's moods of
violence became more frequent and would often be followed by
memory blanks. There are gaps in his memory which he still can't
fill. He was sent to psychiatric hospital but nothing they did
seemed to help. He himself was convinced that his moods and his
violence were more than mental illness and were the result of
demonic control. But, at the time, he gloried in his deeds of
violence. He believed, he said, that 'the worse I was on earth, the
better job I should have in hell'.

Then, one night, he literally saw evil face to face. 'The first
thing I saw in the darkness was an eye,' he told me, 'an eye that
sparkled. Then gradually out of the darkness I saw the whole
person. It was the Devil, seated on a throne.'

'What did he look like?' I asked.

'He was a very good-looking man and he kept repeating,
"Norman, come on to me" over and over. But what was the most
terrible thing about it all was the fear. There was never much I'd
been frightened of, but now – I felt fear, awful fear as I looked at

him and heard his voice. I was horribly frightened and it came to me in that moment that there was only one person who could help me – I knew that – and it was Jesus. I needed Jesus. But I didn't know much about him or how to get to him or call him to help me. Still terrified, I dashed out of the flat and jumped into a taxi to go to my mother's place. All the way there the Devil kept talking to me: "Jump out – kill yourself!" he kept telling me.'

When Norman arrived at his mother's house she was out, but her boyfriend was there. Norman asked him if he knew where there were any Christians and, surprisingly, the man did. He took him to a house where a group of Christian young people were meeting. One of them took Norman to his room. Still the Devil was talking to him. He remembers now how the bed shook as he sat on it. 'You've just to ask Jesus in,' the young man said simply, and Norman knelt by the bed and did so. He described how at once the Devil left him. He felt as if an enormous weight had lifted from his shoulders. He knew that he had made contact with a spiritual world and a spiritual force greater than the world we can see and also greater than the power of the unseen world of evil. The way back to mental and emotional health has been gradual. But the healing and deliverance from evil has been certain and real. The power of God, of goodness and love, restored and rescued Norman from the power of evil.

Julian of Norwich

We know that she was born in 1342 but we do not know when she died and we do not even know her name. She is called 'Julian' – or Lady Julian – after the name of the church in Norwich where she lived for many years. We know about her from her *Revelations of Divine Love* – probably the first book in English by a woman.

Julian lived in seclusion but she witnessed tumultuous times. From 1348 the Black Death raged in England, reaching Norwich by 1349. The death toll was horrific, killing from one third to half of the population of Europe. The plague returned to Norwich in 1361 and 1369 (as it was to return to England every four to twelve years until the last terrible outbreak in London – the Great Plague of 1665). In England as in Europe, the plague was followed by an angry rebellion by serfs and labourers, protesting about poor wages and conditions. Now that there were fewer able-bodied men and their services were in demand, they hoped they might exert force to get better conditions for themselves. But the revolt was put down savagely. On the religious front, the brilliant scholar John Wycliffe attacked clergy and church belief and the Lollards – who were probably followers of his – marched on London. They were demonstrating against some of the lax practices and beliefs of the Church and urging the authority of the Bible, which they wanted to see available in the people's own tongue. There were political intrigues too; in 1399 Henry Bolingbroke deposed Richard II to become Henry IV. In 1413 Henry V became king and fought the famous Battle of Agincourt in 1415. Julian herself probably died in about 1416.

Julian's own story begins when she was thirty. She fell sick and was so desperately ill that it seemed as if she would die. For three days and three nights, she tells us, she lay ill and on the fourth night, when death seemed certain, she received the last rites. She lingered on for two more days and nights before taking a further turn for the worse. Her parish priest was sent for and he held a cross before her saying: 'I have brought you the image of your Maker and Saviour. Look on it and be strengthened.' But her breathing became shorter and shorter and she felt sure that she was dying. Then, instead, all the pain suddenly left her and she felt completely well. It was following this remarkable healing that she received fifteen revelations – or 'showings', as she called them – in quick succession. Then her sickness seemed to return for a short while, after which she had one further vision and was subsequently completely restored to health.

Julian decided to became an anchoress or religious hermit, her cell attached to the church of St Julian in Norwich. There were certain rules governing the hermit's life at that time. A would-be anchorite or anchoress had first to convince the bishop that their calling was genuine and receive his permission. He or she also had to have the means to support themselves. Once the matter was decided a solemn Mass would be held. It was often the Mass for the Dead, since the anchorite's life in the world was now

15

deemed to be at an end. Following that, he or she would be conducted to the anchorage, to remain there until death. Sometimes the anchorage would consist of more than one tiny cell. It might have several rooms and even a little garden. We know from records that Julian had at least two different maids, Sara and Alice, during her time as a hermit. Her maid would shop and look after her needs. As she lived beside a church she may well have had a window through which she could see Mass being celebrated. Another window, curtained off, would allow her to see the occasional visitor, who would come to her for spiritual advice and help. We know that Julian was visited by Margery Kempe, a very extrovert and emotional mystic, who was married with fourteen children, and who found Julian a great comfort. But most of the next twenty years Julian spent in almost total solitude, musing and meditating on the meaning of her revelations. She described herself as 'unlettered' but that may only have meant that she knew no Latin. She could certainly read and write and was familiar with St John's Gospel and St Paul's letters as well as the writings of St Augustine. She left the fruit of her meditations on record; she not only opened up for her readers the meaning of her visions but addressed theological problems and probed the meaning of such universal human concerns as suffering and the love of God. She speaks of God with great tenderness, seeing him as a Mother-as well as a Father-figure.

One of her visions seems amazingly up-to-date and was startling for someone who lived in her day, when the earth was considered the centre of the universe around which the sun and all other planets revolved. This is how Julian describes this 'showing':

He [God] showed me a little thing, the size of a hazel-nut, on the palm of my hand, round like a ball. I looked at it thoughtfully and wondered, 'What is this?' And the answer came, 'It is all that is made.' I marvelled that it continued to exist and did not disintegrate; it was so small. And again my mind supplied the answer, 'It exists, both now and for ever, because God loves it.' In short, everything owes its existence to the love of God.

Today we have seen photographs of the earth viewed from space and we are aware through the discoveries of astronomers and cosmologists that our earth is indeed very small in the scheme of things. Yet along with this glimpse of the minuteness and fragility of earth, Julian grasped that the world was created and is sustained by God. Julian's vision showed her that 'He has the whole world in his hand'. But she also recognised that love is the prime mover. Our world, she tells us, is maintained and secured by that other world we cannot see with physical eyes. And the motive power that sustains and holds everything secure is God who is love.

2

Dreams

How is a dream different from a vision? I suppose the chief difference is that we all have dreams – though some of us remember more of them than others – and they occur naturally at certain stages in our sleep patterns.

A good deal is said and written about dreams and the way in which we can unlock the key of our unconscious minds by listening to what our dreams tell us. Some of what is said seems to make very good sense while other forms of interpretation seem extremely far-fetched. But in a far more direct way, there is no doubt that from Bible times to the present day, God has used dreams to speak to men and women.

I have been interested to hear the stories of a number of people who have experienced God for the first time through a dream. In their case, there has been nothing fanciful or far-fetched about their experience. They have known without a shadow of doubt that it was God who was making himself known to them.

Kriss Akabusi

Kriss grew up in a children's home. He had to go without many of the good things that other children had, so as he grew up he longed to possess the things that others his age could afford. To have money and success seemed to be the worthwhile achievements in life and Kriss set about finding them for himself. Through an army career and prowess in athletics he began to get the wealth and status he had yearned for. And that certainly included owning his own Mercedes car! He had been successful in his marriage too

– or so it seemed. He had a wife he truly loved, yet in spite of himself he found himself being unfaithful to her from time to time. He couldn't really understand why. Nor could he understand why it was that he had so much yet felt strangely unsatisfied.

In his search for something – he didn't know what – he began to read his Bible. In 1986 at the Commonwealth Games Kriss found a copy of the New Testament that had been put on the table beside his bed. It was in modern English, so he could understand it. And the more he read it, the more he came to the conclusion that the Jesus he read about was the person who could meet his deep-seated need. But was it all true? How could he be sure that the Jesus he had read about *was* real? He went on reading but he could find no proof that the person he wanted to believe in was alive today.

Kriss told me about the experience that changed his whole life. In 1987 when he was in the United States, his questions and his anxious feelings somehow came to a head. One night – on 14 April – he felt desperately frustrated; before he went to sleep he spoke to God: 'God, if you're really out there – Jesus, if you're really who you say you are – will you just let me know?'

Then he went to sleep and he dreamed. In the dream he found himself on the bank of a stretch of water. He jumped in and began to swim but the water was rough and turbulent and the current strong. In spite of struggling with all his strength against the current he found himself being taken along with the pull of the water, faster and faster. He felt helpless to do anything to counter the flow. Suddenly – straight ahead – he was confronted by a rapid-moving sheet of water, something like a huge waterfall. (When I talked to Kriss about it he described the uprush of water as resembling a geyser, gushing up from underground.) With his form half hidden by the moving waters, there stood a huge figure of a man; instinctively Kriss knew that man was Jesus. Then Jesus spoke aloud and directly to him, some of the words that Kriss had read – and longed to be true. Jesus said: 'Come to me, those who are weary and heavy laden and I will give you rest. For my yoke is easy and my burden is light.' Kriss just called out 'Jesus!' in joy and recognition.

Then Kriss woke up and sat up in bed. He knew now that Jesus was real and had appeared to him. He was filled with a deep sense of peace, tranquillity and happiness. Before he went to sleep again he wrote down everything that he had seen and heard in his dream. He knew next morning as he read what he had written that it had been no ordinary dream but the answer to his prayer. He had met Jesus for himself.

Julie Carslaw

'I know someone I think you should talk to,' my cousin Andrew told me. He gave me Julie's phone number and we talked. I could imagine her well, although I couldn't see her. She had grown up with her parents and an older brother and sister on a farm in Wiltshire. It was a near idyllic childhood with plenty of freedom and fresh air and her own horses to ride. As a family they did not go to church although she was sent to a Christian boarding-school and believed in God, as a vague, impersonal force. When she left school Julie studied art at Chelsea and was lucky enough to have Elizabeth Frink as a teacher when she took up sculpture. When student days were over, Julie divided her time between ski-racing on the continent in winter and sculpture for the rest of the year. Later she married and settled down to a life mainly concerned with bringing up her children, with her art as a sideline and hobby rather than a demanding career. 'It's not easy to do anything but concentrate wholly on a work once you begin,' she explained, 'and when the children were very young I took on my first and last commission – it was far too demanding to fit in with family life.'

Julie should have been happy and contented, but since the age of fourteen or fifteen she had suffered badly from depression, experiencing one total breakdown. In 1987 she was in a very bad way. She remembers that it was the year of the great storm and it was after that, but still in that same October, that she went to bed one night feeling particularly depressed. She dreamed that as her left hand touched some paper, it caught fire and burst into flame. She knew in her dream that it was because of the sickness within her that was raging so terribly. Then she entered a tunnel. It was underground, very dark and with no light that she could see at the end of it. But as she walked further in she discovered that it came out into a wide cavern and she could see an animal pen, constructed out of sheep hurdles, and inside the pen were two calves lying on clean straw. Standing by was a little girl of about eleven or twelve, dressed in blue dungarees. Julie looked at her and asked desperately, 'Can you help me?'

The little girl shook her head. 'But there is someone I know who can help,' she told her.

Then Julie saw a light on her right, so powerful that it knocked her over, on to the earthen floor. She felt very afraid and asked the little girl to hold her hand. So the child lay down on the ground beside her. Then Julie felt the light pierce her; like a tongue of flame it entered her heart, went through her and came out the other side. It did not hurt her but she was conscious of its powerfulness. At that moment she sat up and woke from her dream. Immediately she roused her husband and told him: 'I've been healed – something wonderful has happened – my depression has gone!'

She had no doubt that it was a Christian dream and she knew that it had changed her profoundly. Six months later, when her mother had a stroke and died soon after, she not only stayed free from depression but experienced an unbelievable sense of peace and of God's love surrounding her. She went to church to give thanks to God, but did not change her life in any other way. Later, when she was staying at a friend's flat in Switzerland, she told her dream to a Christian preacher.

'What have you done about your dream?' he asked her and she told him, 'Nothing.'

He suggested that Julie should make a more definite commitment of her life to God. This was something that her husband had by this time already done, so together they began a journey into spiritual life. Julie has had other dreams, but she has never been revisited, since that first dream, by the depression that had crippled her life for so many years.

Patricia St John

I have not met many saints, but once in my life I was blessed and delighted by friendship with a whole family of them. And, being saints, they were all very much individuals, each carrying their own particular breath of the other, better world. This story is about Patricia, best known for her children's books, such as *Tanglewoods' Secret* and *Treasures of the Snow.* These have been widely translated and made into films, loved now by children of two generations and many countries.

Patricia, like all real saints, was characterised by lightness of spirit and laughter. Being with her was rather like enjoying a glass of champagne. She brought us the sparkle and atmosphere of celebration that those close to God transmit to everyone whose lives they touch. She trained as a nurse at St Thomas' hospital in London during World War II, then went to help her doctor brother Farnham at a mission hospital in Tangier. After his marriage she moved to a mountain town in Morocco, where she could give medical help and share the Christian Good News with her neighbours and those in the surrounding villages. But she and her helper, Fatima, visited the villages only when they were invited. Thorn bushes and dogs who might have rabies protected the villagers from unwanted, interfering foreigners; but when they did invite strangers in, they welcomed them freely with true eastern hospitality. Patricia used to pray, then wait, until for some reason she would be invited to visit and make friends with another group of villagers. There was one village in particular, perched on a hill, across the valley from where she lived, that Patricia longed to visit. She could see it clearly enough from her house, but she could get no nearer than that to meeting the villagers.

One morning, Patricia had stayed the night away in a village she had been visiting and she and her Arab companion, Fatima, set off at dawn. They were anxious to arrive home by nine o'clock – the time lessons began at the school Patricia held for the children of her town. They walked through fields of stubble, and as the sun began to shine through the early mists, they knew that it would soon be very hot. So they were delighted when they saw a local bus coming along the main road, packed with local women. They would not have to walk the eight miles home after all. They climbed happily aboard, and when they were nearing the turning to their town they made their way to the front of the bus and asked the driver to stop. But for some reason he was surly and unwilling to oblige.

'I'm not stopping here,' he muttered, 'it's not a proper bus stop. You can get off at the next stop and walk to the town from there.' The bus chugged on for another five or six miles down the road, before finally grinding to a halt, now a very long way from their home. Patricia had been growing more and more frustrated and impatient.

'We'll never get back in time!' she complained to Fatima.

But Fatima remained cheerful. 'We prayed this morning that God would guide us,' she reminded Patricia, 'so don't be so upset.'

For a moment they stared into the distance, hoping that perhaps a bus might arrive from the other direction to take them back a few miles, but there was none to be seen. But there *was* a solitary figure coming down the hill, which wound upwards from where they were standing. It was a woman and she was carrying in her arms what looked like a bundle of rags. Patricia was perplexed. It wasn't market-day and no woman was likely to leave the village and walk down the hill at any other time. Besides, the women always travelled in groups, never alone. Then Patricia realised that the solitary stranger was coming from the village on the hill; the village she had looked across at so often, with concern and longing.

They waited and watched as the woman came nearer. When she drew close to them she stopped and asked Fatima, 'Is that the English nurse?' jerking her thumb in Patricia's direction. Once reassured she asked to be introduced. Then she gently drew aside the wrappings and showed Patricia the contents of her little bundle. A baby lay there, but in a terrible condition. Patricia had never seen eyes so badly infected. They were closed right up, swollen blue and exuding pus through the matted lashes.

'I have brought her to you,' the woman said.

'How long has she been like this?' Patricia asked.

'For four days,' the woman answered. 'She lies crying with her face to the wall and will not suck.'

23

'But how did you know to bring her here? It's not market-day and there are no others with you.'

'Last night,' the woman said, 'I knew that my child was getting worse. She was burning with fever. I fell asleep heavy-hearted and as I slept I had a dream. In my dream a man dressed in white came to me and said, "Take your child to the English nurse." "But I don't know her and I don't know where to find her," I said. Then the man in white said to me, "Go down to the bridge at the main road at sunrise and you will find her there. She will tell you what to do." So I woke up and took my child and did as the man in white told me to. And you are here.'

Patricia and Fatima walked the five or six miles home without another murmur of complaint, taking the woman and her baby with them. Patricia gave the child repeated shots of penicillin and washed out her eyes and by the evening, when the woman took her child home, she was already looking better. Before she left, the woman invited Patricia to come to see her in her village. That Saturday she and Fatima were able to walk to the village they had so much wanted to visit. They need not have worried about finding the woman and her baby. Everyone had heard her story and the first person they met pointed them to her house. The child's eyes had cleared wonderfully and a delighted, laughing crowd collected to be given the medicines they needed. Then they listened to the stories that the English nurse began to tell them – for the mother asked: 'Have you brought us the way to heaven?'

Catherine Bramwell-Booth

Catherine Bramwell-Booth was the granddaughter of William Booth, the founder of the Salvation Army. And she was a worthy successor to the Grand Old Man. When she celebrated her hundredth birthday in 1983 she was at the receiving end of a great deal of praise and celebration, both from her Army colleagues, and the media at large. There were articles about her in magazines and papers and she was invited to appear on television chat shows. Her minute figure, with its ramrod-straight back; her impeccable Salvation Army uniform, complete with poke bonnet; and her ready wit both charmed and daunted her interrogators. She had a surprisingly sharp tongue and a quick brain and she often left the chat-show host – whether Russell Harty or Michael Parkinson – hoist with his own petard. The viewers loved it and Catherine, accompanied by her two younger sisters, Col. Olive and Major Dora, happily endured the limelight for the good of the cause.

When at last I received Catherine's permission to write her biography it was arranged that I should visit the sisters in the old family home in Berkshire, where William Booth's drum and colours still stood in the dark hall. Then, out of the blue, she suffered a stroke and the meeting was cancelled. But after a while, although she herself was not yet well enough to see me, her two sisters invited me to go down so that they could tell me all they knew about Catherine. So, complete with tape recorder, I used to travel down, take lunch with them in the dining-room – where a place was still laid for Catherine at the top of the table – and I would listen to all that these two charming ladies had to say. They might be old-world and gracious, but they too were mentally sharp, completely practical and although both gentle and courteous, neither was likely to stand for any nonsense or to suffer fools gladly.

One day they turned out an old book which had been published in 1921 but was long since out of print. It consisted of a series of letters written by Catherine and published in a Salvation Army magazine, to various officers who had trained under her and were now facing all manner of difficulties in their new posts. A Salvation Army officer is the equivalent of a minister in other denominations and these young women were facing the trials and problems of coping with a human flock. I was very impressed by the shrewd, practical common sense, as well as the loving concern and spiritual wisdom which these letters contained. When my biography of Catherine was published, this book of letters was republished too. The last letter is unlike any of the others. I believe it must represent a deep spiritual experience – perhaps a dream or a vision – which Catherine experienced in the forest near her home. She called it 'The Law of the Forest'.

In the calm that follows a storm, while the clouds were still driven fast across the sky, the young Catherine sat in the shelter of the wood, listening to the sighing of the wind in the branches. Later, she wrote, she found herself possessed of a knowledge that was unlooked for. She seemed to know that, long ago, the wind was sighing as she had heard it, when a tall pine asked: 'How long?' At last an answer seemed to come, murmured from every side: 'Until the service is completed.' But the pine tree was unsatisfied and continued to grieve for its constant struggle with the winds, its endeavour to provide shelter for the birds and shade for the animals. Instead of growing old to rot and decay it wished that it could have been felled and treated with loving attention. It could have been shaped and polished, treasured and cared for, instead of having to care for others. As the tree continued its complaint, the wind rose and the words were drowned by the noise of the storm. Next morning, the pine had fallen, though no other tree had. The birds and beasts that had depended on that tree for shelter were lost and sad. In due course the tree was taken away, leaving an empty space with only the crushed fern fronds to reveal where it had lain.

The other trees listened, anxious to hear, as an old oak at the centre of the wood brought them his wisdom. He told them that the ancient law of the forest was to serve rather than to be served, to protect and to nourish, to stand firm and strong from year to year, offering shelter and a home to all the birds and beasts that trusted in them. The pine, he said, had ignored the ancient law of the forest to stand firm 'until the service is completed'.

Catherine concluded: 'I do not know how this knowledge came to me. I can picture the tree on whose root I sat listening to the wind in the branches, so clearly do I know that this is the tree that grew up to fill the vacant place. The tree is real enough, and I could take you to it, but as for the rest . . .'

'Can you make anything of it?' Catherine asked her reader. 'If you find an interpretation, write and tell me; but at least we might both appropriate the words, "until the service is completed".' And she herself lived and died according to the law of the forest.

3

Appearings

A friend who is a scientist asked me if I try in any way to verify the personal experiences people tell me about. I explained that my purpose is to tell the stories as I hear them, not to establish their truth by all kinds of tests. In many cases it would be impossible anyway to *prove* that the things they describe actually happened. But what has impressed me most, as I've listened to so many extraordinary experiences, is the utter conviction of the people whose stories I tell that what happened to them *was* real and is valid. In these stories of *Appearings* what struck me was the absolute conviction that the person who appeared was real. The people were substantial – in no way like ghosts or dream figures – and of that they were certain. And the events were recounted by practical and sophisticated 'men' of the world. Perhaps the best test of the genuineness of their experience is the fact that the appearing changed their lives. What they saw and heard was real enough to transform their future.

Fred Lemon

He stood on the platform of a crowded hall, a middle-aged, stocky figure and when he spoke it was with a strong Cockney accent. He began to pray: 'God,' he said, 'this is Fred here. What are you going to do about it?'

I can no longer remember how the prayer went on but I do know that the rest of it was as conversational and assured as the opening phrases. I suspect that the rest of the church audience was as amazed as I was at this unconventional approach, and as

27

curious to know what this man would have to say to us.

The speaker was Fred Lemon and by the time I heard him tell his story he was a respectable greengrocer, living with his wife Doris in London's East End. He used his shop as a marketplace for his new-found Christian faith as well as for selling fruit and vegetables. Fred grew up in London and, like many young men before and since, he quickly got in with the wrong crowd. He drank too much – and that led to violence – and he got into petty crime. One conviction followed another and by 1950 he was in Dartmoor Prison, serving a sentence for robbery with violence. The regime for convicts there was as rugged and unyielding as the stark, stone building, the unfriendly winter climate and the bleak countryside around. Most prisoners accepted that escape from Dartmoor was next to impossible and there was nothing for it but to try to survive the stark routine of that time, until the sentence was served and justice satisfied.

One night Fred turned into his bunk early, mainly because there was nothing else to do. He was not physically tired after a day with little exercise for his body or mind. But the last meal of the day was long over and the light from the gas-lamp was too weak to read by. After a while he dropped off into a fitful sleep. Suddenly, he looked up to see three men standing at the foot of his bunk. At first they seemed ordinary men in ordinary suits. Before he had time to wonder how they could possibly have come into his cell, one of them spoke to him.

'Fred,' he said, pointing to the man at the centre, 'this is Jesus.'

Fascinated, Fred fixed his eyes on the man who stood between the other two visitors and listened for what he had to say. The one who was Jesus began to talk to him, gently and firmly. He reminded Fred of his past – his friends, the drink, the crime, the violence. But he did not single out only Fred's faults. He recalled Fred's acts of kindness and his attempts to reform. Above all, by his words and his manner he gave Fred an overwhelming sense of God's love for him and forgiveness for his wrongdoing. This person, Jesus, loved and forgave him wholly. His last words to Fred were: 'Fred, if you want to be a Christian, you must drive hatred from your heart.'

Then Fred heard a distinct click as the three men passed through the thick stone walls of his cell and disappeared. Next morning Fred knew that he had *not* been dreaming. Jesus had been real and he had come to Fred's prison cell to let him know that he was loved and forgiven. But the sting had been in that parting shot: 'Fred, if you want to be a Christian, you must drive hatred from your heart.' That was the one thing Fred could not, would not do.

During the years of crime – and punishment – there had been many who had treated Fred badly. Prison officers in particular had often used their position of power to make his life in prison a hundred times worse. Hating them and planning to get even and pay them out gave stimulus and purpose to living in this hell-hole. To forgive them was unthinkable.

Four months passed and outside the prison autumn turned to winter. Inside, nothing much seemed to change. But one morning, in the queue to slop out, a fellow prisoner murmured, 'Compliments of the season,' out of the side of his mouth, and Fred realised that it was Christmas Day. He went back to his cell and waited to be called to attend the traditional carol service held in the prison chapel. As he waited, he turned the pages of the Bible to read the story of the first Christmas, told in the Gospels. As he read, he began to imagine the scene as it had been – a smelly, unhygienic stable, with no cleanliness or cheering light. There were no creature comforts at all to welcome the Saviour of the world when he came as a baby to earth. The One who had visited his cell was used to the kind of conditions that Fred had to survive in. But worse had followed. This man, who never did anything wrong, who showed only love and care for others, was cruelly put to death, nailed to a cross-beam of wood and hoisted in mid-air, to suffocate and die. Yet the words *he* spoke were words of forgiveness for those who had ill-treated him. He had prayed, 'Father, forgive them!' So he knew what it would cost Fred when he said, 'You must drive the hatred from your heart.'

For the first time, Fred wanted the icy coldness of his heart to melt. He *wanted* to forgive even the prison officer who had wronged him most. If only he could be free from his hatred! But he could not drive the hatred away by himself. He knelt down on the cold, stone floor of the cell and prayed: 'Lord, I want to give you my heart. Get rid of this hatred inside me. I want to forgive them all.' He began to say over the nicknames of the prison officers who had mistreated him, pausing just a moment before naming the one who had treated him the worst.

In immediate response, he felt the love of God flood into him, melting his hardness and coldness and making it possible for him to forgive and love the men he had hated so bitterly. He knew that the peace the angels sang about that first Christmas had come to him to stay. This time he could not see Jesus, but he knew that he was in the cell with him just as certainly as he had been before, and he would be with him for the rest of his life.

Father Bill Kirkpatrick

We had talked on the phone but we had never met until Father Bill came to our house a few weeks ago. I had read some of his books, including *Going Forth* where he writes about an approach to death and dying that is warm, practical and spiritual. I was deeply moved, too, by the book he edited after the death from AIDS of his long-time partner, Richie McMullen. I was profoundly moved by the love, compassion and gentleness shown by the group of contributors and by Father Bill himself, speaking of their love and compassion for Richie as well as all that they had gained from him. So I was extremely interested to meet the man who now sat in the chair opposite me. He has a gaunt face and a spare frame, and gives an immediate impression of reserve but also of inner strength. I sensed that he possesses a range of hidden reserves of sympathy and compassion that would quickly flow out to the vulnerable and those he perceived to be in need. But I had a strong suspicion that I would not be allowed to see that side of him. As he told his story I began to understand some of the factors that had made him the uniquely special person he is.

I arrived when I shouldn't have done, (he began), and I never knew much about my parents but since there were no one-parent families in those days, I was put in an orphanage at three months old, owned by the Kirkpatricks. Then, when I was seven and the orphanage had to be closed down during the Depression, I was unofficially fostered by Mr and Mrs Kirkpatrick along with one other child – who I think of as my sister. My foster-parents also had their own natural children and a bit later, after being asked to look after some old people, they ran a nursing home for the elderly.

This home became their life-work and for ten years Bill helped. The residents ranged in age from the sixties to some over a hundred years old and many of them were the last of the early pioneer families in the Canadian West. Bill had a deep care and concern for these elderly people. He washed them, dressed them, nursed them; he carried them up and down stairs and looked after them; when they were well enough he took them to the cinema. Eventually an older friend who was chaplain to the nursing home became concerned that Bill was getting too involved and told him to get out while he could and go to England for a year. Bill followed his advice and came to London where he had a string of jobs, ranging from selling pots and pans in Selfridges to being a music copyist for a composer and conductor. Then for three years he was a steward with BOAC – now British Airways. One day during a stopover in Calcutta he saw the terrible conditions of poverty there, and the caring side of him was stirred into life again.

He flew back to England determined to do something to help such people and, in order to have some skill to offer, he decided to train as a nurse. As in every other job he had tackled, he was extremely successful. He became highly proficient and was eventually promoted to a senior post in psychiatric nursing. But he was restless and when he heard that the new Protestant religious centre at Taizé specialised in young men with problems, he decided to go there. He fell in love with the community and asked to stay, but was told to come back again after five years so that he and they could determine whether his response was genuine or merely an emotional one.

Before the five years were up Bill went on holiday to Sardinia. He had been told beforehand that accommodation would be no problem, but when he got there he found there were no hotels with vacancies. So when he wandered into a curiosity shop and found a fellow Canadian behind the counter, he asked his advice. The shop-owner assured him that they would have room to take him in at one of the fishermen's cottages down near the shore, as the husbands were away fishing. His new friend took him to a picturesque little cottage where a small woman welcomed him. Then she hesitated, looking him up and down doubtfully. She explained that at his height his legs would hang over the edge of the bed if she put him in the spare room. So she settled him into the family room instead. All round the room were pictures and statues, but the wall that faced the end of the bed was completely bare. He soon got into bed and went to sleep.

He awoke in the night and saw a woman standing at the foot of the bed. She was the most beautiful woman he had ever seen and she stood holding out her arms but without speaking a word. At the same time Bill felt as if he were surrounded by a deep, palpable atmosphere of love. He was utterly amazed and mystified. Was he dreaming, he wondered afterwards, or did it really happen? His own comment to me was: 'I think I knew it was real but didn't want to believe it.'

When I asked: 'Was it the Virgin Mary?' Bill spoke as if the question was scarcely relevant.

'I don't know – how should I know? At that time I knew nothing about Mary. I know that it was a spiritual experience which took me out of myself. I was somewhere else, but I haven't the words to describe it.' He also emphasised that it was no ghost he saw – the woman was palpably real.

Bill phoned his partner to tell him that he thought he was having a schizophrenic breakdown, then returned to England next day. But the man who was his guru at that time – a Christian Buddhist who was himself a psychiatrist – insisted that Bill needed a priest. Bill had no intention of seeing a priest but eventually they struck a bargain that Bill would see a priest if his friend would also arrange for him to see a different psychiatrist (he refused to accept Bill as his own patient).

Every week Bill visited the Anglican priest, and every week they sat in near silence, the priest saying almost nothing. Yet, wishing to please, Bill went along with arrangements being made for him to be baptised and later confirmed, and then entered on a course of training. This last decision had been made through the persuasive tactics of Canon Stanley Evans, a Christian Communist he had come to know and respect highly. At first Bill assumed naively that everyone who was confirmed went to college, but he soon discovered that he was one of the first batch of students training to be worker priests (now known as non-stipendiary priests). These are people trained and ordained to the priesthood who also continue in the workplace, combining a secular and spiritual ministry. Bill was horrified. He had no love for the Church or for institutions of any kind, but one after another his advisers and his friends confirmed their strong belief that he was destined for the priesthood. Although he had had no formal religious upbringing he had always believed in God, and since all this had come about without his planning, he decided that it must be part of God's plan for him. He knew, deep down, that he had to respond somehow to the vision – or appearing, or whatever it was – that he had experienced in Sardinia.

Before the end of the three years Father Bill was transferred to a standard ordination course and when his training neared its end he had a battle royal over becoming a parish priest. He knew that he was quite unsuited to that vocation so he flatly refused to agree to accept the proffered parish, antagonising more than one bishop in the process. It seemed to him that his life had come to a full stop once again. The hospitals did not want him back because he had helped a colleague who exposed the shameful conditions in the treatment of the mentally ill.

For four years he worked with Centrepoint, the charity which had set up one of the first emergency night shelters for the young homeless in London. During his time with them he helped to develop the project, which is now a large charity, offering emergency help to thousands of young, vulnerable people.

In 1975 Father Bill joined the Anglican order of Franciscan friars and became one of the brothers of the Society of St Francis. He completed four years with them but he knew by then that he could not find his life-work in any organised religion. 'Religion puts you in a box,' he said, 'but spirituality is like a flower – it opens out.'

One day, on a visit to London, he took a wrong turning and

found himself – accidentally it seemed – in Earl's Court. But at once he knew in his bones that this was the place where he had to be. God wanted him to serve him in this place. He had a strong desire to be a kind of hermit, a contemplative who is also there to help others. He remembered that the desert fathers and those who had sought solitariness in past centuries had always been taught that whatever they were doing – meditating or praying – they must remember that anyone who came to them with a need had first call on their time. That person took priority over personal prayer and meditation. That was the kind of lifestyle that Father Bill envisaged. He believes that contemplation always leads to action.

He found just the flat to suit his purpose, but he had no money. He came to an agreement with the estate agent that he would pay the money in a lump sum in seven weeks' time. In an amazing way, that Father Bill sees clearly as the working of the Holy Spirit, the Trust that had supported him during his time at Centrepoint agreed to fund him and he was able to pay the money on the day he had promised it. Father Bill had told the trustees that he meant to live in the flat as a solitary. He would not advertise or canvas 'clients' but wait for those who needed him to come of their own accord. In 1979 he set up his one-man centre in Earl's Court, called Reaching Out. He has lived and ministered to others in that area ever since.

For at least six months after he moved in, nothing happened and not a single person called. Father Bill did no canvassing and made no attempt to attract 'clients'. He simply continued to go to the pub and the clubs, wearing his clerical collar, and chat with the people he met there. He often went for early morning walks at three or four in the morning, to see what was going on. Then, dramatically, the situation changed and within a year or eighteen months of his moving in, the place was buzzing. Over five hundred people had come of their own accord to see him and seek his help. Earl's Court is an area frequented by gays and rent boys.

'They are vulnerable people,' Father Bill says, 'and so am I.' He believes very strongly that all caring is circular. There is no 'them' and 'us'. All are equal in the sight of God and we all receive from as well as give to one another. Father Bill set up the St

Cuthbert Centre for vulnerable people living in bed-sit land as well as Streetwise Youth for young males working at street level in the sex industry.

It was after he had settled there and become known that the AIDS epidemic changed the face of society. Father Bill had spent most of his life nursing the elderly, the mentally and the physically sick, the social outcasts – all who were most vulnerable – and he was already at hand and able to help. Caring for sufferers from HIV and AIDS has been his chief ministry ever since. His training had taught him nursing and pastoral skills, his faith and his own life-story have taught him to love and respect all people. He is able to care for the sick and dying in practical ways, and he is also willing to sit with them quietly when they are dying and say nothing, just be there. 'Nurses and doctors naturally want their patients to get better,' he says, 'they see it as failure when someone dies. I have a different perspective. My job is to help people die with dignity.'

Looking back over his life, Father Bill can see that every part of it has fitted him for the work he has been called to do. Perhaps the rejection by his natural parents made him acutely aware of the deep human hunger for love and gave him an understanding of those who need love and friendship so desperately as their lives are ending. But one of the mainsprings of his ministry is the appearing – the visitation. He has never forgotten the silent, beautiful woman, with her aura of overwhelming divine love. It was this experience that opened his eyes to discover God and to learn to mediate that love to those who need it most.

4

Moments of crisis

We have all had never-to-be-forgotten moments or days in our lives. But for some people one such moment is so important that it changes the whole direction of their future life. The experience may not seem to be a religious one yet it bears the stamp of a message from another world. The change in direction or in lifestyle that follows may be so unexpected or dramatic that it seems to be prompted more by a revelation than an event of the ordinary world. Such moments of crisis can come to religious people but just as often, it seems, to those with no thought beforehand of a world beyond our own. Both kinds of people share their experiences in the stories that follow.

Bishop Jim Thompson

I had often heard the Bishop of Bath and Wells talk on the radio and one day my attention was caught when he told listeners about a crisis in his life. I wrote to the Bishop's Palace and asked if I could talk to him about it. He agreed and I was able to phone him in his study and chat with him about the night that changed his life. By the time I rang off, I had begun to understand why he is nothing like the accepted stereotype of a bishop. His own experience has made him able to understand how ordinary people react and how spiritual experience is not necessarily tied up with churches and cathedrals.

It happened – Jim Thompson's first encounter with the spiritual world – when he was an articled clerk, studying accountancy. He was enjoying life and spent a good bit of his time going round with the group of fellow clerks that he worked with. Out of work hours they would go off together for a pub crawl or dance away the hours to traditional jazz. It all seemed good fun, and he felt that he was getting everything that a young man could want from life.

Jim had grown up in a fairly normal middle-class family that was not very religious. He had been sent off to public boarding-school at the usual age, where he had to learn to cope with being a fat boy. He soon found that clowning about was the best way to deflect the teasing and bullying that inevitably came his way. So the other boys thought that he was more extrovert and ebullient than he really was. In fact he was painfully sensitive but they assumed that his cheery façade reflected a happy and optimistic approach to life. He had to attend school chapel, of course, and went along with what was expected of him by being confirmed at the age of fourteen. But he certainly didn't experience any deeply felt, 'gut' religious experience; confirmation was no more than the usual requirement of formal religion. In fact, even before he left school he was beginning to lose any mild faith in God he might once have had. Over the next few years he grew more than ever convinced that there was nothing in religion. Yet although he did not believe in it, there was something about the Christian faith that left him feeling uneasy. That lingering unease had the effect of making him eager to argue against Christianity with anyone who was willing to take him on. But in spite of his strong antipathy to religion and in spite of the carefree life he seemed to be enjoying with his fellow articled clerks, he still had a deep sense that he could only describe as 'lostness'.

One Christmas Eve he and his friends had been out drinking and they were all a bit the worse for wear. When it was nearly midnight one of the group suggested that they all ought to go to church, so off they went. But when they arrived at the church door and the others began to crowd into the church, Jim knew that he could not follow them. He was clear-headed enough to realise that there would be something not right – somehow out of keeping – about going into a church in the state that he was in. Instead he stayed outside and sat down on a gravestone. The night was cold and he very soon sobered up. He could hear the music and the singing of the carols coming out to him from the church and as he listened he felt terribly alone. It was not just the fact that his friends had gone into the church and he was by himself. He was overcome with a deep sense of being on the outside, in the saddest and truest sense.

Then, with no explanation and no premonition, in the midst of this solitariness and unhappiness he experienced a peace flowing into him. It was peace far more intense than anything that he had ever felt. He had the overwhelming conviction that the struggle – whatever it had been – had ceased, that he was going to be all right and that he *would* find the way. Above all, he knew with absolute clarity and certainty that he was accepted, that he was loved. He knew too, with absolute certainty, that the experience was a spiritual one. He would not remain lost and forsaken, on the outside. He would be able to come in out of the cold.

Jim knows that his experience on that Christmas Eve was a valid one, because the sense of love and acceptance he experienced then has never left him. In spite of events of life which have been hard – even humiliating – he has never lost the sense of God's love and acceptance of him.

Jim went up to Oxford, was ordained and has since become a bishop, first of Stepney, now of Bath and Wells. But he is no ponderous, churchified figure. And when, as so often, he is at the centre of church celebrations – at Christmas or whenever it may be – he never forgets what it was like to be an 'outsider'. The experience on that Christmas night years before has stayed with him. He can identify with all who feel outsiders and he longs to communicate something of the love and peace of the life of the Spirit which first came to him in a cold graveyard and has remained with him ever since.

Captain William Bligh

William Bligh, captain of the ill-fated *Bounty*, has had a thoroughly bad press. He has been consistently portrayed – in words and in the films that have been made of the famous mutiny – as a ruthless, bullying captain who well deserved the fate dealt to him by the mutineers. But the picture we can build up through records of the time presents a very different Bligh.

William Bligh was born in 1854, the son of a customs officer in Plymouth. He had a good education before joining the navy when he was still a lad. Over the years he proved himself to be a skilled navigator and an excellent map-maker. He had the good fortune to sail more than once under Captain Cook, who thought highly of him. Bligh learned about good seamanship from Cook as well as how to look after his crew. At one point on the *Bounty*'s voyage, when the decks became leaky, he gave up his own great cabin so that some of the crew could hang their hammocks there in the dry. He saw that his men had balanced rations, and signed on a fiddler to provide music for country dancing on board as daily exercise.

Bligh's notorious mission – a government one – was to go to Tahiti to collect specimens of breadfruit trees. Although the fruit is fairly tasteless it is nourishing so Pitt's government thought it would provide ideal cheap food for the slaves in the sugar plantations of the West Indies. They chose Bligh to captain a ship and lead the expedition because he was familiar with both Tahiti and the West Indies through his voyages with Cook. He was also an experienced navigator who could be trusted to achieve this mission. After collecting the young plants from Tahiti, Bligh was to transport them to the West Indies to be planted there. A ship was refitted and specially adapted at a cost of over £4,000, with a heated greenhouse to protect the saplings during the cold part of the long voyage. It meant that Bligh was woefully short of space for working crew members and for marines, who normally came on board to provide protection. He had to take a botanist and gardener and they were no help as crew members, nor was the half-blind fiddler. To add to his problems, the ship's doctor was an alcoholic. But there was no shortage of volunteers for the trip. Tahiti was famous for beautiful weather and beautiful women – what more could a sailor want?

Fletcher Christian, who had sailed with Bligh before, begged to come as sailing master. He was the exact opposite of Bligh, who looked unattractive but was punctilious at his work. Christian was inclined to be weak, was sometimes sulky and slipshod in his work, but he was also a real ladies' man, well-connected and educated, with an easy manner.

The newly named *Bounty* set sail and at length arrived at Tahiti, where the men could not wait to sample the delights of the place. Bligh did not join in with them, but he was indulgent and at first he even allowed women to stay on board. Fletcher Christian preferred to live on land with his chosen Tahitian woman. Their stay lasted for twenty-three weeks, but no one complained. Presumably Bligh wanted to make sure that the thousand and more seedlings they had potted up had thoroughly rooted.

They set sail at last, well provided with coconuts and bananas as well as pigs and goats, and at first all went smoothly. Then, one night, Bligh turned in early, but was roughly shaken awake at dawn, the victim of what he later described as 'one of the most atrocious acts of piracy ever committed'. He was bound and closely guarded while the crew argued, and swore and jeered at Bligh and their other captives. Then they herded eighteen of the men, along with Captain Bligh, into the ship's small boat, and cast the boat adrift. The mutineers who remained on the *Bounty* were, in Bligh's view, 'the most able men of the ship's company'.

So why *did* they mutiny? Bligh was by then two-thirds through his mission with every sign of success. Not a single man was ill and the breadfruit plants were flourishing. Bligh had a quick temper and could swear and insult the men sometimes, but unlike most sea captains of the time, he rarely flogged them. Bligh himself pondered about the cause of the mutiny and wrote in his journal:

Perhaps, if there had been marines on board, a sentinel at my cabin door might have prevented it; for I slept with the door always open, that the officer of the watch might have access to me on all occasions, the possibility of such a conspiracy being ever the farthest from my thoughts. Had their mutiny been occasioned by any grievances, either real or imaginary, I must have discovered symptoms of their discontent . . . but the case was far otherwise.

He could only conclude that the men wished to continue their idyllic life on Tahiti rather than return to hard work and life in England. And Tahiti was certainly the mutineers' first destination after they had cast Bligh and his companions adrift. Bligh believed that Fletcher Christian had misgivings about the mutiny, but could not go back once events began to take their course. Bligh records Christian's last words to him: 'That, Captain Bligh, that is the thing; I am in hell – I am in hell.'

When Bligh had been thrown over the side into the ship's boat, his hands were untied and a few pieces of pork were thrown into the boat as well as a few cutlasses. They had already been given a twenty-eight-gallon keg of water and some bread, and a small quantity of rum and wine. They were allowed to take twine, quadrant and compass but no maps or drawings.

Bligh then had to use all his skill and experience, all his good sense and shrewd reckoning. He decided to make for some islands he knew, in order to stock up on provisions. When the wind was right they used sails and the rest of the time they rowed. Bligh aimed eventually to reach Timor where there was a Dutch settlement. His men agreed to subsist on one ounce of bread and a quarter of a pint of water a day so that rations would last out. Bligh wrote in his journal, 'We bore away across a sea, where the navigation is but little known, in a small boat, twenty-three feet long from stem to stern, deep laden with eighteen men.' He divided the men into watches, got the boat in order and then, 'returned God thanks for our miraculous preservation, and, fully confident of his gracious support, I found my mind more at ease than it had been for some time past'.

The voyage that followed was horrific. There were gales and rough seas but at least torrential rain made it possible to catch water. Bligh explained where to find Timor, in case he himself did not survive. The rain squalls left them soaked to the skin and they endured 'cold and shiverings scarce to be conceived'. They wrung out their clothes in sea-water to make them less cold. At night there were no stars to steer by. They suffered extreme cramps and pains. There was sickness and Bligh conserved the small quantity of wine for the worst sufferers. He himself became ill after eating the contents of the stomach of a bird they caught. By 10 June – six weeks after they had been cast adrift – Bligh noted that everyone was looking ill – with 'swelled legs, hollow countenance, sleepiness, slowness of thinking'. But two days later, in the early hours, they sighted Timor – only two leagues away. It seemed unbelievable that they had survived 3,618 miles in an open boat without any loss of life. All that remained was for the weary voyagers to come ashore: 'Our bodies were nothing but skin and bones, our limbs were full of sores, and we were clothed in rags: in this condition, with the tears of joy and gratitude flowing down our cheeks, the people of Timor beheld us with a mixture of horror, surprise, and pity.'

In spite of the efforts of everyone to care for the needs of the travellers, Bligh found it difficult at first to rest. He kept thinking about all the dangers of the voyage and brooding on the failure of his original mission. But above all his mind was 'disposed to reflect on . . . the thanks due to Almighty God, who had given us power to support and bear such heavy calamities, and had enabled me at last, to be the means of saving eighteen lives.'

Jaime Jaramillo

It was Christmas Eve, 1973, and Jaime Jaramillo was strolling along the streets of the Colombian capital of Bogota. He was young and handsome, a university student from a happy and wealthy home, and he hadn't a care in the world. As a long line of cars streamed past along the road, he noticed a little girl tossing a gift box out of a car window. Immediately a small gang of dirty, ragged children rushed into the road to pick it up. Jaime stood still and watched as the small girl who got to it first pounced on the box and picked it up triumphantly. Her eye caught Jaime's and she smiled at him in sheer delight at the treasure she had found. And, pausing to give him that smile, she failed to see the oncoming truck which bore down on her and smashed her against the pavement. When Jaime reached her she was dead.

He was horrified. 'I felt as if I had killed her,' he said, 'because I had distracted her.' He was sure that if she had not paused to exchange that happy smile with him, she would have reached the pavement safely. He picked up the box she had died to capture, and found that it was empty. The child in the car had taken out the doll she had been given for Christmas and thrown the empty box away. The little girl had died for nothing. And she was one of many homeless children begging and running wild on the streets of Bogota. 'From that time,' Jaime said later, 'when I saw that broken body, I realised that I was meant to help street children.'

Jaime was as good as his word. He began at once. It was Christmas Eve, so he would be Father Christmas. The eighteen-year-old engineering student quickly bought some two hundred inexpensive gifts and then spent the hours till sunrise giving them out to the gamines – or street children – that he met all around the city streets.

But that was only a beginning. Jaime determined that he would find a home for ten children within a year. And he was as good as his word. He began to place children in foster homes where they would be cared and provided for. But soon after, Jaime won a scholarship which meant that he had to go abroad for further studies.

The seeds of Jaime's kindness and compassion go back to his childhood. He was born to wealthy parents and life was comfortable, but his parents were also loving and generous, both to their own children and in meeting the needs of others less fortunate. They brought Jaime up in the Roman Catholic faith and taught him to think of others in need. 'From the age of eight, I wanted desperately to be like my father,' Jaime says, 'he is a very good man, who has helped a lot of poor people. My mother too has been a voluntary helper in an old people's home.'

So this young man, who by now was a high-powered business tycoon – a geophysicist and international oil explorer – began to juggle very different lifestyles. Sometimes he is deep in the jungle, working and exploring for oil; often he is in his luxurious, well-appointed office or at home with his wife and two children. But he is equally at ease when he is searching the rat-infested derelict dwellings where some of his street children are found. Sometimes the lifestyles mingle. When he leaves a fashionable, top class restaurant, he is often met outside by a horde of noisy, clamouring street children.

In 1980 when Jaime returned to Colombia from his academic studies overseas, he continued to help the street children. One day he found a little girl lying in the gutter in a pool of blood. He picked her up, against the advice of onlookers who said he'd be held responsible for the accident and have to pay her medical bills. When he took her to hospital they told him that she had suffered an epileptic fit and hit her head against the curb. When he asked her where she lived he was mystified by her answer. She said that she lived *under*, not *on* the streets. He learned that when the police and death squads began to patrol the streets to get rid of these 'unwanted' children, they had fled underground and begun to live in the sewers below. Jaime described the horrific conditions in these rat- and leech-infested underground tunnels. The children try to stay on the ledges, but when the water is high they become trapped and sometimes they fall and drown in the human waste. There is danger from rat bites, from falls and from ingesting the sewage and developing malaria or diarrhoea. When the sewers are flowing fast, there is a white froth on top which the children think is clean. So they wash in it and develop gangrene in their limbs. At nights it is so cold that the children use drugs to deaden their misery.

Jaime began to visit the sewers at night and determined to rescue the children, little by little, beginning with the very young ones and the girls who were pregnant. He invented a way to counteract some of the unpleasantness and dangers of the sewers by wearing a rubber suit and using diving gear with an oxygen supply. One night, in the pitch black, he heard a girl's screams and by flashlight he helped deliver the fifteen-year-old's baby. Then, still in his rubber suit, now blood-splashed, he drove her and the newborn child to hospital in his sports car.

Little by little Jaime rehoused the children. Others helped him but he was the only one to go down into the sewers. That was partly because of the dangers involved but also because the children would trust no one but Jaime. Now, years later, he has at last achieved his target. All the children have been moved out of the sewers to other homes.

For many years, unknown even to his wife, Jaime paid medical costs and other expenses out of his own pocket. 'Charity must be done quietly,' his father had always said. Later he established the Foundation of the Children of the Andes, administered by his wife – once reluctant but now his willing partner in the work. Weaning the children off drugs, teaching them that they are loved and valued and training them to take their place in life are not easy tasks, but Jaime believes and insists that there is hope for these once rejected children.

Jaime Jaramillo does not claim to be deeply religious nor to care for others out of some deep personal psychological need or ulterior motive of his own, but he recognises that compassion and love count for more than money and material goods. 'I believe that we are all born with a mission,' he says. Because of the poignant scene of a small girl's death, witnessed as a young student, he found that mission among the rejected children of the Bogota streets and sewers.

Brother Laurence

Nicholas Herman was born in French Lorraine in about 1626 and served as a footman and a soldier when he was young. He said that he was 'a great awkward fellow who broke everything' while he was a footman, but that was in his young days. When Nicholas was eighteen he went out one day in the middle of winter when there was snow on the ground. Suddenly he stopped still, his attention held by the sight of a huge tree, rising gaunt and bare, its branches cold and leafless against the bleak horizon. As the young man gazed at the tree, there came into his mind a picture of that same tree as it would be when spring arrived. The bare trunk and boughs would be transformed, breaking into fresh green shoots and new leaves. Instead of apparent death there would be abundant life. With that flash of imagination came a deep certainty of the purpose and power of God and through this appreciation of the miracle of new birth in nature, his life, too, was transformed. He was flooded with a deep love for God and a desire to serve him with all his heart and soul. He became strongly aware of God's presence with him and he was to spend the rest of his life joyfully practising the presence of God.

Nicholas did not become a recluse but joined a religious order in Paris, known as the Barefooted Carmelites, as a lay brother. It was his job to serve the community in practical ways. For the rest of his life he worked in the kitchens and looked after the needs of his brother monks. Although he still observed periods of prayer and penance he discovered that he could be just as conscious of God's presence working in the kitchen as he was in the chapel. Television documentaries sometimes give us a glimpse of the charged atmosphere in hotel or hospital kitchens. In the midst of so much heat and bustle there are usually frayed tempers and raised voices. But Brother Laurence, as he was now called, felt as serenely conscious of God's presence in the kitchen as he was when alone and remote from noise and commotion. The heat, the banging of pots and pans, the steam and the greasy dishes could not perturb his tranquil spirit. Always, he knew God's presence with him. 'The time of business,' he said, 'does not with me differ from the time of prayer; and in the noise and clatter of my kitchen, while several people are at the same time calling for different things, I possess God in as great tranquillity as if I were upon my knees at the blessed sacrament.'

He did not always succeed in this calm sense of God's nearness, especially at first. 'Lord, I keep failing,' he would say, 'I can't stop myself. But you can stop me and hold me up.' He felt very sure that experiencing God's presence was something that required practice. God is with us always, he believed, but we must learn to recognise his presence in every part of life.

All that we know about Brother Laurence is gleaned from the writings of M. Beaufort, who was Grand Vicar to M. de Chalons. He wrote down some of the conversations he had with Brother Laurence and kept some of the letters he had written, which were later published. M. Beaufort first met Brother Laurence in 1666, some forty years or more after he had entered the monastery. Brother Laurence explained that all he did sprang from love for God. He did not serve God or his brother monks out of a heavy sense of duty or because he was compelled to obey the rules of the order. He found joy and delight, he said, even in picking up litter out of love for God. 'I engaged in a religious life only for the love of God,' he said; 'whatever becomes of me, whether I am lost or saved, I will always continue to act purely for the love of God.'

He believed in speaking to God simply and without any pretence and advised others how to set about prayer. 'Accustom
yourself by degrees thus to worship him, to beg his grace, to offer
him your heart from time to time in the midst of your business,
even every moment if you can.' He admitted that only with God's
help could he hope to live rightly or carry out his tasks.

One day he told M. Beaufort about a recent ordeal he had had
to face. He had been ordered to go to Burgundy, to buy the
monastery wines. He had no head for business and because he
was lame he found that the only way that he could get about on
the boat was by rolling himself over the casks. But instead of
worrying about it, he reminded God that it was God's business he
was about. And God had helped him.

But M. Beaufort's own comments on Brother Laurence tell us
more than anything else about the man himself. He acknowledged
that since Brother Laurence had found such joy in cultivating the
presence of God, it was natural that he should recommend the
practice to others.

> But his example was a stronger inducement than any argu-
> ments he could propose. His very face did good, such a sweet
> and calm devotion appearing in it as could not but affect
> those who saw him. In the greatest hurry of business in
> the kitchen he did each thing with an even, uninterrupted
> composure and tranquillity of spirit.

The bare tree with its promise of coming growth and fruitfulness
became a symbol of Brother Laurence's own life. His soul
blossomed and came into full leaf through the fruitful power of
God's love. Not long before he died he wrote in a letter:

> If in this life we would enjoy the peace of paradise we must
> accustom ourselves to a familiar, humble, affectionate con-
> versation with him . . . I know that to arrive at this state the
> beginning is very difficult, for we must act purely in faith.
> But though it is difficult, we know also that we can do all
> things with the grace of God, which he never refuses to those

who ask it earnestly . . . Pray to him for me as I pray to him for you. I hope to see him quickly. Adieu.

Sister Gillian Orchard IBVM

When I went to visit Sister Gillian Orchard it was a November morning but – a delightful rarity – it was a bright and sunny day. We sat in comfortable, chintz-cushioned, cane chairs on the balcony outside her room. Below us was a pretty little garden that Sister Gillian enjoys looking after; it was hard to believe that we were in the middle of London. The Victorian house where she lives is home to a group of nuns who belong to the Institute of the Blessed Virgin Mary. I began by asking what the IBVM is and how it began and soon discovered that this was a topic very dear to Sister Gillian's heart. So the story of Gillian Orchard became a story within a story.

Mary Ward

I had vaguely imagined that the IBVM was a Victorian foundation, but its chequered history stretches back to the late sixteenth century. Mary Ward was born in Yorkshire into a Catholic family in 1585, at a time when Roman Catholics in England were persecuted and lived precariously. Mary's grandmother spent many years in prison in York because of her faith, and her cousin was sent to prison for two years when she was a teenage bride. As a child, Mary was sent to live with different family households and spent some time with her grandmother, whose piety was a strong influence. Mary was a shy girl, well trained to behave in the submissive manner expected of girls at that time. So it is all the more remarkable that she was prepared to stand against authority in order to do what she believed God was asking of her. Although she was naturally inclined to fall in with others' opinions and decisions, she succeeded in following her vocation. But the word 'succeeded' makes it seem as if her plans were crowned with success. In fact, when she died, her life-work seemed in ruins.

But Sister Gillian Orchard and Sister Lavinia Byrne and many other members of the movement she founded, are living proof that Mary Ward *did* succeed.

When she was still a young girl Mary Ward felt called to the religious life and her first struggle was to refuse the marriage partners urged on her by her parents. She had to wait until she came of age at twenty-one before she was free to make her own choice to take up a religious vocation. But she had misgivings about the cloistered life of a nun. She wrote: 'I could not conceive how a woman in religion could do any good except to herself alone – a meanness that I resented.'

Mary wanted to live a life wholly devoted to God, but she also wanted to help her fellow men and women. To do that she would have to be living in a community where the sisters were free to move around where there was need and the opportunity to help others. Perhaps Mary had been impressed by the example of her aunt and grandmother who had formed a community with a small group of other women who had been imprisoned for their faith. They prayed, cared for the needs of the poor and supported other Catholics who were suffering for their faith. Mary longed to embrace the austerity of a strict religious order which also existed to reach out and help others. No such order existed.

In 1611, following an illness, Mary's thoughts and aims crystal-lised. The kind of religious order she envisaged for women would be on the same lines as the Society of Jesus, founded by St Ignatius of Loyola some seventy years before. But St Ignatius' Jesuit society had been a revolutionary idea. His order went out and about into the community, teaching and relieving need. And what was revolutionary for men was unthinkable for women. How could women possibly be allowed to leave the safety and seclusion of the cloisters, and move around freely to work where they were needed? More outrageous still, Mary Ward wanted them to be under the direction of a woman rather than the customary male superior.

In an endeavour to toe the line and to try out her vocation in a conventional order, Mary went to the Poor Clares in France. But she knew that was not her true calling so with several close companions she set up a religious community, teaching English.

Although she travelled to Rome to try to gain recognition for her institute, based on the same rules as the Society of Jesus, all her efforts failed. Most looked askance at Mary's 'free-range' nuns, called them 'gadabouts,' 'galopping gurles' or 'Jesuitesses' and believed that they needed to be dealt with firmly. After all, they said, they were 'only women'. Mary Ward believed strongly that in God's sight men and women are equal. 'Women too may do great things for God,' she wrote. 'I sincerely hope that women in time to come will do much for the kingdom of God.'

Mary was condemned and imprisoned by the Inquisition as a heretic, and her institute remained officially dead. She returned to England and when she died in 1645 it looked as though her life-work lay in ruins. But the Institute of the Blessed Virgin Mary survived, although it took centuries to be established as Mary had intended. She had founded the order in 1609 but it was not confirmed by the Roman Catholic Church until 1877. Mary Ward was not recognised as its founder until 1909 and it was as recently as 1978 that the institute was at last allowed to adopt the Jesuit constitution, for which Mary Ward had pleaded. Now the IBVM is divided into three closely connected branches and has spread to many countries.

Sister Gillian Orchard

I was deeply interested in Mary Ward's tale, but now I wanted to hear the story of this present-day member of the IBVM. Sister Gillian read English at London University, then taught English, Latin and RE before becoming head of the boarding-school at Ascot, run by the IBVM.

Life was pleasant and orderly, following the busy pattern of the school year. Then one day, in early September 1980, everything changed. Sister Gillian had spent a happy and satisfactory day working in the school garden, tidying, seeing to some autumn pruning and digging with customary enthusiasm. She loved gardening and made the most of her free time for soon the new school year would begin with its usual demands and pressures. But that night she developed severe stomach pain and began to feel desperately sick and ill. She knew that someone would come to enquire next morning if she did not appear at Mass, so she decided to endure the night. She thought she must have appendicitis. Next morning, a sister came to her room and found her so unwell she sent for the doctor straight away. He confirmed the diagnosis of appendicitis and got her off to hospital. But when the surgeon operated he found to his dismay that Sister Gillian had an enormous, malignant tumour which had burst. A senior surgeon was quickly summoned but after long and extensive surgery her life hung in the balance. The medical staff realised that she had very little chance of recovering.

Sister Gillian can remember regaining consciousness some time later to find tubes and monitoring devices attached to her everywhere. But before consciousness returned she had another, vivid experience. This is how she described it. She seemed to be in a place rather like an underground station and there was a long tunnel stretching to her left. As she looked along it, she could see light – light of a beautiful quality, very bright and warm. Then she looked to her right, and there was another tunnel stretching into the distance in the opposite direction. But within this tunnel was blackness, complete darkness.

In her dream or vision, whichever it may have been, she knew that she had a choice. If she wished, she could choose to take the path of the beautiful tunnel with its warmth and light. Or she could choose to go along the dark tunnel. She could choose – yet she was aware that in another sense she was not entirely free. It was as if she was being drawn towards the dark tunnel. 'I have a choice,' she thought, 'but have I?'

She was choosing yet she was not making the choice. If she chose the dark tunnel, where she felt that she was being drawn, she would be acting entirely by faith – going into the unknown dark. But she also knew within herself that if she chose to go the way of the dark tunnel it would not mean that she had rejected the tunnel of light. Somehow she was aware that the other, beautiful tunnel would still be there, waiting for her, when she was ready for it and her time had come.

She chose the dark tunnel – or it was chosen for her? – and she returned to the world of the living. It took two years of chemotherapy and radiotherapy before she recovered. She endured nausea and sickness, hair loss and the utter weakness of convalescence after serious cancer. After two more years as head of the school she resigned to become chaplain to two IBVM schools. Her counsel and spiritual direction extend much further. She felt sure that there was more work for her to do and part of that has been – and still is – to make Mary Ward's writings accessible to the world today. Her journal and letters cannot be easily understood in their Shakespearean English and with their Latinate construction. But Sister Gillian believes that what she has to say is important and still relevant so she is rendering her writings into contemporary English for today's readers.

Sister Gillian told me how her illness has changed her. Before she was ill she was extremely fit, with a healthy person's slight impatience with illness in others. Now, she believes, she is not 'ruthlessly efficient' as she describes herself as having once been but softened by her experience of illness.

She herself has passed through all the stages of pain, loss, anger, and grief so she can be gentle and understanding with others who are suffering. 'In the last few years,' she told me with utter conviction: 'as I look back on my illness, I see it as all gift.'

5

The Bible

Many people dismiss the Bible as untrue, insist that it presents a vengeful and warlike God and maintain that it is totally irrelevant today. They have probably never read it. For those who decide that they will read it and see for themselves, it's probably best to start off with a translation that gives us the Bible in the kind of language we use today (for example, *Today's English Version* or the *Contemporary English Version)*. In order to understand it we also need to recognise that although the Bible is a unity, it is made up of a whole library of books by many different authors. Not all of them are in the same genre, or written in the same style. Some of it is poetry, some letters, some narrative and so on. The New Testament writings are nearly two thousand years old, the Old Testament much earlier still. But although much has changed in the centuries between, human nature is the same. The men and women in the Bible experience jealousy, love, anger, kindness and ambition – the same emotions that we feel now. They suffered the pain of broken families, knew loss as well as happiness, mourned and celebrated as we do today. The Bible rings true.

The Bible has often been called God's Word. People have believed – and still believe – that the Bible is one of the important ways in which God has spoken to men and women right down the ages to today. We see that in even more of the stories in this book than appear in this section.

John Jeffery

John works for the United Bible Societies, a worldwide group of Bible societies that aim to produce and publish the Bible in many countries where it is not easily available. The headquarters of the British Bible Society has an amazing stock of stories about the effect of reading the Bible on all kinds of people. So I rang them up to see what they could tell me and they suggested that I should talk to John. I arranged to phone him one evening when the children were safely in bed, so that he could tell me his own story.

John's father was killed in World War II, so he was brought up in the southwest of England by his widowed mother. He had no brothers or sisters, but there was a supportive network of grandparents and other family members. His mother was religious and John went through all the normal church rites and rituals, but ended up with nothing more than a nominal faith in God. When he was seventeen there was a huge upheaval in his life. Like plenty of other young people, before settling down to a university course John decided to work with Voluntary Service Overseas, and was directed to Africa. His arrival coincided with the terrible aftermath of the Biafran War. Some of us still remember the harrowing films of starving children that appeared on our television screens. It was the first time that comfortable, well-off viewers in the West had witnessed such scenes of destitution and many people were deeply distressed. John, on the spot, was shaken to the core. He saw sick children dying, when a shilling's worth of medicine could have saved their lives. He remembered all the teaching he'd imbibed that God is love and he turned in anger on that God and cursed him for his cruelty and indifference. That was the end, for John, of any faith he had ever had in God.

When he came back to the UK and went up to university, he felt as if the backbone had gone from his life. With no framework of faith – however nominal – to sustain him, he looked for some kind of spiritual experience and relief in drugs. He got in with a like-minded crowd and began smoking cannabis, then took LSD and amphetamines. In due course he completed his time at university, got his degree and began a career in teaching.

One night, as he was driving south to visit his mother, his car was stopped by police for a routine random check. Unfortunately he and his two passengers were smoking cannabis, and when they realised this the police searched John and found him in illegal possession of heroin. He was put in a police cell and appeared next day before Worcester magistrates. They were unsympathetic and all the harder on him because he was a respectable teacher who they thought should know better. Although it was a first offence, he was sentenced to eighteen months in prison. He was put in a strip cell and left alone to suffer the pains of withdrawal. He knew his career was at an end; his only friends now were other drug users.

John came out of prison after twelve months and spent his discharge pay on heroin. But when he was told that his mother was seriously ill he made his way to her home. He found her dying of cancer with only a short time to live. She pleaded with John to give up drugs. She told him that she wanted to show him that it *could* be done and to do so she herself went without the painkilling drugs prescribed for her. He witnessed the way in which she was voluntarily enduring the pain, because, she said, she wanted to show him how much she cared and to prove that he could kick the habit. She begged him to promise to give up drugs and he gave her his word that he would. But when, soon afterwards, she died, the first thing he did was to lock himself in the toilet and give himself a shot of heroin.

There was no incentive left now for John to change his lifestyle. He quickly became a homeless junkie, constantly being picked up by the police. One day he came to and found himself in hospital in intensive care. The horrible truth was that his best friend had given him heroin that had been cut with warfarin, which is an anticoagulant, with disastrous results. He was on a life-support machine and there were police waiting at the bedside. When a doctor appeared he told John that his right arm would have to be amputated as gangrene had set in. He was sympathetic but he insisted that because John was a junkie it was impossible to give him any drugs to relieve his pain. Before he left he handed him a Gideon New Testament. John would gladly have hurled it back at him if he had been able.

The night that followed was the darkest of John's life. He had suffered the loss of everything that was dear to him and now his right arm was to go. He cried in bitterness of spirit, weeping for all that he had already lost and all that he was going to lose. He was not sorry for what he had done but sad for himself and the misery he was enduring. For the first time since he had cursed God in Africa, John cried out to God for help. After that, he felt strangely at peace and he slept.

Next day the surgeon found that they only needed to amputate two fingers – his right arm was saved. But as soon as he was well enough to leave hospital he went straight to prison. Because he was so bored he decided to pass the time by attending the Bible study meetings that were held for prisoners. Someone let him have a modern version of the Bible and as he began to read it, the verses seemed to leap from the page and take hold of him. He read words that he remembered from Isaiah 41:10: 'Do not be afraid – I am with you! I am your God – let nothing terrify you! I will make you strong and help you; I will protect you and save you.'

It was on Christmas Eve as he was reading from the Bible that the words seemed to meet his own situation and needs directly. He knew then that Jesus was real, that he was alive and that he could trust him utterly for everything he needed. John told me that when he describes it all like that, he realises that his spiritual journey may sound easier than it has actually been. It was very hard at times, he remembers. But when he looks back John can see only God's love. He can see too how God has confirmed his first, tentative steps into Christian faith. He told me about the complete transformation in his life and the joy of a happy marriage and now two sons. He has a satisfying job, too, helping to bring the Bible to people worldwide so that the words that brought him new life can do the same for others too.

Sometimes John travels overseas for United Bible Societies. One day, back in Africa, he was overseeing the unloading of a consignment of Bibles to a particular tribe and he saw a different kind of hunger from the famine he witnessed as a young man. Three lorries arrived at the same time. One brought food aid, another clothes and the third was the lorry with its load of Bibles. To John's amazement the biggest crowd was around the lorry dispensing Bibles. Yet these people who were queuing up were hungry and only half-clad. He asked one African why it was they chose Bibles instead of food and clothes. 'We are used to struggles,' the man replied. 'We have had to manage often without food and without clothing. But this book gives us hope!'

Pitcairn Islanders

When Fletcher Christian and his band of mutineers had dispatched Captain Bligh and eighteen others in the ship's small boat, they themselves headed back by common consent to Tahiti, that island where they had spent idyllic days of leisure and love. Under Captain Bligh's orders, as we saw in Chapter 4, *Bounty* had landed there and stayed for twenty-three weeks, while they potted up the breadfruit plants they had come to collect and waited for them to take root.

The men had enjoyed unparalleled days of self-indulgence on Tahiti – with sun, food and women – and could not wait to return to such a life. In fact, when the *Bounty*, sailing now under Fletcher Christian's command, arrived back in Tahiti, sixteen of the twenty-five mutineers decided to stay there permanently. Meanwhile, the remaining crew collected their chosen Tahitian 'wives'. They also persuaded half a dozen Polynesian men to go with them, accompanied by wives too. These men had no idea that they were going to be treated like slaves by their English captors.

The *Bounty* sailed on for four months and covered almost three thousand miles, before the mutineers found an island which suited their purpose. The mutineers' greatest dread at this stage was that they might be discovered by a passing British ship and brought back to England for trial and almost certain hanging. Pitcairn Island seemed ideal; it was deserted, it had no natural harbour or landing place and was so remote that it was hardly noted on maps. It was inaccessible for days on end when the weather was rough. Even so, for some long time after their arrival, the mutineers stationed one man on watch from a hill-top. They butchered the dogs on board in case their barking might attract attention on the rare occasions when a ship passed close.

After they had unloaded the *Bounty* they were uncertain what to do with the ship. Might it give away their presence on the island? But the matter was decided for them when one of the crew, Matthew Quintal, set fire to the carpenter's storeroom. Soon the *Bounty* was blazing from bow to stern. The sailors watched, horrified, knowing that now they would be permanently cut off from civilisation. They were not just free to begin a new and different life; they now had no choice in the matter.

Gradually they began to create a village, selecting a level area screened from the sea by a line of trees. For a couple of years all went well as they planted saplings, and cared for stock – sharing the pigs they had on board between them. But the British sailors treated the Tahitian men they had brought with them so harshly that they began to plot revenge on their white captors. One day, by stealth and cunning, they attacked the unsuspecting mutineers and within an hour four of them, including Fletcher Christian himself, were murdered. The trouble did not end there; there were reprisals and the murder and bloodshed continued. Four years after the *Bounty's* arrival, only four of the original fifteen who had landed on Pitcairn Island were still alive. But eleven women survived, so babies were born and numbers increased. But within nine years there had been twelve murders and one suicide. Anger and violence were stoked by the home-brewed alcohol they drank freely.

At length only two of the original mutineers were left alive – Neddy Young and John Adams (AKA Alex Smith). Neddy Young realised that he was dying, but he took time and trouble to teach the unlettered Adams to read. They possessed only two books, both of which they had unloaded from the *Bounty* – one was a Bible and the other a prayer book. Adams succeeded in learning to read before Young died in 1800 and he went on reading the Bible. He also went on distilling spirits. One day when he was drunk he had a vision of the Archangel Gabriel, so he believed, poised to attack him with a dart. The dream badly frightened Adams and he began to take to heart the things he was reading in the Bible. He became painfully aware that the wrong deeds he had committed were sins against God. The words of the Bible began to change him. The more he read, the more he determined he was to live in the light of what the Bible had to say. He also decided to teach the Bible to the new generation of Pitcairners. He held church services on a Sunday and as he had some vague recollection of Ash Wednesday and Good Friday being fast days, he decided to be on the safe side and make every Wednesday and Friday fast days for the islanders. It is easy to ridicule Adams' patriarchal role and his over-puritanical piety, but the island was transformed. The population of drunken, murderous ruffians became an ordered, law-abiding and courteous community.

When eventually two British frigates did visit the island, it was decided not to extradite Adams to face trial in England. The officers' report to the authorities stated:

> his exemplary conduct and fatherly care of the whole little colony, would not but command admiration. The pious manner in which all those born on the island have been reared, the correct sense of religion which has been instilled into their young minds by this old man, has given him the pre-eminence over the whole of them, to whom they look up as the father of the whole and one family.

Fyodor Dostoevsky

I still remember, probably fifty years ago, reading Dostoevsky's *The Brothers Karamazov* for the first time. I was so absorbed that I was completely unaware that my train had reached the terminus. I remained in my seat, riveted by Dostoevsky's brilliant story-telling, which seemed more real than the London around me.

Dostoevsky was born in Moscow in 1821. One of his earliest memories is of being held in his mother's arms before the altar of the village church. A dove flew in through the open window, fluttered in the incense-laden air, then flew out of the window on the other side. The small child stretched out towards it, exclaiming, in delight, 'A dove! A dove!' But his mother was dead by the time he was sixteen and two years later his father was murdered.

Dostoevsky' life was packed and fraught with emotion. He seemed to exist on a rollercoaster ride of misery and ecstasy. He was a compulsive gambler and was constantly in debt – often surviving on advances for his next piece of writing, which could never be delivered by the time he had promised. Increasingly frequent attacks of epilepsy added to his anxiety and disquiet. He cared deeply about the sufferings of others and discerned goodness and humanity even in depraved wrongdoers. After training at military engineering school – a highly unsuitable career for someone of his temperament – he was enrolled as a draughtsman in government service. But he did not stay there for long. He knew that his real work in life was to write.

He mixed with a group of socialists – men who questioned the established order and even ventured to criticise the Tsar himself – and although he listened to them and read their writings, he was not himself a political animal. But his movements became known and one morning in the early hours he was arrested and taken to the headquarters of the political police, to join others of his friends who had been arrested too. After weeks of solitary confinement, Dostoevsky was told that along with fourteen others, he had been sentenced to capital punishment by shooting. What he and his fellow condemned did *not* know, was that a high court had recommended to the Tsar that the sentence be commuted. Instead, Dostoevsky was to serve eight years' hard labour in Siberia, followed by military service.

But the Tsar had a fine sense of his own importance and decided to extract every ounce of high drama from the situation. He ordered that the prisoners' sentences *should* be commuted but that the prisoners should not be told. All would go forward as if for execution and the reprieve would be announced only at the very last moment.

There followed the most traumatic experience of Dostoevsky's whole life. On 22 December 1849 he, along with the other condemned men, was woken, dressed in the thin clothes he had worn when he was arrested and taken in a closed coach to a parade ground in a town a few miles away. When the prisoners alighted they could see the sun, a great red ball of fire. People on foot came hurrying to the scene and soldiers stood ready in the square.

A priest, dressed in funeral vestments, told the prisoners to follow him and led them through the deep snow up to a temporary scaffold where they stood in two uneven lines, shivering in their thin clothes. Then a court clerk read out in mumbling tones the charges and sentence on each – 'condemned to capital punishment by shooting'. When the clerk had finished the priest stepped forward to preach the funeral sermon. Then Dostoevsky, with the others, knelt to kiss the cross.

The prisoners were given shrouds to wear – long-sleeved, hooded shirts – and the first three – Dostoevsky stood sixth – were led from the scaffold and tied to three posts. Their hoods were put over their faces. Fifteen soldiers took up their position fifteen paces away, facing the condemned men with rifles at the ready. The order was given: 'Ready, aim!' followed by a roll of drums. As the drum sounded, the rifles were lowered and the men's hoods pulled up. At the same moment a government official leapt from his coach flourishing a piece of paper – the reprieve! The Emperor's little tragi-farce had been played out and the announcement was now made that the Tsar in his great mercy had commuted their sentence to hard labour.

Some of the men threw themselves on their knees, blessing the good Tsar. Several were so traumatised and humiliated by the sham proceedings that they wished they had actually been shot. Dostoevsky felt utterly drained of all emotion.

At midnight on Christmas Eve Dostoevsky's legs were clamped into irons weighing ten pounds in preparation for the journey to Siberia and he was dressed in convicts' clothing. Prisoners were often forced to make the journey on foot but Dostoevsky and his fellow-prisoners were taken by open sleigh, while the bells rang out for Christmas Day.

But when they halted at a transit camp he was met with kindness. Some well-born ladies made it their charitable work to try to relieve the needs of prisoners on their way to labour camp. When Dostoevsky and his fellow-prisoners left to continue the journey, the ladies actually came to say goodbye and see them off. One of them gave Dostoevsky a New Testament. It was all that he had to read in his new brutal surroundings and it brought him that reality of a spiritual world that he desperately needed to experience. He kept it by him for the rest of his life, bequeathing it on his deathbed to his child, Fedya.

As Dostoevsky read the Gospel stories he recognised himself in the men and women who crowded the pages and whose encounters with Christ brought healing, freedom and life. He knew moments of doubt and despair but he also experienced times of lucid calm when he felt infinite love and compassion for his fellow-prisoners. Later he wrote, 'I have composed within myself a confession of faith in which everything is clear and holy for me. This confession is very simple. Here it is: to believe that there is nothing more beautiful, more profound, more sympathetic, more reasonable, more manly, and more perfect than Christ.' In Dostoevsky's last novel, *The Brothers Karamazov*, one of the characters says: 'It is impossible for a convict to be without God.' He himself had found that to be so.

Martin Luther

Martin Luther was born on 10 November, 1483 in Eisleben, and baptised next day – St Martin's Day. In fifteenth-century Germany it was the older sons who were sent out into the world, while the youngest son stayed at home and inherited the farm. So Martin's father Hans, with his new wife Margaret, had left Eisenach in Thuringia, where his parents and grandparents had been peasants, and set out for the county of Mansfeld. There Hans got work as a miner, and although in later years he became a respected and important citizen, while Martin was young the family lived in deep poverty. Martin could remember seeing his mother carrying wood from the forest on her back, to keep their fire burning.

As well as being very poor, his parents were very strict, even harsh. Martin recalled,

My father once whipped me so severely that I fled from him, and it was hard for him to win me back . . . My mother once beat me until the blood flowed, for having stolen a miserable nut. It was this strict discipline which finally

forced me into the monastery, although they meant heartily
well by it.

When he was old enough to attend the village school, life was
not much easier. Martin learned to write and speak Latin from
'ignorant and brutal' teachers. 'The examination was like a trial
for murder,' he recalled. From there he went, at thirteen, to a school
run by a religious brotherhood and by the time he was old enough
to go to university his father could afford to send his promising
son to Leipzig. After graduating Martin began to study law as his
father had wished, but after only two months he gave it up to
become a monk at the Augustinian monastery in Erfurt. His father
was most upset but Martin insisted that he had been warned to do
so by a heavenly vision and stuck to his decision. When he
was twenty-four he was ordained priest but continued studying
theology.

On top of stringent studying, Martin planned a strict regime
for himself. He deliberately endured cold and went without food
until he fainted from weakness and hunger. His upbringing
and his training had made him believe that God was harsh and
demanding. 'When I looked for Christ it seemed to me as if I saw
the devil,' was how he described it later. God seemed fearsome
and unapproachable and he felt himself to be deeply sinful. When
the time came for him to conduct his first Mass he was terrified at
the thought of having to speak to God direct, without any mediator.
Luther was an Augustinian monk and St Augustine had laid great
emphasis on reading the Bible, although not many monks of the
order followed that rule. But Martin did, and although his superiors
did not approve he carried on just the same and came to love the
Bible. He found Augustine's own writings gave him some comfort
too. But he was still overwhelmed by the sense of his own
wickedness and terrified by the harsh, authoritarian God he had
been taught to believe in.

Luther's next move was to the newly founded university at
Wittenberg where he had been appointed by one of his own tutors
and friends to teach philosophy. He used to sit reading in his cell
high up in the tower and it was there that he first read and took
note of the Bible verse that was to change his life – and the lives

of millions of others too. He had begun reading Paul's Epistle to the Romans and came to the verse: 'The righteous will live by faith' (Romans 1:17). The more he pondered on the verse the more he began to realise that the very foundations on which he had built his religion were false. He did not have to achieve a mountain of good works in order to be acceptable to a demanding God. Instead, he had to respond to God in faith or trust, counting on God's freely given love to make him accepted.

But this new understanding of God and of the grounds on which God would accept him did not dawn on Luther all at once. When he was chosen to accompany another Augustinian monk on a visit to Rome, he went sightseeing with all the enthusiasm of a typical tourist while his superior conducted his business. Luther described himself as a 'foolish pilgrim', believing everything he was told. And there were some tall stories going around. In one shrine there was a flight of twenty-eight steps, said to be the very stairway that had been in Pilate's judgment hall in Jerusalem in Jesus's day. Pope Leo IV had granted an indulgence of nine years for every step climbed by a pilgrim on his knees, saying the appointed prayers. (An indulgence was a pardon, absolving the pilgrim from doing penance for his sins and letting him off time in purgatory.) According to the story Luther's son used to tell, his father began enthusiastically to climb these steps on his knees, repeating the obligatory prayers, when he suddenly remembered the verse from Romans. So he hastily got up from his knees and hurried down the stairs he had so laboriously climbed.

Luther became a doctor of divinity and took up the post of Professor of Divinity at the newly established University of Wittenberg in 1518. He lectured on the Epistle to the Romans for three terms. It was during this time that he began to work out the full implications of his new-found understanding of how a person can be right with God. He believed that a person is justified – or put into right relation with God – through a response of faith or trust alone, not by attempting to be good or pay for indulgences. As well as lecturing, Luther began to preach and his sermons were spell-binding.

Trouble came when Luther began to upset the established order. His attitude to indulgences put the authority of Pope and Church in question and threatened to cut off a fruitful source of income. So-called indulgences had begun with the Crusades. In order to encourage people to fight in the Crusades, the Popes offered freedom from doing penance for sins and, later, time off purgatory. Later still that offer was extended to anyone who met the costs of a Crusader. By Luther's time, money given to a number of church causes was said to relieve the donor from penance and time in purgatory – which could be claimed either for themselves or on behalf of dead relatives. Church agents were employed to sell indulgences and some – like Tetzel, who came from near Witten-berg – were unscrupulous. Luther made no bones about preaching against the practice, then advertised a debate about the matter and nailed up his ninety-five theses on the subject to the church door. The Pope decided to 'quiet that man, for newly kindled flames are easily quenched'.

Luther was given sixty days to recant but instead he lighted a bonfire and burned the papal bull and canon law, which set out the practice of indulgences. He had done nothing to help his cause and he was duly excommunicated. When Charles, the new emperor, officiated at his first diet, or court session, at Worms, in 1521, Luther was formally questioned.

The long proceedings were neatly summarised by Luther – who had a splendid sense of humour – in a letter to his artist friend, Carnach: 'All they said was: "Are these books yours?" – "Yes." – "Will you recant?" – "No!" – "Then get out." '

Not only did Luther hear God speak to *him* through the Bible but he translated the Bible into readily understood German so that ordinary people with no scholarship could understand it too. 'I try to speak as men do in the marketplace,' he explained. But it was not always easy to 'clear the sticks and stones out of the way' as he put it and make the Bible accessible. 'Good heavens!' he exclaimed, 'how hard it is to make the Hebrew prophets speak German!' But he also modestly commented, 'In rendering Moses I make him so German that no one would know he was a Jew.'

Martin Luther brought the Bible to many thousands of people in his own lifetime and for centuries after. He believed that the Bible was supremely important. 'We must make great difference,' he said, 'between God's Word and the word of man . . . The Word of God is greater than heaven and earth, yea, greater than death and hell, for it forms part of the power of God, and endures everlastingly; we should, therefore, diligently study God's Word, and know and assuredly believe that God himself speaks unto us.'

6

Angels

'Angels, and belief in angels, are no longer taboo.' That is the opinion of Emma Heathcote, of the theology department at Birmingham University, who is researching 'angel experiences'. In fact, belief and interest in angels seem to be growing, judging by the spate of books, films and television programmes about them. I'm told that more than two million people to date have visited 'Angel Ring', a collection of angel sites on the World Wide Web.

The word 'angel' means messenger and in the Bible angels are God's messengers – sometimes in the form of overwhelmingly brilliant, heavenly beings, but sometimes having the appearance of very ordinary men or women. Their tasks are to carry out God's commands and also to take care of those who belong to God. That description can apply to the heavenly beings we think of as angels but also to men and women who carry out God's work on earth. Sometimes it's hard to tell the difference between the heavenly and the earthly angels. The Bible has accounts of angels whose dazzling brightness terrified their beholders – such as the shepherds on the Bethlehem hills – but also describes visitors in 'plain clothes', who turned out to be supernatural beings with important messages from God.

The writer of one of the letters in the New Testament tells his readers to give hospitality to strangers because in so doing they may well find that they have 'entertained angels unawares'. God's messengers certainly seem to come in all shapes and forms.

John Jeffery

John, whose story is told elsewhere in this book, works for the United Bible Societies. A few years ago he travelled to Kenya on their behalf. While he was there he was free to take time off to visit a cultural centre with his son and the friend who had come with him. Poor roads and the condition of many of the cars made driving difficult and perilous. After their visit, they left the centre and drove to the T-junction where they would join the main road but a continuous stream of traffic kept them waiting on the minor road for a very long time. At last a welcome gap in the line of cars gave John the chance to swing out into the main road. But at that very moment a large black man in Swahili dress stepped out into the road in front of them and held up his hand to stop John moving forward. He was smiling broadly at them, but John, naturally aggrieved, swore at him. He just smiled back at them, but by the time he stepped aside the long line of traffic had resumed and John was left to wait once again.

At last there was another gap and John joined the steady procession of cars making for town. But a little further down the road they saw the aftermath of a horrific accident. In the mass of buckled metal John recognised a car that had moved into the gap John's car would have filled, but for the intervention of the smiling man. If he had not intercepted them, the boys and John himself would have been tragically involved in the pile-up. John is convinced that the person he cursed unawares was an angel, who saved his life and the lives of the two boys with him.

Ron Newby

Ron grew up in the industrial northwest of England and began his working life as an apprentice in a big chemical firm whose plant dominated the area. He attended Sunday school as a young child and later joined a church where an elderly couple had been responsible for much of the work. When they retired and moved to a seaside town they invited Ron for a week's holiday. During

the week, as he took a stroll along the front, he came to a beach
hut where an elderly man was sitting. Ron thought it strange to
find him there because it was a cold blustery day outside the
holiday season. But he stopped when the old man seemed to want
to talk with him. A Bible was resting on the man's knee and as he
looked keenly at Ron he said: 'I have a verse from the Bible to
give to you.' Ron listened as the old man read out: 'Take this child
and nurse it for me.' He thanked him automatically and walked
on, mystified.

Ron knew enough Bible stories to recognise where the quoted
verse came from. They were the words of Pharaoh's daughter to
the woman who was Moses' mother. The princess had rescued the
baby Moses from the bulrushes in Egypt and was looking for
someone to care for him. But the words coming from the old man
and quoted to a young lad seemed utterly bizarre and irrelevant.
Ron decided that the person he had encountered was probably a
bit confused. But he did not forget those strange words in the
years that followed.

Ron soon left the chemical plant and began work in a children's
home. One of a large family, he had always looked after his own
little brothers and sisters and was glad to look after other children
too. After many twists and turns he sat for exams, gained a degree
and qualified in social work. He was regularly promoted and
finally reached a very senior position in a leading children's
charitable society.

One day a missionary nurse in his home church talked to the
youth group Ron led about the needs of an orphanage in North
Africa. Ron and the youngsters decided on a sponsored walk to
raise funds for it and there, he supposed, the matter would rest.
But he gradually became more involved in the work. Then, some
time later, a horrifying television news footage showed the plight
of children in Ethiopia. Ron was deeply distressed and phoned up
a well-known charity, begging them to do something to help. Their
reply was: 'We're stretched to capacity. *You* do something about
it.'

Ron had experience and expertise in management as well as
childcare. But to plunge into organising Christian aid himself
was a big step. Then, all at once, the words of the old man from

many years before seemed to come home to him. They sounded remarkably like the voice of God. 'Take this child and nurse it for me.' He felt certain that God was asking him to look after abandoned and needy children. So, with his kitchen table as his only office equipment, Ron began the work of Global Care, which, mainly through Ron's tireless efforts, has now reached out to meet the desperate need of children in very many countries of the world. But Ron has never forgotten the personal emphasis – 'Take *this* child . . .' Every individual child matters to him. The motto of Global Care has been from the beginning: 'We can't change the world, but we can make the world of change to one child.'

Ron has changed his mind about the strange old man in the beach hut on a cold day at the seaside years before. He was not mad. Ron is convinced now that he saw and spoke with an angel.

The Angel of the North

The largest statue to date in the United Kingdom and probably the largest man-made angel in the world towers from its hill-top site over the gateway to Tyneside in the northeast of England. Its outstretched wings welcome the ninety thousand motorists a day that pass by on the A1 road and it can also be clearly seen by travellers on the nearby railway line. The Angel of the North is as tall as four double-decker buses and has a wingspan bigger than a Boeing 757. It was the work of the sculptor Antony Gormley and the construction was carried out by a firm of steelworkers in nearby Hartlepool. It is made of a special weather-resistant steel which contains copper. In time the surface will oxidise to form a patina, which will increasingly give the Angel warmth and a rich, red-brown colour.

The sculptor believes that those who see the Angel should be free to interpret its meaning for themselves but there are many ways in which the Angel of the North will reflect and symbolise both the past and present of that area. The hill top where it stands covers disused mine workings and the Angel is a visible symbol of the hidden toil and courage of the men who mined there. The industry of the north, demonstrated in steel, shipbuilding and coal, represents one facet of the indomitable spirit of humankind. But the Angel stands sentinel over more than the industrial life of the region. All around and to the north lie relics of the Celtic faith of past generations. This is the country of Cuthbert and Caedmon, Hilda and Bede. The Angel also celebrates the deep and precious heritage of Christian faith in Britain.

When Antony Gormley spoke about the angel he was planning, he said: 'The face will not have individual features. The effect of the piece is in the alertness, the awareness of space and the gesture of the wings – to give a sense of embrace.'

One of the people who lives in Gateshead told me about his own feelings for the Angel. He remembers the day he moved to Gateshead. It was a dark, winter morning and the rain was falling. As he approached the spot where the Angel now stands, he wondered why on earth he was coming to live there. It all seemed so bleak and forsaken. That was five or six years ago and now, in the course of work, he often passes the same spot. But now the Angel stands there, wings outstretched, and for him, it has made all the difference. 'Nearly always there are two or three people standing close to the Angel, often holding out their own arms as they mirror the Angel's protective gesture. And when I see the Angel, I feel that I belong and that it is welcoming me home.'

Not everyone approves of the Angel and not everyone who sees it will agree that it has spiritual significance. But many believe that the Angel of the North symbolises the spiritual world that can protect and embrace us all, interpenetrating the world of men and women. We belong both to the spiritual world and the everyday, material world and the Angel of the North reminds us that the two worlds can and frequently do flow together.

William Lester

When I talked to the Rev. William Lester over the transatlantic telephone, he sounded at least twenty years younger than his self-confessed eighty-three years. He told me the good news that he was to be married the following month – to the sister of his late wife. He sounded a brisk, no-nonsense man, with both feet firmly on the ground, yet the story he had to tell me makes sense only in terms of a spiritual world. He believes that there is such a world and that it touches and intermingles with our own very closely indeed.

William Lester is a minister in the Presbyterian Church. (Although he has been officially retired for eighteen years, he still has the pastorate of a small church.) When he was a young man he worked with the inter-denominational Latin America Mission with headquarters in Costa Rica, and went as a missionary to Colombia. He ran a small Bible institute in the town of Sincelejo, where there were no more than about eleven students at the time. Every weekend the students would go out on preaching missions to the small surrounding towns. Monday was their day off, so many of them travelled back to the institute that day. One Monday a student returning home had to change buses at Corozel. But unfortunately for him, there was no transport going his way. The place was packed with people making their way in the opposite direction, to go to the bull-fight. The student decided to make the most of the time on his hands and began to give out tracts – small leaflets about the Christian gospel. One was taken by a man very much the worse for drink. He also admitted that he could not read. But he took the tract that was offered and stuffed it into his pocket. And that was probably the end of that as far as the student would have guessed.

But the man remembered the leaflet and asked his brother-in-law to read it to him. They read it through together and decided that they would like to get hold of a Bible to find out more. Once they had a Bible, a little group began to collect to listen to the brother-in-law reading from it. But they had to admit that they could not understand much of it even when it was read out to them. So they sent to the Bible institute, asking for someone to come over and explain this new teaching to them. William Lester went himself, once a week, talking to them as they crammed inside the crude hut with its bamboo walls. There were empty holes for windows and door, so the pigs and chickens joined the forty to fifty people who crowded around to listen to him. The fifty grew to sixty or seventy interested listeners, but by this time the brother-in-law began to object to the informal meetings and refused to read the Bible to them any more. A small splinter group began to oppose Lester and one night in particular they made their animosity very clear.

When the little meeting was over for that night, William Lester and the student he had brought with him got into their car to drive back to the institute. Suddenly they screeched to a halt. Just in time they had seen a large tree lying across the road, right in their path. They got out, and with a machete they cut up the tree and carted the pieces of wood out of the main roadway. Then, without more ado, they continued safely on their way home.

It was at least a year later when things began to happen in the small town. People began to change. As William Lester put it, 'God began to work.' It was then that one of the men came up to William Lester.

'I want to tell you I'm sorry,' he began. 'I tried to kill you – and I would have done so if you had not had so many men with you.'

Lester was completely baffled and asked the man to tell him when all this happened.

'Don't you remember?' the man asked him. 'One evening as you were going home in your car, you came across a tree right across the road. I put that tree there in order to stop you. I knew you would have to get out to move the tree and that was when we planned to kill you. But when we saw how many men you had with you we did not dare to touch you.'

'But there were no men with us,' Lester insisted, 'there was only me and my student.'

But the man shook his head vigorously. 'But we all saw them clearly,' he insisted. 'There must have been eight or ten of them and they were the tallest men we ever saw. They were dressed in white. But what we could not understand,' he went on, 'was what happened to them. You see, the moment you and your student got back into the car, those tall men in white disappeared. We never saw them again. But they saved your lives.'

Anne Hobbs

Anne is a friend of mine who, with her husband, heads up a Christian organisation that runs weekend seminars for marriage enrichment. Her parents were not churchgoers and she did not have a religious upbringing, but they did send her to Sunday school, although when she was about twelve she drifted away and didn't go to church again. But she was an avid reader, so as a young child she spent happy hours in her bedroom at the top of the house, reading what was available, which was the Bible and a well-thumbed set of children's encyclopaedias. Both thrilled and fascinated her.

We were sitting comfortably together in my living-room the other day when she told me about the angels in her life. Anne was only seventeen when she became ill and a brain tumour was diagnosed. The blackouts and other symptoms she was experiencing made that the most obvious diagnosis.

'One day,' she told me, 'I was actually in the doctor's surgery when I passed out. The next thing I knew, I woke up to find myself alone in a tiny room in the hospital. The doctor had called an ambulance and there I was, so ill and exhausted that I didn't even know whether I wanted to go on fighting whatever was making me feel so ill. I really can't tell you whether I fell asleep again after that, or whether I slipped into unconsciousness. But I do vividly remember the dream – if it was a dream – that came to me then. I was being carried in the arms of someone I knew to be an angel.'

'How did you *know* it was an angel?' I asked her.

'I just knew, without being told,' she answered. 'The angel didn't have wings, but we were flying out of the hot, stuffy atmosphere of the hospital room into clear, fresh air; and we were flying towards a light. I wish I knew how to describe that light. Usually light is something you experience only with your sense of sight. This light was extraordinarily brilliant and somehow I was perceiving it with every one of my senses. I didn't just *see* it – I could smell it, hear it . . . It was wonderful, wholly desirable, and every part of me, my whole being, reached out towards it. I was tempted just to relax and to allow myself to be carried on towards that light. But there was a part of me that resisted. Because in spite of the absolute beauty of that light, there was something awesome and terrible about it too. And then, I was so young! I was engaged to be married and I wanted a bit of happiness before I died. I talked to the angel who was carrying me: "I'm too young," I told the angel, "I don't want to die yet – just let me get married and have a few years of happiness and I promise I'll devote my life to God." Then I woke up or came to. And from that time I gradually began to recover. It wasn't immediate, but the blackouts and the sickness grew less and less, until, quite soon, I was completely better. But I didn't keep my promise to devote my life to God – not then and not until many years and many events later. Yet that experience changed my life for ever, I think. I learned to enjoy the present, not to count on the future. And everything – the beauty of spring and summer – all seemed precious and important because I had learned that life can be brief – nothing can be taken for granted.'

'I think there has been another angel in my life,' Anne went on. 'Do you think a dog could be an angel?' Then Anne told me the story of the angel-dog called Kim.

'It was a particularly difficult time in my life. My marriage had broken down and I was left on my own to bring up two small children, aged seven and a half and six years old. I also had to earn enough to support them, so I decided to go to college to become a teacher. I had no family anywhere near me so no one to turn to for help. But there was another young mum along the road and she became a good friend. We would look after each other's children.

'One evening, after dark, I was going along to this friend's house to collect my children – she'd been looking after them for me. Suddenly, a man loomed up out of the darkness, and stood in front of me. He said, "You never notice me, but I see you." Then, to my horror, he began to tell me all the places I'd been to in the last few days. It was terrifying – he'd got it all right. He knew so much about me and my movements, and he was right – I hadn't even noticed him.

'I was very shaken when I arrived at my friend's house and I told her about it. I was still frightened when I walked the children home so I prayed, then I put them to bed and tried to get on with my studies. But I knew I was very vulnerable and I felt so alone.

'It was midnight a few nights later and I was in bed, when I heard drunken singing in the front garden. I looked out and it was the same man singing under the window. What shook me was the fact that he was singing that song, "Here's to you, Mrs Robinson" – you see, my name then was Robinson. Well, I threw some water over him and he went away.

'A few days later I got home from college just after the children had got back. They were clearly frightened. They said that a man had knocked loudly at the door and pushed open the letterbox to shout through to them. He'd said that they were to let him in because their mother had said that they could. Of course I'd always told the children not to open the door to anyone so they hadn't done so, but it was very scary for them.

'I knew it was the stalker again. Later on that same evening a woman who lived up the road arrived at the door. (She kept rabbits and so did we, so we used to look after each other's rabbits when needed.) She'd got a dog with her – and she was using a bit of string for a lead. She told us that this dog had turned up out of the blue. She'd tried everywhere to find where it came from and asked all around, but no one knew anything about it. She was afraid that if she handed the dog in, it would be put down, so she wondered if we would give it a home. We did. We tried out all sorts of names and the dog seemed to answer to "Kim".

'It wasn't long before the stalker came to the front door again and I was at home. Again he banged on the door and lifted the letterbox flap to call through. But Kim was there in an instant, growling and snarling and jumping up at the flap. The man soon made his escape. That dog protected me and the children wonderfully. Every time I saw the man, Kim's fur would bristle and she would growl and strenuously defend me. It made me feel so safe. And in the evenings Kim would lie on my feet as I sat at the table studying. She was so warm and comforting.

'This went on for the best part of a year. Then the man stopped coming. My friend along the road had made some enquiries and discovered that he had a record for violence against his wife and had once thrown a paving-stone at someone. So for all we know he may have been back in prison.

'It was one evening soon after that Kim went out of the front door – that was unusual for her. And she never came back. She disappeared into thin air – she went as suddenly and mysteriously as she had come. The children were terribly upset, of course, but we never saw her again. And we never saw the man again either.'

Irene von Treskow Ahrens

The Rev. Irene Ahrens seems to have a penchant for angels. A few years ago some angel collages that she had designed, as part of a book of about angels for her daughter, were exhibited at the prestigious London Pentagram Gallery. So when the Post Office, who knew her reputation as a designer, decided on angels as the theme for the 1998 Christmas postage stamps, they asked Irene to design them. 'But the angels in the collages were too wild,' she told me. 'The ones on the stamps are like those painted by medieval artists.' She drew my attention to the fact that on every stamp the angel is looking downwards. 'You see,' she explained, 'although it is nowhere shown, the focal point is the manger with the Christ child in it. All the angels are looking at him.'

Irene von Treskow – the name she retains as a designer – came to England from her native Germany in 1984 because of her husband's work. She was at a low point at the time and when a young man that they met and came to know asked her if she had given her life to Jesus, she realised that this was just what she should do. 'In my case,' she told me, 'it was just what I needed and it led to my becoming a Christian.'

Irene had designed a hundred book jackets for Faber and Faber and worked for Saatchi and Saatchi under a very famous art director. But by the late 1980s she began to feel that God was calling her to the Anglican ministry. All her colleagues thought she was quite mad but her boss gave her all the help he could. 'If you really feel that is what you should do,' he told her, 'I'll support you.'

Irene is now a curate, with very little time for the design and art work she once excelled in, but she was happy to have the opportunity to put the angels on everyone's Christmas mail. 'The theme is very appropriate to Christmas,' she told *The Times* newspaper, 'as the angels had a major part in adoring Jesus and spreading the good news.'

'We encountered our own angel once,' she told me, 'though he was dressed in sturdy peasant clothes and drove a VW Beetle.' Irene's husband had been very ill with meningitis and as a result he suffered from epileptic fits. It was Christmas Eve 1983 and they decided to go for a walk through the snow, along the steep path of the little private road that led from the Swiss chalet where they were staying. Suddenly her husband sat down abruptly on the railing that fenced off the path from the steep hillside that fell away below. Irene realised with a pang of fear that his dizziness marked the onset of a fit. She dared not risk his falling from the rail and down the steep hill, so she quickly pushed him on to the ground, where he lay in the snow. It had been 4 p.m. when they set out and by now they were an hour's walk from the chalet and it was already dusk.

Irene waited for her husband to become conscious again and then told him that she would go back at once and fetch the car, but he was still very weak and confused and begged her not to leave him. He lay there in the snow while the darkness deepened around them. Irene was at her wits' end not knowing what to do. Suddenly, she heard the sound of an engine, puttering up the steep road. She could hardly believe her ears, because this was a road where no cars could be expected to come. But sure enough, a little VW Beetle came into sight and Irene dashed out to stop the driver in his tracks. He looked at her grimly at first but when she explained their situation he immediately agreed to drive them both home. It turned out that Peter was a neighbour, who owned the field next to their chalet, which explained why he was using the private road. But that he should be driving their way at that time on Christmas

Eve seemed more wonderful than chance or coincidence. For the two of them, and for the little community in which he lives, Peter became – and still is – '*Pierre L'Ange*'.

7

Moments of knowing

When a man or woman claims to have had an experience of God that is purely subjective, we cannot prove that what they say is true. But we can mark any changes that follow in the course of their lives and draw our own conclusions. It may be easier to assess the claims of people in the recent or more distant past – like those in this group – where we can stand at a distance from them and view the whole span of their lives and achievements.

These men and women came to a recognition of God and spiritual realities through a sudden or gradual intuition – what could be called a moment of knowing. In every case it involved saying 'Yes' to life and going forward in the direction that they knew from that time on to be the right one for them. Their moment of knowing gave them insight and courage to accept life and, apart from the ups and downs that are part of being human, they were able to live the rest of life with a sense of assurance and an acceptance of their particular vocation.

Margaret Fell

Margaret Askew was eighteen when, in 1632, her bridegroom of thirty-four brought her to Swarthmoor Hall, the large house in Cumbria that his father had built. Margaret came from a well-to-do family and her new husband, who had recently been called to the Bar, seemed set to go far. The match was a good one; they had nine children and seven girls and one boy survived to grow up in a happy, family home. Thomas was a success as a Justice of the Peace and a Member of Parliament and later became a Judge of

Assize. This meant that he was often away from home on his judicial circuit, but there were always happy homecomings to look forward to. Thomas was a moderate person who did not like extremists – an unusual standpoint in those ruthless, turbulent times in English affairs. He was not involved in the execution of Charles I and although he held important office during Oliver Cromwell's Protectorate, he was not wholly sympathetic to him. He was tolerant in religious matters and appointed William Lampitt, an Independent minister, to the living of the local church, which was in his gift. Thomas Fell lived out his religion in fair dealing and kindness and care towards others.

Margaret must have led a busy life as wife of the lord of the manor, and mother of a large family with a husband often away from home. The Fells were hospitable and plenty of visitors came and went. But in the midst of an active life Margaret still had time to think. In spite of being deeply religious, she felt dissatisfied. She was looking for something that seemed to elude her – a depth of genuine experience that would give certainty and meaning to her life. Margaret was not alone in her spiritual hunger. There were many other people in that part of the country – calling themselves Seekers – who were also looking for a faith that would satisfy them. Margaret hoped that the many preachers they entertained at Swarthmoor Hall might satisfy her quest for truth.

One day, when Judge Fell was away on his Welsh circuit, and Margaret was out, a visitor arrived. He was George Fox, and although a stranger to them, the daughters of the house made him welcome and looked after him in their mother's absence. William Lampitt, the local minister, was also visiting Swarthmoor Hall at the time and it wasn't long before Lampitt and Fox began a heated argument. There were all kinds of strange religious sects springing up at that time and Lampitt did not trust the beliefs of these newfangled Quakers, who had been attracting many followers in that part of the country. By the time Margaret arrived home Lampitt had gone and Fox had cooled down. But the girls told their mother all about the argument. That evening George Fox talked to Margaret and the family, answering all their questions. Next morning Lampitt called again; he felt responsible for the

Fell family while the Judge was away. This time both men kept calmer.

Fox stayed on at Swarthmoor Hall and Margaret became more and more affected by what he had to say. A day or two later when a 'lecture day' had been arranged at the church the Fell family tried to persuade Mr Fox to go with them. But he refused and instead he paced the fields before he changed his mind and suddenly decided that he should go to the church after all. As he arrived he heard the congregation singing and carrying out their worship in what seemed to him a purely mechanical and uninspired way. It was against the law to interrupt a church service but anyone could ask to speak after it was over and George Fox asked permission. When he spoke the contrast with all that had come before was overwhelming. His words came across powerfully and with the genuine ring of truth.

Margaret Fell was touched to the core of her being. As Fox spoke about the inwardness of true religion – that what matters is Christ in the heart – Margaret was convinced that at last she had found what for so long she had been seeking. She stood up in her pew, remained standing for a while, then, as suddenly, sank down and began to weep. Every head was turned in her direction. The villagers could scarcely believe their eyes. Was this the way for the wife of the lord of the manor to behave in church? A local magistrate who was in the congregation insisted that Fox should leave the church, but Margaret protested to the churchwardens and Fox was allowed for a time to go on preaching. But many churchgoing people declared that Fox's new teaching was almost blasphemous and in the end the objectors had their way. Fox was thrown out into the churchyard where he went on preaching to the crowd that soon gathered round him. That evening he spoke again to the whole Fell household at Swarthmoor Hall.

By now Margaret was wholly convinced that what she was hearing was the truth and her daughters and some of the servants were convinced too. But Margaret's joy and relief were tinged with anxiety. When she looked back on that time she wrote: 'I was struck with such a sadness, I knew not what to do, my husband being from home. I saw it was the truth, and I could not deny it; and I did as the Apostle said, "I received truth in the love of it." '

George Fox left but two other Quakers arrived and they helped to deal with the excitement his visit had caused and to calm the situation. They reassured Margaret, who had fallen into a state of anxious depression. When news came that Judge Fell was on his way home a deputation set out to meet him – the minister William Lampitt and some of the local leaders. When Judge Fell saw their grim faces, he was sure that something terrible must have happened to one of his family. But they had come to forewarn him of the infamous George Fox and the disastrous effect his visit had had on his household. The Judge reserved judgment but he felt concerned. Back at home, Margaret was anxious too. She wrote: 'Any may think what a condition I was like to be in, that either I must displease my husband or offend God . . . but I desired the Lord that I might be kept in it.'

George Fox was summoned back to Swarthmoor Hall, and he and his fellow Quakers spoke movingly to Thomas Fell, who was a wise enough judge of people to recognise their sincerity and uprightness. He never became a Quaker himself, but he did nothing to stop his wife and family from joining them. He himself offered Swarthmoor Hall as a meeting place for the Friends, as they were also known, and would sometimes listen to all that went on, though he and his groom still rode over to the church for Sunday services. William Lampitt tried in vain to influence his patron against the new movement, but with no success. Judge Fell gave the Quakers protection through his hospitality and his influential standing in the district. Once, when Judge Fell was away from home, Lampitt planned a demonstration which ended in some of the Quakers, including George Fox, being beaten up and wounded. They came to Swarthmoor Hall, where Margaret and her daughters dressed their wounds. Margaret would plead on behalf of Friends who were imprisoned and she set up a relief fund for them and their destitute families. Once she went to see the new king – Charles II – to beg for Fox's release from prison, assuring him that the Quakers were 'a people that follow after those things that make for peace, love and unity'.

Judge Fell died in 1658 and for eleven years Margaret remained a widow. More than once she herself went to prison for her faith, while her daughters carried on her work. Then, in 1669, Margaret

Fell and George Fox were married. They were happy in the short times they had together between Fox's travels and Margaret's own missionary journeys. Margaret was in prison when Fox was ill but his stepdaughters nursed him. After Fox's death, Margaret lived on into the reign of William and Mary and an age of religious tolerance. In the wisdom of her old age she tried to curb the quirkiness and fussy insistence about dress and speech that was creeping into some Quakers' way of life. She realised how easily the first spontaneous rapture of the movement could give place to deadness and formalism. She remembered her own moment of knowing and her first encounter with the truth as George Fox had proclaimed it and she reminded his followers that clothes and outward details 'will not make them true Christians: it's the Spirit that gives life'.

Dag Hammarskjöld

Dag Hammarskjöld was born in Sweden in 1905 and grew up to live a life marked by great outward success. He was healthy, well off and belonged to a neutral country which meant that he was exempt from the horrors of World War II. His father came from a long line of soldiers and government officials and his mother from a family of scholars and clergy and he seemed to inherit the best gifts of both. He had a brilliant career as a student at Uppsala University and by the age of twenty-eight he was an assistant professor at Stockholm University. He went on to be chairman of the Bank of Sweden and Swedish Foreign Minister from 1951 until his appointment as Secretary General to the United Nations in 1953.

He described his job there as being 'the curator of the secrets of eighty-two nations' and once said that being Secretary General was like being secular Pope. He must be utterly fair-handed, without favourites or special confidantes. It was certainly an extremely demanding and exhausting job and also a lonely one; it left little time or scope for personal friendships. During his office with the United Nations he played a leading part in setting up the UN emergency force in Sinai and Gaza and at the time of his death, he had been engaged in negotiations over the Congo crisis. He needed to be tough, physically and mentally, because quite often he would work an eighteen- or twenty-hour day, and sometimes that pressure would continue for weeks on end.

But in spite of appearances, Hammarskjöld was *not* a tough person, not in the sense of being thick-skinned or insensitive. Outwardly he was the competent and energetic man of action but within he had the imagination and soul of a poet. He also had the extreme sensitivity that goes with such a temperament. We know something about his inner life from the fragmented journal that he kept. After his death it was found in his New York house, together with a letter addressed to Leif Belfrage, a Swedish Foreign Affairs Secretary. Although – or perhaps because – he was such a private man, he felt some need to share his inmost thoughts. He was half ashamed of this need. He wrote: 'How ridiculous, this need of yours to communicate! Why should it mean so much to you that at least *one* person has seen the inside of your life? Why should you write down all this, for yourself, to be sure – *perhaps*, though, for others as well?' He certainly gave Leif permission to publish these fragments as a kind of 'White Book' (or government paper) concerning, he said, his negotiations with himself – and with God.

We can imagine him scrawling these intense, analytical musings when he was almost sick with exhaustion and lack of sleep, his mind burdened by the international problems that weighed heavily on him. We get a glimpse of his courage in one extract where he describes, in the terms of a climber, the time 'when the morning's freshness has been replaced by the weariness of midday, when the leg muscles quiver under the strain, the climb seems endless, and suddenly, nothing will go quite as you wish' and adds, 'it is then that you must *not* hesitate'.

He realised that a person's public image bears no real resemblance to the true person within:

Around a man who has been pushed into the limelight, a legend begins to grow as it does around a dead one. But a dead man is in no danger of yielding to the temptation to nourish his legend, or accept its picture as reality. I pity the man who falls in love with his image as it is drawn by public opinion during the honeymoon of publicity.

He never embraced that public image; in the *Markings*, as he called his often random, jotted notes, there is nothing to nourish the legend of the Hammarskjöld who was in the limelight. He is always ruthlessly honest about himself.

His journal tells us nothing about the fascinating experiences of his life as an international arbitrator; in its pages he reveals instead the interior workings of his mind. The *Markings* show us at first a man who is ill at ease with himself and tortured with life. In an early entry he wrote: 'What I ask is absurd: that life shall have a meaning. What I strive for is impossible: that my life shall acquire a meaning.' But at some point he *did* find meaning and the answer to his questioning. He discovered a purpose and goal in life. Piecing together the terse, often enigmatic entries, it is possible to grasp something of what made him able to respond with such courage and integrity to his difficult vocation. He learned to exercise what could be called the 'Yes' response. In spite of melancholic and at times almost suicidal tendencies, Hammarskjöld had an experience of God which helped him to respond positively to life. In an entry on Whitsunday 1961 (he died in September of that same year) he wrote:

I don't know Who – or what – put the question, I don't know when it was put. I don't even remember answering. But at some moment I did answer *Yes* to Someone – or Something – and from that hour I was certain that existence is meaningful and that, therefore, my life, in self-surrender, had a goal.

Hammarskjöld enjoyed the writings of medieval mystics with their emphasis on renunciation, but he found the perfect pattern for human living in the Gospels. He recognised in the life and ultimate death of Jesus the perfect surrender of a person to the will of God. He set himself to follow that pattern, giving himself to serve others. He knew that for Jesus that way of obedience led to the cross and he felt intuitively that his own life and self-giving for the nations of the world would end in death. He recognised that, unlike the mystics whom he admired, he was not called to a life of solitary contemplation. He believed that other models suited the twentieth century. He wrote, 'In our age, the road to holiness necessarily passes through the world of action.'

He believed that his own gifts were given to him by God, to be surrendered in humility and trust for the working out of God's purposes. For him the present was what mattered. Past and future were not in his hands, but every day he could – and did – renew his self-giving. 'Each morning we must hold out the chalice of our being to receive, to carry and give back,' he wrote. He was deeply aware of God's presence with him in all the stress and tension of international diplomacy. More than once he writes simply: 'Not I, but God in me.'

Hammarskjöld seems to have had a foreboding of his death, aware that it would be untimely. A previous Secretary General, Count Bernadotte, had been assassinated by extremists and perhaps he foresaw a similar fate. In the event he died in an air crash – seemingly accidental – but some have since queried the circumstances and suspected that it might have been deliberately engineered. He had written: 'Do not seek death. Death will find you. But seek the road which makes death a fulfilment.' And scattered throughout *Markings* is his repeated 'Yes!' both to life and to death.

> Night is drawing nigh –
> For all that has been – Thanks!
> To all that shall be – Yes!

John Wesley

It is not surprising that John Wesley was a deeply religious young man. His mother Susanna had lavished constant care on the spiritual training and education of her large brood of children and John – or Jacky as she called him – had been the object of her particular concern. He believed that God had preserved his life from a fire when he was five for a very special purpose.

John grew up to demonstrate many of the best qualities of both his parents. He was short – as was his father – and always neatly dressed and cheerful by temperament. He claimed that he 'did not remember to have felt lowness of spirits for one quarter of an hour since he was born'. He had splendid organisational skills and he was meticulous over details; there was never a scrap of paper or a book out of place in his study. He was also warm-hearted and had a sense of humour, like his father. Above all he was a prolific and splendid preacher. For over forty years he travelled the roads of Britain, covering an average of eight thousand miles in a year and preaching in small out-of-the-way places as well as in the big towns and cities. He changed the face of Britain by transforming the lives of thousands of ordinary working people through the gospel he preached.

John grew up to be a very religious man. He lived up to the stringent rules his mother had laid down and even went further, carving out for himself a strictly disciplined lifestyle. While he and his brother Charles were at Oxford they formed the Holy Club, whose members devoted themselves to an ascetic way of life and also to social work among prisoners and others in need. They were teased and taunted mercilessly by their fellow-students for their extreme religious lifestyle.

After Oxford, John and Charles planned to sail for Georgia, as missionaries to the native Americans. But their mission was *not* a success. John knew that for all his religious endeavours there was something lacking in his own life and experience. When he arrived back in England he remarked sadly: 'I went to America to convert the Indians; but, oh, who shall convert me?' He was soon to find the answer. On board ship going to America, the brothers had met a group of German Moravians. These were Christians with a simple evangelical faith and great missionary zeal. Their sincerity and genuineness made a great impression on John, so when he met another Moravian, back in England, he was ready to listen and learn from him. Peter Boehler encouraged John to dwell on God's *grace*, rather than trying to win God's acceptance by a life of good works and religious practices. Grace, he explained, is

God's love freely given to those who don't deserve it and can do nothing to earn it.

John began to preach this doctrine and told his congregations that God's love and forgiveness are freely given to those who turn towards him in repentance. But this new concept of God's undeserved and unconditional love had still not touched his own life and experience. Nearly three weeks after Boehler had left the country, on 24 May, John Wesley wrote in *Journal* that he set out to go 'very unwillingly to a society in Aldersgate Street (in London) where one was reading Luther's *Preface to the Epistle to the Romans*.' During that auspicious day all kinds of small 'clues' had alerted John to what was about to happen. For example, before he left home he had read these words from his Bible: 'Thou art not far from the kingdom of God.'

This is how John Wesley describes the experience that followed:

About a quarter before nine, while he was describing the change which God works in the heart through faith in Christ, I felt my heart strangely warmed. I felt I did trust in Christ, Christ alone, for salvation; and an assurance was given me that He had taken away my sins, even mine, and saved me from the law of sin and death. I began to pray with all my might for those who had in a more especial manner despitefully used me and persecuted me. I then testified openly to all there what I now first felt in my heart.

John Wesley's life and his preaching were completely transformed. In prisons and in London churches he began to tell others of 'the glad tidings of salvation'. Dry theology and cold religious practice had been transformed by his warm and living experience of the love and forgiveness of God. The 'brand plucked from the burning' became a living fire throughout the land.

C.S. Lewis

Most people who have heard of C.S. Lewis picture him as the genial writer of the Narnia children's books or as the romantic, tragic lover of the film *Shadowlands*. But when he first became known to the ordinary public Lewis presented a very different image; he was a rarity for that time – a respected intellectual who was also an orthodox Christian and a popular communicator. I still remember, as a very young teenager, listening spellbound to his broadcast talks on Sunday afternoons in 1941 and 1942, during the darkest days of World War II. Here, I discovered, was Christianity that was infectious, interesting and understandable. It was also intellectually respectable. I still treasure my 1942 copy of those published radio talks and my other well-used, once hot-off-the press copies of early C.S. Lewis books. I would not part with them to any avid collector of first editions.

C.S. Lewis – Jack as he was known to family and friends – was born in 1898 and he grew up in Ireland, a sensitive, imaginative boy, the younger son of two parents of very different backgrounds and temperaments. His happy early days were soon shattered by the death of his mother from cancer when he was still a child. Wretched days at a boarding school – in the Dotheboys Hall mould – added their quota of pain and unhappiness. Later he went as a boarder to the home of a tutor in Surrey, where his eccentric teacher set about strengthening his intellectual muscle and opening his eyes to the delights of Homer and the classics. His tutor was a rationalist but by this time Lewis had already settled into an atheism of his own. When World War I broke out, he was conscripted into the army, but when he was wounded, and therefore discharged, he was free to take up his reserved place at Oxford. He added a degree in English to his Oxford arts degree known as 'Greats' and soon settled comfortably into the role of a bachelor English don, basking in the stimulating friendship of other intellectual and literary men.

In spite of his rationalist beliefs, Lewis had a strong sense of the magic and mystery which were at the heart of the legends and poetry he studied and loved. There was something more too. Ever since he was young he had experienced – unbidden and elusive – moments of deep and overwhelming joy. He could remember one morning when a large parcel of books had arrived as a Christmas present from his father and how the promised feast of reading that lay ahead somehow mingled with the pleasure of a winter walk across the hills. He could recall the sudden moment of joy, but nothing he did seemed able to bring back the magic and happiness of that moment. He began to realise that such moments of joy never come to order but occur unexpectedly and of their own accord. And yet, the memory of the joy was a joy in its own right too. He discovered that 'what I had felt on the walk had also been desire, and . . . in so far as that kind of desire is itself desirable, [it] is the fullest possession we can know on earth'. To try to rekindle the 'thrill' – to set out deliberately to create it – is to misunderstand its meaning and purpose. The joy is not something to be called up or manufactured for its own sake but is always a by-product; in Wordsworth's phrase, it is an 'intimation of immortality', a brief ecstasy belonging to the world beyond our own, for which we are all homesick, whether we know it or not. The unexplained yearning such moments of joy create is not satisfied, Lewis discovered, by sex or by any other human pleasure.

But these discoveries did not disturb Lewis's intellectual beliefs. He kept the rational side of him strictly apart from the side that gloried in myth, imagination and poetry. He was profoundly thankful that he *could* keep the boundaries intact – he certainly wanted to be safe from divine interference.

One day, on a station bookstall, he bought a book by George Macdonald, and, as he began to read, he discovered that Macdonald had woven his own Christian belief into the world of fairytale and myth. What Lewis found even more surprising was that instead of spoiling the magic of his tales, Macdonald's 'holiness', as Lewis described it, seemed to turn everything to gold. As he read he was, so he says, carried 'sleeping across a frontier'. It was as if he had died in the old country of rationalism and unbelief and come alive in the new country; and it had all happened without his ever remembering how it had happened. This 'magic' of Macdonald, unlike the myths and legends he himself had loved and cherished, did not leave him feeling that the rest of the world was desert. It stood the test of solid reality, as down-to-earth as the food on the table and the fire in the grate.

It was many years before Lewis related this new joy he had experienced to the spiritual world of the Christian God. He was deeply influenced by the writings of George Macdonald and also influenced by some of his friends and colleagues, whose own intellects and imagination had been transformed by their Christian faith. Nevill Coghill and J.R.R. Tolkien were both Christians and fellow-members with Lewis of the Inklings, the literary club of kindred spirits in Oxford who met to read and talk about their writings.

One 'coincidence' after another seemed to challenge Lewis' disbelief in God, yet he maintained that God still left him free to choose whether or not to commit himself to faith. He describes in *Surprised by Joy* how he faced the first big choice on top of a double-decker bus, going up Headington Hill in Oxford. He was, he says, somehow given the chance to unbuckle and remove the armour he had worn so defensively to protect himself against the inroads of belief in God. In that moment he chose to undo the buckle, to unloose the rein. More was to follow. He began to feel increasingly the steady approach of the Spirit – as he described him – which he had tried to elude. One night in his room he was brought face to face again with the reality of an Unseen Power. Struggling and unwilling, he surrendered. He admitted that 'God was God' and he knelt and prayed. It was not a moment of peace and bliss; he described himself as being dragged, kicking and screaming, into acknowledging the reality and the right over him of the God he could not see. But this moment of relinquishment to God was not a Christian conversion. He acknowledged the existence of a Power – of God – but nothing more.

His further moment of knowing took place one sunny morning when he was being driven to Whipsnade Zoo in Buckinghamshire. He admits that his memory of it all is hazy. What he *did* know, with positive finality, was that 'when we set out I did not believe that Jesus Christ is the Son of God, and when we reached the zoo I did'. He does not remember engaging in any deep theological reasoning nor experiencing any great emotion – only certainty and assurance in a final moment of knowing. Lewis had stopped running away. It seemed that God had finally caught up with him and he knew that he could not escape. But Lewis discovered in Christian faith the freedom, love and meaning that had eluded him until then. This, for him, was the most important moment of knowing and of joy.

8

Suffering and tragedy

When I was a child, World War II was in progress and people used to say, 'Why does God allow war and let innocent people suffer? Why doesn't he strike Hitler dead?' Those two questions sum up the age-long human response to the problem of suffering. First of all, if God is a God of love, why does he let innocent people suffer? And second, if he is all-powerful, why doesn't he deal with those who cause it and put an end to it? Many people conclude that if there *is* a God, he is either loving and powerless or powerful and unloving. They are more likely to decide that there is no God and that pain and suffering are a by-product of the evolutionary process. It's just a lottery whether or not you are a victim.

Religious people often add their own pennyworth which is far from helpful. Some describe God as the one who sends trouble and suffering to test people. Others murmur that there must be a purpose in it and expect to bring comfort to the sufferers by such a vague assurance.

I talked to Professor Stephen Morley from Leeds University, a psychologist who has specialised in the dynamics of pain and pain relief. I know that he is a Christian believer, but he is also a scientist and the ones I have spoken to have been very even-handed, not trying to manipulate facts to fit their faith. 'The pain falls on the just and the unjust,' he observed. 'For some it leads to bitterness and unbelief and for others it opens up a broader world. For these people, pain helps them to get life into context – they get their pain into context too. Others certainly become embittered.' He refused to say on the evidence that pain brings people closer to a spiritual dimension. Pain *may* be the way into greater spiritual awareness but it can just as easily lead to greater disbelief and bitterness. Suffering helps some people to grow as human beings while it causes others to shrivel and be diminished.

C.S. Lewis called pain 'God's megaphone' – a means by which God makes people listen to important things that they would not otherwise hear above the racket of everyday life. I've certainly heard the comment afterwards from people who have been through some kind of suffering: 'I wouldn't have been without that experience, I learned so much.' And that response comes as often from those who are agnostic as from those with a faith.

Karim

Karim's mother and father were peasant farmers in Syria. Although they had thirteen children only four survived. Infant mortality is high where there is an ignorance of hygiene and a lack of medical care. Karim was the youngest of the four who lived and he was still young in 1946 when Syria gained independence from French rule. The new Syrian government was determined to do its best to provide education for ordinary citizens – French schools had catered only for an elite group. But there were still school fees to pay and not many parents could afford to give their children an education. But Karim's parents were determined to send him to school, so he was the fortunate one chosen from his family. He knew how fortunate he was and how much his parents had sacrificed to give him this chance in life so he was determined to succeed for their sake.

In fact he did so well that he was awarded a scholarship and place at the university in Damascus. This was a very unusual achievement and there was great celebration and excitement as Karim travelled to the capital to begin his student studies. Like all students he and his new friends enjoyed university life as well as getting down to work. But Karim was fired with enthusiasm to help not only his family but his people. He knew that there was little hope of justice for most of his countrymen. Most were unable even to write a letter, let alone plead in the courts, so he determined to study law in order to be able to help them. But after less than a year at university his plans were rudely interrupted.

The Middle East was in turmoil and from the time of its independence Syria had been preparing for war against Israel. The government bought arms from the then Soviet Union, and Soviet personnel came to the university looking for likely lads to train in military service. Karim was one of the young men chosen, along with some of his student friends, and told that he was to go to Russia in order to train to be a fighter pilot. He had no choice in the matter. He was given a few days to go home and prepare for his new life and say goodbye to his family, who were very proud of him. They were proud that he had been chosen and that he would be training in order to fight for his country. The little group of students left for Russia and their training began. As well as flying lessons, they learned some Russian and were given an attractively presented dose of Communist teaching too.

Then one day, out of the blue, Karim was told to report to his commanding officer. He had no idea what was afoot but he was told that he was to be sent straight back to Syria immediately. All kinds of thoughts went through his mind. Perhaps something had happened to his family – was his mother ill or dying? But when he arrived at military headquarters in Damascus he was immediately put into handcuffs and a lengthy interrogation began. He gradually learned that while he had been in Russia an attempted coup had taken place in Syria. It had been ruthlessly crushed by the military and the leaders had been dealt with. By complete chance, Karim had the same surname as the rebel leader. He knew nothing about him and was certainly not a relative, but he *was* suspect, however much he denied any connection, so at the age of nineteen he was thrust into prison for no crime at all. Looking back, he tells me that he was one of the lucky ones. Other suspects were shot on the spot or consigned to prison for life.

He was released after six months, but he had nowhere to go. His mother, worn out with grief and frustration, had died before his release and there was no place for him at university now. He decided to leave the country and go to neighbouring Lebanon where he found work as a hospital porter, with his accommodation provided.

He had been at the hospital a year when a group of British

nurses arrived in Lebanon. They came as a Christian team, planning to visit the Middle East, spending six months in different countries, helping in the hospitals. One of the nurses was allocated to Karim's hospital and in spite of not knowing a word of each other's languages, they managed to communicate very well. When she left, his nurse friend gave Karim her address in England and two years later he decided to come to England to visit her. 'I came for thirty days,' he told me, 'and I have stayed for thirty years!' At that time it was easier for overseas visitors to find work, settle down in the UK, and eventually be offered British nationality. Karim started off as general factotum at a boarding-school – a job which involved working all hours with only one half-day off a week. But he stuck it out and also began to teach himself English. The friendship with the nurse blossomed and before long they were married. They lived in the house which had been provided for her as district nurse and midwife.

Karim had various jobs; he worked as a porter in the hospital, an assistant in an ironmonger's shop, in a factory, and finally on the railways, working shifts. But in spite of everything he was very happy. His wife remained a true and committed Christian, but she never at any time tried to put pressure on Karim to follow her religion. A baby daughter was born in 1966 and later a second daughter was born. At last life seemed to be going really well. Then, one terrible day, his wife discovered a lump on her breast. An urgent mastectomy followed and she no longer felt well enough to work full time. They realised that they might have to move from their house, so they bought a small one of their own and carried on as best they could. But his wife grew worse, and the treatment she was receiving was horrific. Karim was still working shifts and things seemed impossibly hard. But during this gruelling time, friends from his wife's church began to visit – and not just to pay social calls. They set to and did the hundred and one things that needed to be done. Karim had not met them before and he could not understand why they showed such kindness and love to them all in such practical ways.

In spite of all the treatment, Karim's wife died in 1984. Karim was grief-stricken. He had somehow to manage the household and his two teenage daughters on his own and carry on with his shift work on the railways. But to his surprise the friends from the church still came and they helped in every way they could. They never tried to persuade him to go to church, but Karim wanted an opportunity to thank them all, so he asked the church pastor if he could have two minutes at the next Sunday service in which to express his thanks to everyone. He had never been to this service before but he felt that this visit would somehow round off and complete the whole event. It would certainly to be a one-off. But, strangely, when the next Sunday came round he felt a strong desire to go back – and the same happened the following Sunday too. He told himself that it was a kind of addiction, brought on because of his feelings for his dead wife. When they sang the hymns and songs she had sung he could imagine he heard her lovely voice. He enjoyed meeting those who had been so kind to them through all their trouble. Although they were warm and welcoming, no one tried to put pressure on him to make some kind of acceptance of their faith.

One morning – it was 14 November 1984 – there was to be a special service. Karim found it hard to describe his feelings about that morning, but he told me that there was something special about the whole atmosphere of the service – a kind of godliness and reverence that hung in the air. During the service, several people went quietly around praying with others. One man came up to Karim, put his hand on his shoulder and began to pray for him. Karim experienced a shock, as if electricity was going down his arm, and a warmth flowed into him from the man's touch. He felt somehow transformed and as he left the church an elderly lady looked hard at him and said, 'You are smiling! It looks as though you have the Lord in your heart!'

'Yes, I have!' Karim answered as he walked away.

As he cooked the lunch and then cleaned his car he thought again and again, 'Why ever did I say that? What did I *mean*?' He tried to debate the question. In his heart – his deepest emotions and awareness – he did feel different, but in his head – with his mind – he could not recognise that something had happened to him.

He did not sleep much that night and next morning he was up early to start his shift as a guard on the early train to London. It was 5.20 a.m. when the train arrived at one of the stations on the route and he got out of the train to check on passengers leaving and boarding. His attention was arrested by a poster on the station wall. The wording seemed to stand out, large and clear, as if it was an urgent message written for his eyes alone. He knew that it was a Bible verse. It read, 'Jesus said: Come to me, all of you who are tired from carrying heavy loads, and I will give you rest.'

Karim immediately gave his own reply. He said: 'All right, Lord, if you're really there, I'm tired and I'm stressed and I want that rest you promise. Please give it to me.' At once, he told me, he had a wonderful sense of peace and relief. There was no more debate about the how or why of it all; he knew beyond doubt that he had met Jesus. That peace, and that joy, he told me, has never left him in the years – increasingly happy ones – that have passed since that day.

Amy Carmichael

When I was a child I learned about a very special home in India where children grew up and were cared for. The girls and boys whose photos we saw seemed always to be laughing and smiling; it seemed idyllic. They lived in Indian-style cottage homes, with a church – called the House of Prayer – at the centre and the complex contained schools, workshops, offices, a book-room and a hospital in the style of an Indian village. There were vegetable plots and a farm with a dairy herd. None of the helpers was paid in money; staff contributed what skills they had for the benefit of the six or seven hundred that made up the 'family'. As a child I knew nothing of these details but felt in my bones that the Dohnavur Fellowship, as it was called, was a happy and 'good' place. I was also aware that the children who now looked so contented and loved had not always been so. I knew that they had been rescued and brought to this haven of happiness but I did not understand anything more about their past or just what they had been rescued from.

At the heart of the Dohnavur Fellowship was Amy Carmichael, an Irish woman born in 1867. When she was still in her teens she began to feel concerned about the young people in her neighbourhood who had not had much of a chance in life. She ran a Bible class for the mill girls and taught the boys in Belfast at a night school. Later she worked for a time in the slums of Manchester until for the first but not the last time, her health gave way. She was never to be robust or tough physically, but her inner strength and drive, motivated by her love for people in need, gave her the will to endure and succeed. She spent fifteen hectic months as a missionary in Japan but that ended in illness too and she was ordered back to England. But when an opportunity came for her to go to India, she was only too eager to seize it. She set sail in 1895 – at the age of twenty-eight – and was never again to set foot in her own country.

At first, after learning the language, she used to go with a team of Christian Indian women to visit the villages. But in 1901, when she was still in her thirties, something happened that was to change the whole direction of her life's work. A little seven-year-old girl – Pearleyes – ran away from a Hindu temple and asked to be taken to Amy Carmichael, whom she called 'Ammal, the Servant of Jesus'. At that time it was the custom for children to be given to the temple in order to be 'married' to the god and to spend their life there as cult prostitutes.

Pearleyes' father had been a scholarly Hindu landowner but when he died her mother took her to visit a temple and stay with the temple women for a while. But Pearleyes ran away and by walking and hitching lifts on bullock carts she managed to reach her home, two days' journey away. The temple women came after her; they frightened and bullied her mother into returning Pearleyes to them. This time she was more closely guarded but she managed to escape again. A kind woman found her and took her home for the night before taking her to Amy next day. 'My name is Pearleyes,' the child told her, 'and I want to stay here always. I have come to stay.'

When Amy and her helpers heard what she had to tell of the lot of these children in the temples, they were determined to provide a refuge for more children at risk. Getting information was a slow and delicate job. Some of the children, it seemed, were offered to the temple because of a vow or family custom; in other cases a widow or deserted wife would hand over her child because she was not rich or influential enough to marry her off in a match suited to her caste. In fact, high-caste children who were without protectors were always at risk. In time, more children were brought to Amy Carmichael and her helpers and the Dohnavur Fellowship was established.

Amy Carmichael had never been strong and in 1932 she had an accident which left her housebound until her death in 1951, nearly twenty years later. She was now unable to take an active part in the work and she suffered a great deal of pain, yet her room was still the centre of the Dohnavur Fellowship and the mainspring of love and power for the life of the whole centre. In spite of her suffering – or perhaps because of it – she experienced God's peace and faithfulness herself and was the means of radiating these values to everyone in the complex. She spent a great deal of time in prayer and in writing – letters, poems and books. She believed firmly that trial and suffering were a necessary ingredient of life for anyone who would be a channel of God's love. And love she reckoned to be the supreme value. She wrote:

> More and more I feel that love is the golden secret of life. The very air of heaven is love, for God is love and love never fails. So go on loving not only the loveless but the unloveable, the difficult, the perplexing, the disappointing – unto the end.

The Dohnavur Fellowship still functions, although all its members are now Indian nationals. The dedication of children to the temples is now illegal, but Dohnavur still provides a home for children who might otherwise be exploited. The hospital treats patients living nearby, from every religious background and social group.

Frances Young

'I am no saint!' Frances Young writes about herself, but at the very least she is a most remarkable woman. She is a theologian and professor in the University of Birmingham as well as holding the office of Pro-Vice-Chancellor there. But that is only half the story of her day-to-day life. She is an ordained Methodist minister, who sees part of her vocation as preaching and speaking to ordinary non-academic gatherings. Over and above all that – and with huge bearing on her work – is her home life.

When Professor Young and her husband looked forward to the birth of their first child, they knew very little about babies – like many academics. Looking back, Frances Young thinks that was why, when others sensed that all was not well with their new little son, Arthur, she had no inkling of the real situation. No one said anything for some months and she has never forgotten the shock when first she was told the truth about Arthur's condition. In one way it explained so many things – his reluctance to feed, his failure to respond to noise or voices, even though his hearing is unimpaired. But it was a long time before the full extent of his handicap was recognised.

Although some advances have been made, Arthur is still unable to talk, to dress himself and he is still in nappies. Caring for him takes many hours of effort and sometimes Arthur is anything but co-operative. When he was young, his mother found it desperately painful to see her child in a state of terrible distress and – because he could not communicate – to be quite unable to discover the cause. The problems grew worse when Arthur began to have severe epileptic fits that had to be controlled. When two more children were born – both of them boys who are healthy and free from handicap – the sheer hard work of coping with new babies, then toddlers, as well as Arthur, was overwhelming. Frances Young writes warmly of the help and support she has received in relief care and day care too, but is also honest about the problems of delay and red tape that make life doubly difficult for parents trying to cope with disablement in the family.

As a theologian, Frances had studied and thought through the deep problem of suffering, coupled with belief in a God of love. She could have written able, academic papers from her study that would have been sound, competent but wholly theoretical. Instead, she worked through in practice the problem of undeserved suffering, enduring bitterness of heart and daily personal struggle. Her book, *Face to Face*, is an almost disturbingly honest account of her own emotions, of Arthur's needs and of her struggle to align her belief in God with the experiences of her own life. She has produced a theology of suffering which is powerful because it is anchored in reality and truth.

Frances Young thought that she had accepted the fact of Arthur's deep handicap, but she discovered that at a deeper level she had done nothing of the kind. She still preached and she was not being insincere, because at one level she *did* retain her faith in God. Yet she felt that God had abandoned her. She writes that she was at that time unable 'to accept the existence and love of God at those deeper levels where it makes a real difference to one's life'. That was the rub. Her faith no longer warmed and motivated her, strengthened and encouraged her on her difficult journey. At the place in her life where God should be, she felt only despair and an internal blank. She realises, looking back, the sheer emotional stress of coping with a severely handicapped child while also pursuing a demanding academic life. These pressures must have contributed to her sense of blackness and despair. But she also knew that her theoretical, well-reasoned theology of God and suffering had not been resolved on a practical level. She had not forged her own, personal made-to-measure faith – very different from the off-the-peg samples on offer. Many of the theological theories on offer just did not fit the particular facts of Arthur's condition.

Then, one day, Frances had her own moment of knowing. It was only a brief flash, and she no longer remembers what time of day it was or how it occurred within the context of life in the family. Yet it was a fundamental breakthrough. She *can* remember the particular chair she was sitting on and the fact that she was sitting on the edge, ready to go off and do something about the house. Then, at that moment, she had what she calls a 'thought-flash' that came to her out of the blue. A voice in her mind said: 'It doesn't make any difference to me whether you believe in my reality or not.' That was all. But the words stunned her; she felt as if Someone was putting her in her place. In one way it was all very ordinary – nothing dramatic happened and she just stood up and got on with what she was doing. But, she writes, 'I have not seriously doubted the reality of God since that moment.' She herself cannot determine why that moment of insight and knowledge of God was so important. After all, she knew that God existed independently of his creation – it is a theological fact. But in that moment she became shatteringly aware of what she describes as the 'aseity' of God. The word, from the Latin '*a se*' meaning 'of himself' describes God's ability to be, without depending on human belief for his existence. God, she recognised with absolute clarity, is beyond anything she could project on to him – he just *is*! She realised that God needs no defender and the knowledge released her from her doubts and somehow absolved her of responsibility. Through her suffering and through Arthur, she learned to know God in a new way and at a deeper level.

John Skidmore

John walked up the path towards our house, smiling and relaxed. 'You look just like your photo!' he said reassuringly and I warmed at once to this man, looking younger than his thirty-four years, but with typically confident Australian charm. He had been in England for twelve years, he told me later. It was natural for people of his generation to want to come to the UK, he explained, because school education, including history, was all British-centred when he was at school, so he wanted to come to Britain and explore it all for himself.

John and his older brother had grown up in a stable, happy home with parents who loved them and encouraged them to be independent. His parents had been brought up in a Christian tradition but were not themselves religious or churchgoing. They taught their sons to respect others and to have moral standards but believed that it was up to the boys themselves to choose religion, if they wanted to, once they were adults.

John left school – which he had thoroughly enjoyed – and went off to Hawaii for a year before going to university on a scholarship with a computer company. His father encouraged him to apply, while he could, for a visa which would make him eligible to live and work in England should he want to. He came, in due course, just for a working holiday but got homesick so went back to

Australia. But rather to his surprise he found that, once back, he could not settle there either – England seemed to be pulling him. So eventually he returned to England where he has been ever since.

About four years ago John was working in Bristol. He had a very good job in computing. He was successful, happy with his colleagues and got on well with those working for him. He kept on his London flat and used to go back there at weekends. Everything seemed to be going fine. Then he fell ill. He had never known a day's sickness in his life but now he seemed to have got a really bad dose of flu. It just wouldn't clear up, and although he struggled on, he felt no better. As he had no experience of being ill he just thought, 'So this is what people feel like when they have flu.' At weekends he rested and slept, too tired to bother to travel back to London.

But one weekend he felt so ill – he couldn't even seem to breathe – that he thought he had better get back and see a doctor. When he arrived and phoned the surgery it turned out that his own doctor was away, so they promised to get a locum to visit him. The locum arrived the next morning. She took a good look at him and asked, 'Have you been tested for HIV?'

John thought the idea ridiculous. 'Of course not!' he told her. But the doctor had experience of AIDS both in this country and overseas and without delay she took a blood sample. Then she told John that she was sending him to hospital straight away. There was no doubt that he was suffering from pneumonia and no time must be lost in getting treatment. As John looks back he is deeply grateful for her swift action. He knows now that if the treatment had been delayed one more day he would not have lived. As it was, he became worse and two days later he 'died' in his hospital bed as a high fever developed and his temperature rose beyond control. He remembers that night, lying there in bed and suddenly, after all the pain and suffering of the past days, feeling really well. He thought, at the time, that the fever must have subsided, but he thinks now that it may have been when he 'died' because he can also remember a flurry of activity as nurses dashed to get help. There were cries of 'O my God – get the doctor!' and staff crowded round his bed.

'It was strange – I could see it all and yet I couldn't see it. I thought perhaps I had been dreaming, but when I asked the nurses afterwards they confirmed that it had happened just as I had remembered it.

'And that was the time when I got my messages. I call them messages because I don't know how else to describe them. I didn't hear a voice and I didn't see a vision. It was just as if these thoughts came into my mind – but very strongly, there was no doubting them. It was thoughts being put into my mind that had never been there before. The first message was that everything was going to be all right. There was a condition – it came across very strongly that I must never attempt to commit suicide. (I don't understand to this day why that part of the message came across so strongly.) The other part of the message was that there is a purpose for me – "you won't ever know what this purpose is, but you must believe that this purpose is very strong and there is a reason for your being here. You mustn't give up under any circumstances, because it could reflect on others. So you don't have to worry." It was so strong and so positive.

'You can imagine how worried I'd been up to that time, very, very stressed, desperately trying to work things out in my mind. Some people actually have a breakdown when they are told that their life is in the balance. They'd given me two or three months to live at the most – I had very advanced AIDS. But suddenly all that stress and tension was released. I knew everything was going to be fine and that knowledge in itself was healing. I no longer had that psychological problem so my body was free to get better. It was a most unusual message of healing and it just felt so good. Absolute peace. Afterwards I asked the nurses if someone had been sitting by my bed and had said these things to me. But they confirmed that no visitor had been near or spoken to me; there was nothing to explain it.

'Friends and family who came to see me were devastated. I told them the doctors said I hadn't long to live, but that I didn't believe it – but *they* didn't believe *me*! They thought I hadn't taken in what the doctors had told me, that my mind had gone. And it was so difficult to explain to anyone what had happened. So I put the whole experience aside for six months. And gradually I did get better. Then an uncle from Australia visited me and he understood at once. He'd had a similar experience after an industrial accident. He told me, "You need to find a path. It will come." '

John tried various paths, but he thinks now that he has been going the long way round. He tried various lines of enquiry before he realised that there was a church at the end of his road and he has started going there. He also met Father Bill Kirkpatrick.

'I've found a lot of answers to my questions in church,' John said, 'but I'm in a very early stage of a whole new way of thinking. I used to question everything and feel frustrated. Now I'm learning to accept. I should have died three and a half years ago and the doctor is astounded because I shouldn't be here now. I'm realistic enough to know it may not last, but I have faith to believe that it's lasting this far for a reason. I feel privileged. Maybe I shall understand in the future. Before I was ill I used to love money, leisure, work – I was just selfish and never thought about developing my spiritual side. I didn't even know I had a spiritual side. Everything is new now. God's taking me on a new path. That illness was the best thing that ever happened to me.'

9

Love

I suppose that 'love' is one of the most used and most abused words in the language. We use it to include a fondness for chocolate, an affection for a pet and for that closest human emotion that binds two people together for life. But even when we use the word love to define the relationship between people we may misuse it – making it a high-sounding substitute for lust, sexual desire, infatuation or even possessive self-interest. Love can be courageous and self-sacrificing but it can also be jealous, cruel and destructive.

Jesus's disciple John (who is the probable author of the letters in the New Testament that bear his name) tells us that not only does love, in its best and purest form, *come* from God but that God *is* love. And the men and women down the ages to our own day who have seemed to reflect God most clearly are the ones who have shown his kind of love to their fellow men and women and to the world God made.

Raj Kumari

I first saw Raj on television and was struck with her beauty. Then I realised that it was not just the loveliness of her features that held my attention but something warm and beautiful that surrounded and possessed her and seemed to reach from her to those around. The only name I could find for that indefinable quality was love. And I was right. Love is the keynote of Raj's experience of God. When I visited her flat, near a main London train terminus, she told me her story.

108

Raj is the youngest daughter of Indian Hindu parents, who settled in an English Midlands town where they had their family of four daughters and three sons. All her life Raj had longed for love and acceptance. In her parents' culture girls were not wanted as sons were; added to that, Raj was darker-skinned than her siblings and this too was thought to make her less beautiful. She felt desperately unloved and longed to win her father's acceptance and affection, but he brushed off every attempt she made to capture his attention or approval. The rest of the family followed his lead and Raj became the one to be picked on, bullied and beaten. When her birthday came round there was no cake and no celebration. Only her eldest sister tried to take her side and give her some protection. But when Raj was still a child, that sister left the family. She went through an arranged marriage to a man she did not know, but left her bridegroom immediately. In the family's eyes she had disgraced them and was as good as dead. Her father turned his anger and bitterness against Raj, flinging insults at her and insisting that she would one day do the self-same thing.

Raj determined all the more to give her father no cause for reproach and when the time came to leave school she enrolled at college, to train as a nursery nurse. Unlike her other sisters, she did not date boyfriends but kept within the accepted pattern for a young Hindu girl. But she was given more and more work about the house to do and with the burden of so many household chores she could only complete her college projects by staying up at night. The late nights gave her father something more to complain about. When her brothers punched her and swore at her, even her mother took their side.

At last Raj could bear it no longer and – more as a cry for help than a suicide attempt – took an overdose. She was found in the morning and her life saved, but all her father said was: 'A shame it didn't work.' Now Raj knew that there was nothing she could do to change his feelings towards her, so she decided to leave college and go to work. She found a job in a shop and worked all hours in order to be away from home. Gradually she saved up enough to leave home and move into a flat with a friend. The family did not even notice as she gradually moved her belongings and finally left. After only two weeks they stopped even trying to find her.

Raj began to make up for lost time by doing all the things that her parents would have forbidden. She cut and permed her hair, used make-up, began to smoke and went clubbing. She hoped and believed that she would find love, marriage and a family with a man who would love her truly in return. So when her first relationship went wrong, she felt sadly disillusioned. She still looked and longed for love, but none of the boys she went out with seemed ready to be loving and faithful.

Then Malcolm came along. At first Raj was not interested in him, but he was persistent, calling on her several times within a week. She began to think that perhaps at last she had found someone who really did love her, especially when he mentioned marriage and asked if she would come to London with him to meet his family – mother and sister. Since Raj had a week's holiday coming, she agreed to go. At the end of the week away Malcolm told her that he was not returning north but staying in London. She was free to go back, but he also asked her if, instead, she would like to stay with him. Raj happily agreed to stay, hoping that at last she had found true love. But soon Malcolm told her that he was in trouble. He owed a lot of money and he was afraid that his creditors would kill him if he didn't repay them. Raj was very concerned and offered at once to try to raise the money through her friends, but Malcolm had other ideas. If Raj would only work in the sauna massage parlour, he said, she would soon earn enough to clear him of his debts. Used all her life to pleasing others at her own expense, Raj reluctantly agreed. One thing soon led to another and before long Malcolm had installed her in a Soho flat with a maid to sit with her, to make money for him. She still described him glowingly to others, trying to keep up the pretence that he was a loving, faithful boyfriend, but often she would only see him when he came to collect the money she had earned for him. Yet Raj still loved him dearly and yearned for him to love her in return.

Sometimes the door bell would ring and Raj's maid would answer the door to find Heidi, the girl who lived in the flat above, standing on the step. Heidi was a Swiss girl who had worked the clubs and pubs herself in the past but had now become a Christian and wanted to share her faith with the prostitutes living near her.

Raj was not interested, but she was to learn later that Heidi and her friends at church had begun to pray, not so much for Raj as for her pimp, Malcolm. And then what seemed impossible happened.

Malcolm and two friends were back in their home town one day, walking together along the street. Suddenly, all three saw clearly in the sky the figure of Jesus on the cross. Malcolm heard a voice saying to him, 'Stop what you are doing.' He was totally shocked by the experience. He went to pieces, had a complete breakdown, and even tried to take his own life. After he had recovered some kind of equilibrium, he went back to Raj and told her that she must stop her work as a prostitute. He put an end to his own involvement in drug-dealing and voodoo and began trying to live a strictly moral life. Sadly, Raj explained, he seemed to experience nothing of God's forgiveness, feeling only remorse and a need to make amends for his wrongdoing. Raj stayed with him, loving him still. '*You've* got God,' she told him, 'but *I* want love!' She took a job in an Oxford Street store and even made contact again with Heidi. But when she tried to read the Bible and pray it all seemed meaningless.

One day, in February, Raj was feeling more cheerful. She had bought a Valentine card for Malcolm and hurried home to put it on his pillow. Just then the phone rang. It was Malcolm's sister. 'Could you move out of the flat for a bit?' she asked Raj. 'Malcolm has a child and the child's mother is coming to London. She wants to stay with Malcolm so you can go to his brother's.'

Raj was bitterly hurt and she was also very angry. Always, throughout her life, she had tried to please others, and to make any sacrifice rather than fail to do as others asked or demanded. But now, she decided, she would be compliant no longer. She made up her mind to go back to prostitution – but this time to earn big money for herself. She rang her maid, but was told that the girl was asleep, so in desperation she rang Heidi and poured out the story to her. At once Heidi said, 'Come and stay with me – come tonight!' But Raj was still loath to leave Malcolm and decided to wait till morning. The night that followed was to be the most terrible yet the most wonderful in her life.

Now that her anger had been aroused, all the sadness and injustice of the past years seemed to well up from deep within her.

For years she had succeeded in pushing down the feelings of pain, the memory of hurts and rebuffs, the beatings and the unkindnesses. But now, one after another, the memories flooded her mind, rising up from her innermost being. She sobbed and cried endlessly as she relived the grief, the pain and the rejection.

On and on the weeping went and on and on the bitter memories flooded back, until she seemed to be voiding from her memory everything in her whole life that had made her so unhappy. At two o'clock in the morning she suddenly heard a voice – and she knew that it was the voice of God – saying to her, 'Raj, stop crying.'

Without stopping to think she answered: 'I can't, God!' Then, naturally and spontaneously, she poured out to God all her sadness and unhappiness, suppressed and endured for so long. 'I've had enough of trying to find love,' she told him, 'I am ready to hand over my life to you.'

It was then, at that moment, that she became aware of a love that seemed to enfold her, warm and palpable. She was utterly unprepared for the experience. No one had ever told her that God was like that. Malcolm had spoken of broken laws and the need to make reparation, but nothing of a God who loved and forgave. In the wonder and warmth of that love Raj knew that there was acceptance, forgiveness and all that a good and loving father would give. She felt embraced, wrapped round and utterly cherished and blessed in the love that flooded through her. As the love embraced her she felt her own anger and bitterness dissolve. The wonderful forgiveness that she was experiencing seemed to flow out in turn towards those who had wronged her. Soon, to her own amazement, she felt able to go to bed and sleep peacefully.

In the night it had snowed and next morning Raj packed her bags and stepped out into the whiteness of the world to walk to Heidi's. Through Heidi she met friends who gently cared for her and taught her more about the God who had encountered her with his overwhelming love.

St Francis

For most people St Francis conjures up pictures of a nature saint, a man in a brown habit surrounded by an assortment of tame animals and birds. Many remember singing 'All creatures of our God and King', words adapted from Francis' *Canticle to the Sun* where sun and moon, animals and death itself are addressed as his brothers and sisters. But any image of Francis as a harmless, sentimental, nature-loving saint is misleading and only half the story.

Francis was born in Assisi in Italy in 1182, when his thriving merchant father was away on a business mission to France. His mother baptised him Giovanni, after Jesus's close disciple John, but when his father returned he renamed him Francis, in honour of his trade trip – which must surely have been a successful one. Francis grew up in very comfortable surroundings. His father's cloth trade flourished and his parents could afford to give him a good education, as well as fashionable clothes and the chance to enjoy himself. Francis was a sociable young man with plenty of friends and he certainly had good times with them. Like most young people of the time, his head was stuffed full with the popular ideas of courtly love. According to this code, young men were spurred on to brave deeds and chivalry by romantic love for some beautiful but unobtainable lady. Courtly love demanded chastity and obedience for the sake of the beloved and the young man was expected to perform acts of valour for her sake.

When Francis was still a teenager he went to war and fought for Assisi against Perugia but he was captured by the enemy and spent a year in prison. Even *his* irrepressible high spirits were quenched when he developed a high fever and he regained his freedom a much sobered man. But he still expected to find his fortune as a soldier and a knight and in 1204 he set out to fight in the papal army. But before he got far, resplendent in bright new armour, he met a knight of noble birth who was so poor that he could not afford any knightly regalia. Francis insisted on giving the poor knight his own armour but after resuming his journey and going only another twenty- five miles, he had a dream. In his dream he heard a voice asking: 'Where are you going?'

Francis answered that he was going to Apulia to become a knight. The voice asked: 'Which is it better to serve, the master or the servant?'

He understood then that God was calling him, not to be a soldier and knight in the ranks of an earthly ruler, but to serve God himself. He asked: 'Lord, what do you want me to do?'

'Go home,' the command came, 'there you will be told what you are to do.'

Obediently, he returned home, still uncertain what his future was to be.

Francis threw a party to celebrate his homecoming but his friends sensed at once that he had somehow changed. They asked him teasingly if he was in love and Francis admitted that he was. But he did not tell them that the object of his love was not some lady of noble birth but the one he called Lady Poverty. He knew now that fine clothes and extravagant living did not bring happiness. Although he had no need to live as a poor beggar he was going to choose a life of simplicity and self-giving out of love for God. He had begun this stripping of himself for love when he gave the poor knight his precious new armour. He would go on stripping himself for God's sake and for love of others for the rest of his life.

In the broken-down little church at San Damiano was a crucifix. Francis used to go into the church and gaze at it, filled with love and gratitude to God as he reflected on God's great love and self-giving for him. His love grew steadily stronger as he spent the months that followed in solitude and prayer.

Francis made the journey to Rome and outside St Peter's he gave away all the money he had, then changed places with a beggar and spent the day dressed in the beggar's filthy rags. He would live the rest of his life as the faithful champion and lover of Lady Poverty. On the journey home he met a leper. Francis had always loathed and shrunk from the hideously deformed lepers that roamed the countryside, but now he went up to the man with a gift and kissed his hand. The leper took Francis into his arms and kissed him on the lips. Once more back in the dilapidated church at San Damiano, kneeling before the crucifix, he heard the voice of Christ say to him: 'Francis, my Church is in ruins – repair it.'

For the moment, Francis took the words literally. He began to repair the church building, and even stole and sold a bale of rich cloth from his father to provide the money that was needed. But the priest at San Damiano was too frightened to accept the money and Francis' father was soon hot on his heels. Francis withdrew into the woods, sheltering in a cave. He chose to abandon the comforts and sophistication of wealthy town life and live simply, close to the earth. He felt at one with the country around him and all it contained. Because he was free now from all the artificial and material trappings he had once had, he began to experience a deep sense of the oneness of God's world. Francis' love and care began to embrace everything in nature and to extend to all that God had created.

After his stay in the cave Francis went home to meet his father and an angry confrontation followed. Francis told his family that he was God's servant now and as a mark of his renunciation of the old way of life, he stripped naked in front of his father and the bishop who was present. The bishop gave him an old tunic to wear and Francis chalked a cross on the back of it. Now he had divested himself of everything he had once owned and held dear and he embraced poverty, not because it was forced on him but because love had made it the most rewarding and joyful way of life. More and more men, and women, flocked to join him in the simple life of preaching and prayer, loving and giving.

Years later, when he was dying, the brothers laid him on the ground, naked as Jesus had been on the cross. He died as he had lived, free from self and possessions and open in love towards God and his whole creation.

Dame Thora Hird

'I just wish that everyone could be as happy as we were!' Thora Hird was talking to me about her fifty-eight years of marriage to Scottie, and she really meant what she said. Many people know her for her brilliant acting, or for her sympathetic presenting of *Praise Be!* on BBC television, but she is probably loved and admired chiefly because her spontaneous warmth and generosity seem to come to us personally, across the air waves into our own living-rooms.

In her autobiographies – *Scene and Hird* and *Is it Thora?* – she tells fascinating tales of her childhood in seaside Morecambe and the loving family life she enjoyed. Perhaps because she received love freely, she has been able to give it, not only to her parents, her brother, her adored husband, her daughter and grandchildren but also to her enormous and admiring audiences. Her acting skills are superb and always carry conviction. We are moved to laughter or tears – sometimes both at the same time – because she herself and the characters she portrays have the unmistakable ring of truth. We know that she is showing us her heart, and it is one of kindness, love and generosity to others. She is never small-minded or mean and her laughter is never unkind.

Thora Hird's Sunday-evening television programme *Praise Be!* consisted of favourite hymns requested by listeners, which she introduced with warmth and sensitivity. She told me that after each programme she used to receive sackfuls of letters, many of which touched her deeply. 'I just used to feel like crying when I read some of them,' she said, 'but Scottie used to look across and say, very gently, "Now then . . ." ' and her tears would be checked. Her husband could not bear to see her distressed, but Thora was aware of how fortunate she was and she felt deeply for the many lonely people who wrote to her as well as admiring the faith that helped them to endure.

In 1994 Scottie had a massive stroke. When Thora came back from visiting him in the hospital one evening, she sat on her bed and prayed, 'Please take him, God!' She could not bear to see him so changed and so utterly lifeless and unresponsive. That was at half past seven in the evening. At 2.20 a.m. she had a phone call to say that he had died. She hurried back to the hospital but when at last she returned home again she sat quietly on the bed once more, and once more she prayed. 'You'll have to help me, God,' she said. She knew that she had no resources in herself to cope with this enormous loss.

'Within five minutes or less,' she went on to say, 'I found myself thinking of all the laughs we'd had together, all the jokes we'd shared. I was so grateful! In fact, I never did have "the big cry", though I came near it once. My daughter Jan and I went on a pilgrimage to the holy places in Jordan. We were standing on the top of Mount Nebo, where Moses looked out on to the Promised Land that he would never enter. We could see right over to Galilee. There was a little church there, very old, looking as if it was made of wattle and daub. There were no pews, just forms, a pulpit and a couple of bentwood chairs. Jan said, "This is my Daddy's church" and it seemed like that to me. There was nothing special about it except that it seemed so full of love. Then I felt that feeling at the base of my stomach, and I knew I was going to cry. But at that moment I heard a voice, not ten inches away from me, saying – "Now then . . . !" I know I didn't imagine it, it was so real and close.' And just as Scottie's 'Now then!' had checked her tears in the past, so his gentle words checked them again then.

Thora Hird's experience of God is practical – it is expressed in prayer, a constant live link with God – and it is also received and given through love. She told me that she wished that others could know the love that she has experienced. But by showing love to others, known and unknown, she *is* giving them a share in the love she has enjoyed all her long life.

Festo Kivengere

By Festo Kivengere's own reckoning, he was born in Uganda in the year of the Great Cattle Plague. But further education was to separate him for a while from his home and his tribal beginnings. In 1939 he returned to his home town of Rukungiri. He had successfully finished his teacher training and now, complete with certificate and with a post promised in the school he had once attended as a pupil, he made a triumphant journey back. But he was in for a surprise. Dramatic changes had been taking place in the town in his absence. While he had been away at college, a religious revival had swept through the town; the women could be heard singing hymns about God's love as they went for water to the well, and neighbours sat in little knots talking and laughing as they shared their experiences of God. Festo was not well pleased. His uncle, who was district chief and strict enough about church-

117

going also disapproved strongly of this new, intrusive religious fervour. Festo himself was an agnostic, not so much on grounds of reason but because he preferred not to have too much to do with a God who might interfere in his life.

But the new enthusiasm was bursting out everywhere and it amounted to a lot more than emotion or repeating the right words. People had begun to put right the things they had done wrong in the past and to own up to lies they had told, sometimes years before.

Festo's tribe were cattle people. They not only counted their wealth in cows but loved their cattle as they loved their children. Festo knew the names of all his father's 120 cows, bulls and calves by the time he was three years old. One day a man arrived where Festo's uncle, the chief, was holding court. He was followed by his servants, driving eight cows. The visitor, who was known to be wealthy, approached the chief, who asked him whose cows his servants drove. 'They are yours, your honour,' the man replied.

The chief looked puzzled but the cattle owner explained: 'When I was once looking after your cattle I told you we had been raided, but that was a lie. I had stolen four of your cows – and those four are now eight. I have brought them back to you.'

'Who discovered the theft?' the chief asked and the man replied, 'Jesus did. He has forgiven my sins and given me peace. He told me to return the cows that are yours.'

The chief was dumbfounded but when Festo asked him later if he was pleased to have these extra cows he shook his head. 'No,' he said, 'because if I were to be as honest as that man I would have to give back a hundred cows to their rightful owners.'

Signs of the revival spread and multiplied and Festo grew increasingly uncomfortable. Even his young niece tried to persuade him to find the peace and happiness they were now enjoying. But although he still felt no love for God and rejected all the religious enthusiasm bursting out around him, he knew that he was miserably unhappy. He wanted to keep control of his life and yet his whole repetitive routine of work-play-eat-drink-sleep began to seem meaningless. He wondered if life was worth living or if he should end it all.

One day, as he cycled home he saw a friend cycling towards him on the dusty road. He called out excitedly to Festo and stopped beside him. His face was glowing as he poured out his good news. 'Three hours ago Jesus became real to me and I know he has forgiven me. Now I want you to forgive me too,' he told Festo. Then he mentioned three occasions when he had wronged him. Still bursting with exuberance, he cycled off, whistling, and Festo pedalled wearily home, depressed at the sight of his friend's joy.

When he reached his own room he knelt by his bed and tried to pray: 'God, if you happen to be there, as my friend says, I am miserable. If you can do anything for me, please do it now . . . Help!'

He described what happened next and what he saw:

In front of me was Jesus. He was there real and crucified for me. His broken body was hanging on the cross, and suddenly I knew that it was my badness that did this to the King of Life. It shook me. I thought I was going to hell . . . all the wretchedness of my life came out. But then I saw his eyes of infinite love which were looking into mine. Could it be that he was clearly saying, 'This is how much I love you, Festo!'?

That love was wholly unexpected, but it filled my room, and I was convinced. In spite of what I was, I knew I was accepted . . . whatever Jesus did on the cross, it was for me.

That was the beginning of Festo's own life of loving and giving. He found his life work in the church rather than the schoolroom, becoming Bishop of Kizegi in Uganda, and founding and leading some of the evangelistic teams connected with African Enterprise. But he never faltered in his commitment to showing love and forgiveness. Even through the persecution of Idi Amin's reign of terror, and the murder of his friend Janani Luwum, Festo was able to forgive. He wrote a little book called *I Love Idi Amin*. He was able to tell the world: 'Our only weapon is love.'

10

Miracles

At the beginning of his book on miracles, C.S. Lewis observed:

> The question whether miracles occur can never be answered
> simply by experience. Every event which might claim to be
> a miracle is, in the last resort, something presented to our
> senses, something seen, heard, touched, smelled, or tasted.
> And our senses are not infallible. If anything extraordinary
> seems to have happened, we can always say that we have
> been the victims of an illusion. If we hold a philosophy which
> excludes the supernatural, this is what we always shall say.

If we have already decided that there is no spiritual world and no
supernatural power at work in our world, we are not likely to be
convinced by accounts of miracles. But some people, whose minds
are open to the possibility of God, have found that he has broken
through to them through a miracle that they have experienced or
heard about from reliable witnesses.

Malcolm Muggeridge

'We would be delighted to have a visit from you . . . would you
ring us so that we can arrange a day that suits us both?' It was
1985 when I received the letter and I was elated at the chance to
meet Malcolm Muggeridge in person. I had long admired his wit
and his brilliance in the written word and on television (in spite of
his avowed dislike and distrust of that medium). Now I had the
opportunity to talk to him about the book I was writing on

Catherine Bramwell-Booth – the 100-year-old granddaughter of William Booth, founder of the Salvation Army. Malcolm Muggeridge had interviewed her himself and obviously admired her stalwart Christian spirit as well as her quick tongue and keen sense of humour. As my train rattled through the spring country-side of Sussex, I was full of expectation about the meeting that lay ahead. And it was as stimulating and rewarding as I had anticipated. Malcolm and Kitty, his wife, sat on either side of the fireplace in a barely furnished cottage. Kitty, a niece of Beatrice Webb, was not only clever but warm and kind. We talked of many things and before I left, Malcolm had generously offered to write a foreword to my forthcoming book, completely without charge.

Malcolm Muggeridge was born in 1903, in part of the London dormitory town of Croydon. His father, who was an agnostic, held strong socialist views and would 'preach' regularly in the open air. The family belonged to the lower middle class – a suburban group which they despised, lavishing their admiration on the working classes – 'the people'. In due course Malcolm went up to Cambridge but he did so to fulfil his father's dearest wishes rather than his own, and he worked no harder than was needed in order to gain a pass degree. In spite of his scepticism and agnostic outlook, friendship with Alec Vidler in particular gave him some insight into Christian faith. Vidler went on to become a leading theologian and he and Malcolm remained lifelong friends. Even at that stage in his life, Malcolm began to realise, as he put it, that there was a bridge spanning the chasm between 'the black despair of lying bound and gagged in the tiny dungeon of the ego and soaring upwards into the white radiance of God's love – and that this bridge was the Incarnation'.

After Cambridge, he embarked on a varied journalistic career which included being a foreign correspondent, a newspaper editor and later doing a stint as editor of *Punch* magazine. A spell in Soviet Russia opened his eyes to the reality of life in a Communist state and cured him of the ideals he had grown up to cherish and admire.

Muggeridge made the journey to faith slowly. (He was finally received into the Roman Catholic Church in 1982, when he was nearly eighty.) In many ways it was the influence of other

Christians that finally convinced him of the truth of the spiritual world. He told me how much his son's Christian living had influenced him. Len Muggeridge's Christianity was at the opposite extreme from the Roman Catholicism his father finally embraced, but Malcolm was deeply impressed by the faith he saw in action in his son's lifestyle.

The other profound influence on Malcolm was Mother Teresa. He said: 'Words cannot convey how beholden I am to her. She has given me a whole new vision of what being a Christian means; of the amazing power of love, and how in one dedicated soul it can burgeon to cover the whole world.'

He first interviewed Mother Teresa for BBC television in the mid-1960s and was amazed at the audience response to this small, nervous woman. Something of the magic of her simplicity and love conquered the usual falsifying effect of television and brought home to hundreds of viewers the truth and reality of this woman's faith. Muggeridge was keen to go to India and film her as well as the work of her Sisters of Charity among the sick and dying on the streets of Calcutta. The BBC agreed and Malcolm and the film crew, led by skilled cameraman Ken Macmillan, were given five days in which to record their images and impressions of the work for a fifty-minute documentary. It was a very tight schedule, because two to three months shooting would be the norm for this length of film. Their time restriction meant that there would be no time to redo anything that did not come out well first time round. In the event everything went with unusual smoothness and with none of the customary bickering and disagreements among the team.

But there was one problem. Part of the work of the Sisters of Charity is to pick up the dying from the streets of Calcutta and bring them to the building given to Mother Teresa, where, as she put it, they could 'die within sight of a loving face'. But the light within this building was very dim, lit only by small windows high up in the walls, totally unsuitable for filming in. The crew had one small light only and no time to fix up the kind of lighting needed for successful filming. Ken decided to film the courtyard outside, which was bathed in sunshine and where some convalescing patients were sitting, to make up as far as possible for the filming inside, which he was certain was bound to be a failure. In his book *Something Beautiful for God* Malcolm Muggeridge describes what he is certain is 'the first authentic photographic miracle'. When the film was processed, the footage taken in the sunny courtyard was surprisingly dim and rather confused, but the part Ken took inside the building 'was bathed in a particularly beautiful soft light'. Ken insisted that technically, the result was an impossibility. To prove the point, he used the same stock in the same kind of light in his next filming assignment in the Middle East. The result was completely negative.

Muggeridge himself was convinced that the camera revealed the luminosity of love. He compared it to the light that artists depict as haloes around the heads of saints. Everyone agreed that the light in that part of the film is exceptionally lovely. The room might be filled with the stench and squalor of dying people from the dirty Calcutta streets, but the love of God reflected to them from those who cared for them was greater and more powerful than any darkness or gloom that the place held.

Muggeridge records his sadness that even for those who are 'believers', miracles seem to be unwelcome these days. But, he writes,

> I record the matter here in the hope that in years to come, Christian believers may be glad to know that in a dark time the light that shone about the heads of dying derelicts brought in from the streets of Calcutta by Mother Teresa's Sisters of the Missionaries of Charity, was somehow recorded on film.

Corrie Ten Boom

'What an improbable, unbelievable, unpredictable impossibility!' That was the way an architect described the tall crooked house in the middle of Haarlem which was watchmaker's shop and home to the Ten Boom family. And the architect was delighted, for his plans were to create a hiding-place for Jewish people who faced the threat of exile and death and a house like that provided all the right opportunities.

The house had begun as two houses, back to back, but the wall between the tall narrow houses had been knocked down to make one house, with a corkscrew staircase between. The shop premises were below and the living space above. It was a home where children were always around. Once Corrie and her brother and sisters were grown up, numerous other children in need were cared for and brought up in the crooked house. Corrie's grandfather had opened his shop in 1837, and now her father and his family were known as the finest watchmakers in Holland.

But in 1937, when they celebrated the shop's centenary, a heavy cloud was looming. Corrie's brother, Willem, a church minister, had been watching with alarm the rise of Hitler and his persecution of the Jewish people. The home for elderly Jews that Willem had built in Hilversum was fast filling up with young people as well, escaping from Germany while they could. When war finally came and the Dutch were under German occupation, anti-Jewish activities began in Holland too. Shops carried signs saying 'No Jews served here'. Once, when a synagogue was set on fire, the fire engines let it blaze, taking care only to prevent the flames from spreading to the nearby buildings. The next indignity was to force Jewish people to wear a six-pointed yellow star with *Jood* (Jew) written at its centre. Not long after, the situation worsened. Sinister trucks drew up in the town square, and terrified men and women who were wearing the yellow star were herded into them.

One day German soldiers raided the Weils' furrier's shop, which was across the way from the watchmaker's shop, and threw out the bewildered Jewish owner. The Ten Booms took their neighbour in, then managed to smuggle him away to safety. Jewish people began to be afraid to be seen on the streets and Corrie used to deliver their watches to them after they had been repaired, to save them risking the streets and calling at the shop themselves. Gradually the Ten Booms' home became a haven for the trail of frightened, threatened Jewish men and women who began to arrive at the watchmaker's shop seeking refuge. Somehow Corrie improvised ways of providing a safe hiding-place for them, using her own ingenuity to keep them hidden from the German authorities.

Eventually her nephew introduced her to a leader of the official Dutch underground movement, whose members had many contacts and knew more reliable ways of protecting the threatened Jews. One of their number was the architect who visited the shop in Haarlem to devise a safer hiding-place. He ignored the nooks and crannies and ready-made hideaways that Corrie showed him. These would be too obvious, he said; the police or German soldiers would go straight to them. After searching the whole house he decided to build a false wall in Corrie's bedroom, which was right at the top of the three-storey building. The space between the two walls would provide a temporary hiding-place for several people. Once built, the new wall was skilfully smeared and stained to look as old as the other walls.

For eighteen months the elderly watchmaker and his two daughters kept their secret safe, but one day, when Corrie was lying ill in bed with flu, the house was raided. The seven Jewish refugees remained undiscovered in their hidden compartment, but Corrie, her sister Betsie and their father were arrested and taken to the police station. After questioning and further delays, they were separated and taken to prison in Scheveningen.

Terrible days and months followed. Later Corrie was to hear that her father had survived prison for only ten days and in spite of her grief she was thankful that he had been spared further pain and distress. When, at last, they were transported like cattle by freight trucks to Germany, Corrie had the joy and relief of being reunited with Betsie. But two nights in the open, one during heavy rain, had seriously affected Betsie's already poor health. Before being allocated to their quarters, every prisoner was stripped and searched. Corrie prayed hard about her treasured Bible, a woollen sweater and some precious vitamin drops that she badly needed to smuggle into the building. She knew how desperately Betsie needed the warmth of the jumper and the vitamins to help her survive. When Corrie finally went past the guards she was the only prisoner not to be searched and her precious treasures went with her into the building where they were to sleep.

It was a huge room, made to hold 400 but occupied by 1,400 – with more women arriving daily. The women slept on tiers on wooden slats. Sometimes the weight of too many closely packed bodies was too great and the slats broke, plunging the women on to those on the tier below. The conditions were horrific, but as soon as they arrived Betsie reminded Corrie that they should give thanks for *everything* – and insisted that their thanksgiving to God should include even the fleas that caused them so much trouble. Corrie grudgingly agreed. (Later Corrie was to discover that it was because of those tormenting fleas that guards refused to come to their building, giving them the freedom to read the Bible and pray with all who wanted to join them.)

The first night they were there, quarrels kept breaking out as women argued over their share of space, and shouted and swore at one another. In the midst of it all Betsie prayed for God's peace to reign. Amazingly, the quarrels began to die down. The short tempers and frayed nerves seemed to settle and grow quiet and more friendly comments were exchanged and even some good-humoured laughter could be heard. As time went by many of the women in that grim and dreadful place gladly joined Corrie and Betsie in the evenings as they read out loud from the Bible, sang and prayed. Women of all denominations and languages united to sing and pray, and translate the Bible for one another. Verses that they knew well came alive for them as freshly as if they had been written yesterday – and written especially for them.

Every day Corrie carefully measured drops of vitamins from the bottle for Betsie. She would have liked to hoard them for Betsie's use alone, but how could she refuse to give a dose to the many other sick people who shared the building? Soon there were fifteen or twenty other women receiving the vitamin drops every day. Anxiously, Corrie held the little bottle up to the light, trying to see how much was left and how soon the supply would give out, but the dark glass gave no clue to what remained. All she knew was that every day, enough drops came to meet the needs of all those women who were sick and in need of them. Corrie was puzzled until Betsie reminded her of the woman in the Bible whose supply of oil did not fail while famine lasted and suggested that she should stop looking for answers. Still the number of sick women increased and still enough drops came from the little bottle to supply them all.

Then, one day, a friendly Dutch woman guard managed to

smuggle them some vitamin compound that she had filched from stores. Corrie was delighted but decided before she started on the new supply she would use up the contents of her little bottle. But the bottle was empty and no matter how much she turned it upside down and shook it, not a drop came out. Corrie believed with all her heart that in the stench and despair of that flea-ridden building, God had been present in the gift of his peace, in his living Word, the Bible, and in the miracle of the life-giving vitamins that lasted as long as the need remained.

John Wimber

'I'm just a fat man trying to get to heaven' is how John Wimber described himself when he first preached in England in 1981. But that description does not do him justice. He *was* built on the grand scale but with his impressive head of white hair and full beard, he seemed to possess the *gravitas* as well as the looks of an Old Testament prophet.

John Wimber was born in Illinois in 1934, with no kind of spiritual background or heritage. He used to say that he was a fourth generation *un*believer. His father left home when he was still a toddler and his mother brought him up alone until she remarried and went to live in California. As he grew up John discovered a great love for music and considerable aptitude for it too. He learned to play the saxophone at school and joined various jazz bands. As well as belonging to a number of jazz clubs, he had made a lot of money before he was thirty by successfully directing, orchestrating and recording music. In 1962 he formed a group in Las Vegas called the Righteous Brothers, which soon topped the charts. John himself provided the saxophone backing. When he was twenty-one he got married, but six years later, when their third child was on the way, the marriage was on the rocks and he and his wife, Carol, split up for a while. It was at this time that John had what he called his 'desert experience'.

One day, in despair, John drove out into the desert to try to think things out. There, in the solitude and silence he prayed, even though he was appealing to a God he had never believed in. When he got back to his hotel he found a message to say that his wife had phoned. He couldn't believe that something had happened so quickly in response, he was sure, to his prayer. He rang her back and after talking together for a long time they both agreed that they should give their marriage another chance.

It seemed to John that his cry to God had been answered and he became alert, ready for any other signs or signals that might come to him from another world. When he heard that a stand-in drummer for the Righteous Brothers had become a Christian his interest deepened. He and Carol met others who were Christians and before long they joined a church themselves. Soon they were deeply involved, so much so that John gave up his musical career, studied theology and trained to be a pastor. The church to which he was first appointed soon grew in membership from 200 to 800. After a while he became a recognised specialist in the field of church growth and was invited to advise churches right across North America. But John Wimber is best known not for his teaching on church growth nor for his use of music in church worship but for his belief that evangelising should always be accompanied by 'wonders and signs'.

He came to this belief gradually and he would describe his early experiences with characteristic humour. When he first became a pastor of a church he preached a series of sermons from Luke's Gospel. In the Gospel accounts, Jesus's teaching and preaching about the kingdom of God go hand in hand with his miracles of healing. People in John's congregation who listened to these sermons began praying among themselves for one another's healing. John felt alarmed when he first heard about this, but then he began to wonder if the frequent link between preaching and miracles in the Gospels might indicate that the Church should accompany evangelism with healing too. So after he had preached his sermon, he began to invite anyone who wanted healing to come forward. The result was disastrous. Nothing happened and no one was healed. Some people actually left the church because they disagreed with what he was doing. John began to wonder whether he had been mistaken.

Then, one morning, one of the new members of his church asked him to come to the house and pray for his wife who was suffering from a high fever. John went, but with little expectation of success. He laid his hands on her in a rather half-hearted way, prayed, then turned to her husband, ready to explain to him why it was that people were no longer healed as they had been in Jesus's day. But he realised that the man was not listening to him; instead he was looking over his head, and his face was beaming. When John turned round he saw the reason why. The wife he had prayed over had got out of bed, and now seemed completely well. 'What's happened to you?' he asked incredulously. 'I'm better!' she replied, and invited him to breakfast.

John drove home jubilant. God *had* healed. He felt more than ever convinced that just as healing and preaching the good news had belonged together in Jesus's ministry they should go together today. Healing became an integral part of John's evangelism and in the Vineyard churches which came under his leadership.

Those who knew John Wimber witness to the fact that his healing ministry was always linked with love rather than displaying power. He listened, accepted and dealt with people lovingly. Compassionate and sensitive care, rather than miraculous cures, characterised his dealings with those who came to him for healing.

John Field

When is a coincidence more than coincidence? When is it a miracle? Probably we'd all have our own views but the story John Field had to tell me sounded far more than a tale of improbable good luck.

John's parents were both members of the Salvation Army, but any Christian influence that may have rubbed off on to him very soon disappeared when he grew up and joined the RAF. He was in the Royal Air Force Police, a dog handler who trained dogs (using kindness and repetition, he assured me). He played football for the RAF so Sunday was taken up with other things than church-going. He followed the same Sunday routine when he left the service after nine years – but kept playing football. He knew he had the right temperament and talents to be a good sales rep, so for the next thirteen years he worked as a salesman for a very large company based in Blackpool. When the depot closed John did not want to move the family and interfere with the children's schooling, so he joined a greetings card firm and now works from home as one of their sales directors, travelling around the north west of England.

It was through his wife Sandra, invited to church by a friend, that he became a Christian. He had thought he was one already – just too busy to go to church or do anything about religion – but a visit to her church made him think differently. A snap decision to go to hear Billy Graham preach clinched the matter. John Field became a Christian for real.

One day, a new friend from the church asked if he would be willing to go with him to drive a minibus to Romania. Norman was a supporter of Global Care, a children's charity that had set up a home for Romanian children who had been rescued from the appalling conditions of a state orphanage. The children were grouped into two families of eight each, with their own house-parents, living in a house and going to school like children in normal families. All the children had been certified as too mentally handicapped to be educated, yet now, with love and family care, they were beginning to flourish in every way, some coming top of their class at school.

Norman and John set off for Romania, driving in four-hour shifts and taking four days to complete the overland trip. When they arrived the children rushed out in great excitement. The sight of a brand new minibus was an event and they happily piled in for a trip to the town.

John and Norman were cheered to see the happiness of these children but badly shocked by what they saw of the conditions at the state orphanage which they also visited. John was determined to do anything more he could to help these children. The following year enough money was raised to pay for diesel fuel and for accommodation on the trip out. He managed to get hold of a truck and one December day he set off, taking his wife and daughter with him, with food and Christmas gifts donated by children in English schools, packed lovingly into individual shoe boxes for each child. The plan was to spend Christmas with the Romanian children, then head back, spending New Year with friends in

Germany and arriving home in time for an important sales meeting John was due to attend in early January.

From the word go things seemed to go wrong. They were held up for eight and a half hours before they had even crossed the Romanian border because they were told that one necessary document was missing. After that delay John had to drive non-stop to avoid the danger of their load being pilfered. Trouble was beginning to erupt in Bosnia and a succession of trucks and lorries screeched past them in the opposite direction, almost grazing the passenger side where Sandra was sitting (their truck was right-hand drive). When they arrived, customs officials refused to unseal the lorry until after Christmas.

Finally, their mission accomplished, John and Sandra left for the journey home, having first had to fill up with diesel fuel. John thinks that probably it was dirt in the fuel that caused clogging and the string of breakdowns that followed. They broke down twenty-six times on the journey home but on almost every occasion there were what John described as guardian angels to protect them. The first time the engine petered out they were still in Romania, in pitch dark with no street lights, but a stranger they met offered them a bed for the night and knew a mechanic friend who would fix the truck in the morning. So the delays continued, the truck spluttering to a standstill with alarming regularity and needing a mechanic to clean it and set it to rights again.

All this cost time and it also cost money and by the time they reached Budapest their store of ready cash had been exhausted. So when they waited to collect their truck at a repair garage yet again they had no money with which to pay the £280 or so that was owing. It was useless to flourish cheque books or credit cards – nothing but cash payment would be accepted. John stood still, at a complete loss as to what to do next – other than to pray. At that moment another customer, who was also waiting to collect her car, came across to him and said in perfect English: 'Let me pay your bill.' John was completely nonplussed to hear someone speak his language, let alone offer to pay his bill. The woman explained that she taught English and had an English boyfriend living in Essex. She would happily pay what they owed if John would send a cheque for the right amount to her friend in

Chelmsford, once they got back to England. She then took John and Sandra home with her and gave them a meal and a night's lodging before they set out again on their way.

In Germany, as snow was falling, they had a more serious breakdown and when they pulled off the motorway their handbrake froze. They could scarcely believe it when the smiling face of the pastor friend they had planned to stay with for New Year appeared, arriving somehow when he was most needed. They had to abandon the truck for yet another expensive repair job while their friend drove them to his home.

At last they were ready for the last lap of their journey back. In Germany they had been able to use a credit card to pay the heavy bill, but there were two big problems still to be faced. First, the many delays meant that John had missed his important sales meeting and, second, they were about one thousand pounds out of pocket.

When they got back there was a message telling John to meet his boss at a chosen point on the motorway. He arrived apprehensively and the director said: 'First of all, John, we are very sorry that you missed the meeting, but we know it was in a good cause and so that is all right. The second thing I have to tell you is that you were chosen as Sales Representative of the Year and I have a trophy here for you – and a cheque for one thousand pounds.'

John firmly believes in miracles.

11

Science

'Why is it that most people think that science and religion don't mix?' I asked the Rev. Dr Bill Knight. He is now a team rector in Berkshire but previously specialised in high-energy nuclear physics. He had worked at the prestigious international research centre in particle interaction in Switzerland.

People who think science and religion are in conflict are about a hundred years out of date (he replied). The end of the nineteenth century and the early twentieth was a triumphalist period for science – just as earlier centuries were for religion. There was this feeling that science could do anything. That's now been shown to be a fallacy. Science is very good at investigating but it has its own presuppositions and there is no more justification for accepting these than there is for accepting the presuppositions that come from philosophy. The world is intelligible in different ways. Science is about mechanism – how things happen – not about purpose. The Bible is only wrong if it is thought to be making scientific statements.

Scientific research requires a sceptical approach. Although suppositions must be made and much is intuited, everything must be regarded sceptically until it is confirmed in the light of further evidence or more experiments. Some scientists carry this attitude of scepticism into every part of their lives. But religious faith requires a different approach.

A recent survey indicated that 50 per cent of scientists believe in the existence of a God, some as the result of their scientific work.

Many scientists with religious faith have found that their faith has been expanded and set on new paths of discovery through what they have learned from scientific investigation. Albert Einstein said: 'Religion without science is blind. Science without religion is lame.' We need them both.

Blaise Pascal

Blaise Pascal's sister was probably telling the plain truth when she wrote: 'As soon as my brother was old enough for talk he gave tokens of an extraordinary mind . . . which surprised everyone . . . He was always far ahead of his age.' From earliest years he gave clear indications of genius and at the age of sixteen he wrote a scientific treatise that showed brilliant and original thinking.

Blaise Pascal was born in 1623, in a France well on the way to recovery after years of bitter war and disruption. He was the middle one of three children, with an older and a younger sister. His mother died when he was only three years old and – unusually for the time – his father undertook the education of the three children himself. Etienne Pascal seems to have been a wise and enlightened teacher. He taught the children by reason rather than by rote. For example, he explained the principles underlying language study, so that the children could grasp foreign languages in a methodical way. He carefully timetabled the age and stage at which Blaise should embark on different subjects so that he should not be pressured. He himself was keen on mathematics but in order not to tax his son too much or too soon, he decided to postpone teaching him geometry until Blaise was sixteen; no books on the subject were allowed in the house, nor was the topic discussed within the family.

But the story goes that one day, when Blaise was twelve, his father came into the room to find him surrounded by diagrams he had drawn. Blaise had discovered the principles of geometry for himself. He had had to invent his own terms to describe straight lines and circles – he called circles 'rounds'. When his father found him he was in the middle of trying to prove that the three angles of a triangle add up to two right angles. He had reasoned that it must be so and was now working out the proof.

The family had lived in Paris since Blaise was eight years old, with all the benefits of contact with intellectual circles and academic studies. But when he was seventeen, the family moved to Rouen. Etienne was appointed the king's representative to assess and levy taxes but when he took over the job he found affairs and figures in a terrible mess. Blaise helped him sort things out and decided that a *machine* was needed to do the wearisome adding, subtracting, multiplying and dividing. So he invented a calculator that could do all these things and come up with the final result. Within five years he had produced fifty models of calculators – all of slightly different design – and he sent one as a gift to the chancellor. It was a simple machine, small enough to carry around – and it worked! By 1652 he had produced a standard commercial model which went on sale.

But before this time arrived the whole Pascal family had undergone a profound religious experience – though each one was affected in a different way. In 1646 Etienne had an accident; he was hurrying out to try to stop a duel and he slipped on the ice. Two brothers came to help him and stayed with the family for three months, bringing healing to Etienne and influencing the whole family through their teaching and Christian lifestyle. Blaise began to study his Bible – so thoroughly that in time he could quote any passage from memory, giving his own translation into French as he went.

Blaise Pascal had never been thoroughly fit and when he was only twenty-three he fell ill through overwork. Five years later his father died. One sister was already married and the other sister carried out her long-cherished wish to take the veil and enter a convent. Pascal was now free from family responsibilities and entered enthusiastically into the life of the court and the brilliant society of the day. He revelled in the intellectual stimulus and frequented the salons of great ladies to enjoy the pleasure of fine conversation. They, in turn, were delighted to show off this brilliant young celebrity. But in spite of his success and the dazzling prospects ahead, Pascal admitted that he was unhappy and un-settled. The world of culture and the intellect did not satisfy him. He confided to his sister, Jacqueline, who was now a nun, that he was sick of the follies and amusements of the world. His conscience was troubling him too. God seemed far away, and he described this seeming absence of God as 'the void within the void'.

Pascal began again to read his Bible and to pray. Then, on the night of 23 November 1654, he had an experience of the spiritual world which was to stamp his life indelibly and remain imprinted on his memory until he died. He had a vision, which he timed meticulously as lasting for two hours. The moment it was over, Pascal seized paper and pen and quickly wrote his account of it. Later he copied the words on to parchment. The original paper is still in existence and the strange mixture of Bible verses, philosophy and devotional words written there has been endlessly analysed by all kinds of people who have reached all kinds of conclusions. No one can claim to give the true explanation but what *is* certain is the effect that this encounter with the spiritual world had on Pascal himself. In 1657 a colleague wrote: 'It seems difficult to get hold of M. Pascal as he is immersed in devotions; but all the same he has not lost sight of mathematics.' But now, added to his devotions and his mathematical studies was a deep joy – a hilarity – which his sister's grave religious order could not wholly approve.

In 1658 Pascal was absorbed in a mathematical problem which Galileo had said was insoluble and which had totally baffled Descartes. He finally achieved the impossible and solved it. His sister Gilberte said that he did so when he was unable to sleep because of toothache. (He was ill that year but would not allow his illness to interfere with his work.) Pascal did not publish his solution but instead advertised a competition for scientists to solve the problem within three months. Not surprisingly, no one did, so Pascal published the solution himself. But he never signed his work from the time of his vision – was he trying to avoid the temptation of personal pride?

He made further attempts to fight pride. He wore an iron belt with small spikes next to his skin. In 1660 he gave up all his luxuries – his horse and carriage, beautiful tapestries, and most of his books except the Bible. Then he deserted his beloved mathematics and science in order to identify with the poor and help relieve their needs. He began a society for providing public vehicles on the streets of Paris. It was a great success, but he sent the profits he made to hospitals and a relief fund.

All his life Blaise Pascal sought for truth. When he was a child, someone at the dinner table struck their porcelain plate with a knife and he noticed the sound that it made. He also noticed that the sound stopped when the plate was touched. At once, his sister recalled, he wanted to know why. From that observation he went on to question and make further experiments in sound. Always, he searched for meaning and for truth. But he discovered that in science itself, reason is not enough. Geometry had to be given a start in the form of initial propositions, which could not be proved but had to be accepted. Pascal believed that these first principles are not guesswork or uncertain facts, but are just as true as the things that can be proved by reason. They are the product of a different kind of knowledge which is known not by reason but by what Pascal called '*le coeur*' – the heart. He wrote: 'Reason has to trust these intuitions of *le coeur* and has to base upon them every rational argument.' In matters of religious faith, Pascal believed also that God's grace was needed as well as man's intellect: 'It is the way of God, who does all things gently, to put religion into the mind by reason and into the heart by grace' and 'it is the heart that feels God, not the reason'.

Pascal died in 1662, at the early age of thirty-nine. Yet he had achieved almost impossible feats in science and mathematics as well as arguing powerfully in religious debate. But it was his vision – found sewn into his doublet when he died – that gave life and meaning to his superb powers of reason. The joy and peace that his vision brought never left him. His *Pensées* (*Thoughts*), often jotted down as fragments and not prepared for publication, survive to remind us of the spiritual vision of the great man of science and reason.

Maureen Palmer

The Rev. Canon Dr Maureen Palmer is Sub Dean of Guildford Cathedral but I sat in her office on a sunny summer day not to talk to her about the Church but about her scientific vocation. I suppose I had not been prepared for the person who sat opposite me – a small, quick-moving, smiling woman, busy but clearly giving me her whole attention. Although Maureen is now a full-time cleric, she has not shed her scientific background and involvement and I was keen to hear her story and to discover how she combines Christian faith with scientific study. I learned that she is Warden of the Society of Ordained Scientists and that there is a large number of scientists who are also clergy.

Maureen was brought up in a churchgoing family – in fact church dominated the first few years of her life. But as she grew older she felt very confused about what God was really like. She imagined him as two-faced. When she asked who had made the flowers and the animals she was told that it was God – so he must be good and generous. Yet he seemed to have a stern and punishing face too, for it was God, she was told, who would be cross if she was naughty. He seemed to be the invisible police-man on her trail. But when she was four years old everything changed. Their home was badly bombed and her father was never the same again. He had been a churchwarden, but from that time he seldom set foot in church again. She continued going to church with her mother but when they moved house they went to a different church. A great deal used to be said about sin and Maureen decided that God was both boring and demanding, a spoilsport, waiting to stop her doing anything she was enjoying.

One day, she went to play with a friend whose father was a doctor. It was a memorable and important day in Maureen's life, for it gave her the first exciting glimpse into the world of nature and science. The doctor let her look down his microscope at sections of leaves, stems and flowers. A whole new world opened up. This kind adult friend listened to her and answered her questions seriously. He gave her a little book called *Exploring Nature*. She began to collect specimens of spiders and beetles and dissect any that she found dead. Sadly the friend and her doctor father moved away but Maureen's interest in natural history continued and by the time she was fifteen she was deeply immersed in all things scientific. Her church involvement continued too

– but the two interests were kept apart, in quite different compartments.

When Maureen went up to university to study science she still believed in God in spite of the arguments against his existence which she heard. But she seemed to need him less and less. He had been crowded out to become the God of the gaps – necessary only when there was no other answer to give. Then Maureen had a very serious illness which led to her losing her faith altogether, or at least she lost the kind of faith she had grown up with. But gradually, in its place came a stronger faith, one which did not yet have answers to all her questions, but one which was part of her whole life. Maureen realised that it was not possible to live an honest and whole life all the while that she kept her science and her faith in two separate compartments. Somehow she must integrate the two, even though it might take her a while to sort out some of her queries. In fact she recognised that there were some questions she might never be able to answer.

She began by looking at the stories of creation in Genesis alongside what is known scientifically about the beginnings of our world and of life on earth. It was a while before she realised that the Bible stories are not concerned with factual information about the beginning of the world but with the relationship between God and his creation. She began to recognise that while science is putting forward a hypothesis and testing it by experiment, Christians are asking questions about ultimate meaning which cannot be answered by experiment and observation.

But Maureen has also found ways in which scientific discovery actually helps Christians to understand some of the ultimate questions they are asking. Scientists have demonstrated that our universe is in a constant state of change and evolution. It is, in fact, an inventive universe. This provides a very different picture of God from the absent landlord – or the watchmaker who set our universe going at a particular point in past time and then sat back, no longer involved. The God of the changing universe is the God who is at all times in relationship to his created order, holding it in being through his love.

In the incarnation God limited himself by becoming human. In Jesus, he lived, suffered and died. So God is not 'impassable' or unaffected by human beings. He is involved in the suffering of the universe. God allows the creation to be a free process and he emptied himself and became human so that this freedom could exist. Jesus, in his humanity, reveals and demonstrates the self-limiting and self-sacrificing relationship of God to the created world. God still suffers with those who suffer in his world.

In this and other ways Maureen has discovered new insights into God and the spiritual world through her studies in science. But she is the first to admit that she does not have the answers to all her questions – scientific or theological. God is, after all, the God of surprises. One piece of the mosaic may slip happily into place, but there are always other spaces that as yet remain unfilled.

Angela Tilby

The Rev. Angela Tilby is very elusive and that's not surprising because she combines several professions in her very busy life. She presents programmes on the BBC, lectures at a theological college and is also an honorary curate in an Anglican church. I finally managed to track her down and talk to her about her book, *Science and the Soul*. Angela wrote it when she was producing a series of television programmes called *Soul*. The series aimed to explore ways in which religion might respond to new areas of scientific thinking and discovery, especially in the field of cosmology and the study of consciousness. I missed the programmes but read the book with enormous interest and enjoyment.

It is surprising to discover that Angela Tilby is not a scientist herself. Yet in her book she succeeds in helping ordinary people like me to understand scientific concepts better than I have ever done before. As a student Angela specialised in classics and then read theology at Cambridge. She went on to be a radio producer, later moving to television and producing for the BBC such popular and prestigious series as *Everyman* and *Horizon*. She met a good many scientists and scientific journalists in the course of her work and became very interested in science and in what makes scientists tick. She recognised that they have to grapple with the problem of putting across their subject to lay people who have very little background knowledge – the same sort of challenge that theologians face today.

When she was still a young radio producer a colleague told her that she ought to find out about Heisenberg's uncertainty principle. Heisenberg was a leading physicist and Nobel Prize winner, who formulated his uncertainty principle as long ago as 1927. But his findings were deeply disturbing to many scientists, undermining, it seemed, all former beliefs that the universe functions according to fixed laws.

The uncertainty principle relates to quantum mechanics, which is the study of the behaviour of subatomic particles. A subatomic particle is a part of an atom, even smaller than the atom itself. Much reliance has always been placed on the fact that nature behaves predictably, true to its own laws. But the shocking discovery emerged that subatomic particles seem not to do this. A quantum particle exhibits both wave and particle properties and it sometimes behaves like a wave and sometimes like a particle. It seems impossible to predict which way it will choose to behave. Einstein, whose theory of relativity had revolutionised Newtonian physics, found Heisenberg's theory impossible to accept – 'God doesn't play dice' was his comment. Some scientists still maintain that there *are* laws at work, it's just that they have not yet been understood or calculated. But others – scientists who are Christians as well as those who are not – welcome the excitement and the freedom that this concept of uncertainty offers. Instead of a predetermined, mechanistic universe we are up to our necks in a creative, evolving world of openness and possibility.

But Angela Tilby realised that the uncertainty principle also opens up new ways of thinking about God and the way in which he plans and acts. New research that undermines concepts and laws taken for granted for centuries can be disturbing but it can also be liberating. It can open windows on to new thinking and understanding. Scientific exploration has not negated God's existence but thrown new light on him. It certainly puts paid to the one-time picture of God as the watchmaker who set the universe going, then sat back and let it function by its own mechanism. If the universe is unpredictable and evolving God must still be at work in its activity.

On a personal level, Angela had been involved with many Christians who believe that God has a fixed and unalterable plan for their lives. His will is like a blueprint which it is their responsibility to find and follow, with disastrous results if they fail to do so. But the uncertainty principle encourages Christian believers to trust a God who is deeply and continuously involved with every human being even as they are caught up in the thick of life. The accidents, the chances for good or seeming ill that befall us, even the choices we make, are all raw material in which God too can be involved. Whichever way life goes, God is willing to work with us in our lives just as they are, always able to evolve something good and beautiful that can reflect his greatness and glory. Fatalism and determinism go out of the window. Choice, freedom, and the gentle, guiding and creative work of God's Spirit are present to take its place.

Fraser Watts

Susan Howatch's Starbridge novels have met with enormous success. She was already a popular writer when she experienced the great change in her direction in life which is described in another part of this book. She wanted, she told me, to do something worthwhile with royalties from the Starbridge novels and wondered about the possibility of endowing a lectureship in the field of science and theology. It was not chance, she feels sure, that led to a meeting at just about that time with Dr John Polkinghorne, the eminent mathematical physicist and theologian at Cambridge. When Susan made the suggestion to him, he told her that he and a colleague had actually written to suggest the need for such a lectureship only days before. Susan was encouraged to go ahead with her scheme and in 1994 a lectureship in theology and natural science was created in the Faculty of Divinity at Cambridge. And the very first person to be appointed lecturer was Fraser Watts, who is both a research psychologist and an ordained clergyman.

The Rev. Dr Fraser Watts – to give him his full title – read psychology and philosophy at Oxford and then worked in the field of clinical psychology, doing research and lecturing for the National Health Service. He then joined the Medical Research Council at Cambridge and worked for twelve years, mainly in the area of information processing in emotional disorders. Since he was a boy he had felt called to become an ordained clergyman but somehow time had passed and he had made no move in that direction. But when he was forty he began to think seriously about his postponed vocation. He imagined how he'd feel when he came to retirement age if he had left the call unanswered. So he trained for the Anglican ministry, and was ordained as a non-stipendiary minister, which means that he combines honorary work in the Church with a secular job. He remained with the Medical Research Council until his appointment as the very first Starbridge lecturer in theology and natural science.

I asked him first if there were any ways in which it is difficult to be a Christian and also a psychologist. He admitted that there are two broad ways where psychology can sometimes sit uneasily with religion. The first is in what he calls the 'nothing but' theory of humankind. Fraser Watts explains more in his chapter of the book he edited called *Science Meets Faith*. According to the 'nothing but' theorists, men and women are 'nothing but survival machines for our genes' – we have 'minds that are nothing but computer programmes' and we ourselves 'are nothing but our nervous systems'. Fraser Watts believes that these views are suspect when they are treated as scientific certainties. In fact he would argue that they are ideological rather than scientific assertions. It is necessary to make certain assumptions when beginning research, but the 'nothing but' theories do not fall into that category. Nor are the 'nothing but' theories legitimate conclusions resulting from scientific research. In other words, the 'nothing but' theories are unscientific. Worse still, they are bad science because as unjustified presuppositions they run the risk of distorting open-minded enquiries.

Study of the mind and consciousness is of intense interest – even excitement – nowadays. One scientist describes consciousness as 'just about the last surviving mystery' and another comments that 'understanding consciousness with the conscious mind is a wonderful giddy idea'. Fraser Watts believes that it is important and exciting from a religious as well as a scientific point of view. It is because as human beings we possess consciousness of a very special kind that we can reflect, use language, make judgments and, indeed, be spiritual beings. Through our consciousness we can interpret life in religious terms and can come to know God and the spiritual world. Fraser Watts is happy to agree that although mind and consciousness are real and distinct properties, they are grounded in the physical brain. He suspects that new laws will emerge about consciousness different from those that apply to the brain. But he cannot be happy with the dogmatic statement – made in advance of proper research – that we are nothing more than a bundle of neurones.

I asked Fraser Watts about the second difference of opinion between Christians and some psychologists. Freud, and some of his followers, he told me, dismiss belief in God as no more than the fulfilment of a human cry for emotional and psychological reassurance. Men and women feel the need for some kind of emotional support, so they have invented God to meet that need. This argument cannot be proved in the light of the very limited and specialised group of patients who consulted Freud. They were by no means a cross-section of humanity but intellectual, upper middle-class members of *fin de siècle* Viennese society. They were also psychologically sick else they would not have been his patients. Judged on the evidence of such people it could well be argued that some people who are inadequate do feel the need to create God in order to provide themselves with a prop or crutch. It is true, too, that there are a number of such people in most churches. But if the basis of the Church's belief is its mission to show God's love and care it is likely to attract those most aware of their need for support and compassion. The large number of healthy, successful and emotionally robust people who also believe in God could just as easily disprove the theory that God is a human invention to meet personal inadequacy.

It seems that as in so many other branches of scientific study, science neither proves nor disproves the existence of the spiritual world. We need to be wary of protagonists from both sides of the divide who try to proclaim scientific theory as proof for their own ideologies.

12

Prison

In some ways these people who were prisoners have a lot in common with those who tell us about their spiritual experience through solitude. The difference, as Terry Waite points out, is that prisoners have solitude forced upon them. Because they have not *chosen* to be alone, they have to acclimatise themselves to the situation and come to terms with an unsought solitude. In most cases they are living in uncongenial, often squalid, conditions, devoid of decent food, warmth or sanitation. I wonder very much how I would endure such circumstances, let alone turn them to spiritual good. But many people in our prisons as a result of crime also find the benefit of time to stop, think and reflect on their life up to that time. Many of them too have a deep spiritual experience, as chaplains and prison visitors confirm. Solitude and time to reflect can open a window to new experiences of God.

Terry Waite

I still remember the shock waves that followed the news that Terry Waite, the Archbishop of Canterbury's special envoy, had been taken hostage in Beirut. I was off on a fortnight's holiday abroad and fully expected to hear news of his release before we got home. But he was to spend 1,763 days in captivity – over four years – and most of that time in solitary confinement. For the months before his capture, his tall, often sombre, six foot seven figure, had been a familiar one in our newspapers, during his years of negotiating on behalf of hostages. Now he was one himself.

Terry Waite was born in 1939 and grew up in the Cheshire

145

countryside, where he and his family occupied the large police house and garden allocated to his father as village policeman. Like his father, he is sensitive, intelligent and enigmatic. In solitary confinement he had only too much time to ask the questions: 'Who am I? What am I?' and as we read his autobiography, woven so graphically into the account of his years as a hostage, we wonder the same. In spite of his struggle to be honest and open, we have to acknowledge in him all the complementary and conflicting ingredients contained in every complex and mature human being.

After serving in the Grenadier Guards, Terry Waite was accepted for the Church Army, where he helped for a time in a hostel for down-and-outs, and then travelled the country running village missions. Later he was transferred to the education branch of the Church of England where he began to fulfil his true potential. Gradually, his growing skills and abilities began to be in demand all over the world. Apart from lightning overseas tours, he and his family – he was now married, with young children – lived in Rome, then in Uganda. When his children were nearing their teens, he returned to the UK, working first for the British Council of Churches before becoming the Archbishop of Canterbury's special envoy.

Before his capture in 1987, Terry Waite was due to meet American hostages in Beirut. A man known to Waite, who had previously taken him secretly to visit hostages, arrived at the hotel and drove him rapidly through the night-time streets of Beirut. When the car stopped and he was bundled into another car, then blindfolded, he began to feel certain that he himself had now been kidnapped. After two days of waiting and uncertainty, he was driven to a building and pushed into an underground, white-tiled cell, seven feet by ten feet and in places too low for him too stand upright. There was a heavy steel door fastened with thick iron bars. He guessed that he was in one of a network of underground cells, nicknamed by the hostage Terry Anderson as the 'Lebanese gulag'.

From that time on, in spite of changes of location, the same terrible conditions prevailed. Cockroaches and mosquitoes abounded. The room was shuttered and barred, so that no air or light could penetrate. The monotony of solitude and the passing of unmarked time was only broken by the once daily walk – blindfold – to the toilet and washroom and by the arrival of sparse rations of the same plain food. Whenever a guard entered the room Terry Waite had to pull down the blindfold which he wore in readiness. The dark, the absence of colour or visual stimulus – the solitariness – would have sent many men mad. Right from the start, in order to maintain his sanity, he made three resolutions: he would indulge in no regrets, no sentimentality and no self-pity. Only so, he believed, could he survive.

In his solitude he remembered the words of a friend, some time before. She had told him that in seeking the liberation of the hostages, he was in reality seeking his own liberation. He wondered if, paradoxically, it would be in prison that he would begin to find that liberation. And what would liberation involve? Freedom from fear, darkness, anxiety?

Dark and light, powerful symbols that occur so often in the Bible, became pregnant with meaning. Light represented truth and honesty as opposed to self-deception and lack of integrity. He wrote later, 'It's painful to be introspective, to see myself in the light of truth. In this solitary dark space the light of truth shines brightly, so brightly that it hurts.'

He was very conscious of himself as 'an ordinary man, chained to a wall, and attempting to struggle through another day of boredom and uncertainty'. Occasionally his guards gave in to his urgent request for books, but only rarely, and the longed for book, when it came, could turn out to be anything from a Mills and Boon romance to Dostoevsky's *The Brothers Karamazov*.

He longed to write, but with no paper and ink, he decided to write his book, *Taken on Trust*, in his head. He re-enacted all the emotions of childhood and of his many experiences up to that time, as he recounted to himself, in detail, the story of his life. He found sustenance and joy, as well as suffering, remorse and self-blame, as he created in his mind the story that he would one day, he hoped, put down on paper. As he went from one chapter of his life to the next, he courageously allowed the spotlight to focus on each part in turn, reflecting on his past with courage and honesty and with all the time in the world to spare. It seemed to him that his experience in captivity was a mirror image of his inward experience. One day, he writes,

> A ray of light enters the room through a minute space between the metal window cover and the wall. Gently it pierces the darkness. It shines with a steadfast intensity and gives me hope. Light is stronger than darkness. Hold on to light. Let it strengthen you.

All his life he had been intensely active. In later years particularly, he had boarded one plane after another, flying all over the world, seeing people, people and more people, attending meetings, dealing with delicate situations and pushing himself in faster and faster mode, higher and higher gear. Now, suddenly, everything had been taken from him and he was left entirely alone, without activity or company. But he had the self-awareness to recognise that this period of solitude was important if he was to digest and resolve the years of action. 'If I can embrace solitude as a friend,' he concluded, 'I might find healing.'

Often Terry Waite's faith was low. He admits, 'There doesn't seem to be a great deal of faith in me. At least the faith that gives me security.' And, 'My faith has been exposed for what it is – uncertain, questioning, vulnerable.' In one time of great distress and illness he doubted the efficacy of prayer. With an honesty that is painful to overhear he confesses, 'I am a long way from the heart of the religion I profess. I hardly know the meaning of love.' As he stripped off layer after layer of the public figure and of the person he had admitted to being, he recognised that much of his heroic action and selfless deeds had been motivated not by love but by the desire to please, to be accepted. Now he wanted to 'grow up'.

'Comfort won't come from without,' he concluded. 'I must find my own inner harmony, my own internal balance.' And he did. His terrible years of captivity, which for many of his temperament and experience would have brought about total breakdown and dissolution, enabled him to strip off the superfluous layers with which we all protect ourselves from too much reality. He sloughed off what had been external and unreal in his faith and reached his own centre. He could say, 'the outer and the inner journeys have at last met' – he had become a whole person in the fullest sense. For all its pain, Terry Waite's book is also one of triumph, for through his ordeal he was able to affirm: 'I am truly happy to have discovered that suffering need not destroy; it can be creative.' And, he adds, 'I would wish that for all who feel oppressed and without hope.'

I had been deeply moved by Terry Waite's book so I was delighted to be able to chat with him in person. We talked about loneliness first. 'It's a state of mind,' he said. In his imprisonment he had learned to turn loneliness into creative solitude. It's an accepted fact that extroverts are sociable creatures who like the company of others, whereas introverts like solitude and want to be alone. But Terry Waite thinks that we can be too hasty in assessing others and putting them into one category or another. 'My friends thought I was an extrovert,' he said, 'but that was not the whole story.' He agrees that although we all need time alone as well as needing one another, many of us find it difficult to make time for solitude, which is so necessary for our refreshment. 'In my case, solitude was forced upon me,' he said. 'Sometimes it seemed as if the time was being wasted – so many apparently useless thoughts. But all that was going on in my mind was part of a gradual movement.'

I commented on the honesty of his account – his refusal to pretend that his faith was stronger than it was. He believes that Christians should not pretend to feelings they don't have, or experiences that are not wholly genuine, even though it may seem that they are slipping below the expected standard. He acknowledges that his faith was not always high but he added with utter conviction: 'Even when circumstances were bleak and my physical condition was deteriorating, I still recognised that I was in the hands of God – I had hope.'

Dietrich Bonhoeffer

Inside my well-worn paperback copy of Dietrich Bonhoeffer's *Letters and Papers from Prison* I discovered a small cutting from

The Times newspaper of 4 April 1985, which I had pasted in. It reports the fortieth anniversary of Bonhoeffer's death, marked by a special ceremony in Flossenburg, Bavaria, the place of his execution. Another cutting from the same paper, too large to paste in, reported in July 1998 the unveiling in Westminster Abbey of the statues of ten modern martyrs. All ten were chosen for 'their openness to death for the glory of Christ' and one of them is Dietrich Bonhoeffer.

He was born in 1906 in Breslau – which then belonged to Prussia – one of a large and happy family. His father was a distinguished professor of psychiatry at Berlin University and his mother's grandfather had been a professor of church history. Young Dietrich played with the children of his parents' fellow academics.

So with inherited abilities and a stimulating upbringing, it's scarcely surprising that he himself went up to Berlin University in 1924, qualified in theology in 1927, and was regarded by his teachers as a brilliant and outstanding student. After further study in New York, he was appointed lecturer in systematic theology in Berlin University. But, unlike many churchgoing people in Germany, Bonhoeffer was not prepared to immerse himself in the academic world and turn a blind eye to what was happening in the world outside. He clearly recognised the dangers lurking in the new Nazi philosophy and made no bones about saying so. In 1933 he denounced Hitler and his policies on the radio. He came to England to take charge of the German congregations in London. He felt that he must warn his fellow Germans about the complacent attitude of many Christians in Germany to the Nazi philosophy. He also warned the Church in the West about what was going on in his motherland.

He returned to Germany but in 1936 he was banned from teaching by the Nazi authorities. He was a gentle man who had always been a pacifist but he began to realise that he must give his support to resisting Hitler. Through his brother-in-law he became increasingly involved with other responsible Germans who were trying to oppose the Nazi doctrines. In 1939 he was on a lecture tour in the United States and friends there – knowing war might come – begged him to accept a permanent post and stay on, but Bonhoeffer was convinced that he ought to return to Germany. He took one of the last ships to sail before war broke out and once home again he spent his time encouraging like-minded Christians, writing and supporting the resistance movement.

The Gestapo forbade him to write, lecture or make speeches of any kind and would not let him remain in Berlin. But somehow he managed to continue his work until, in April 1943, on a bright Monday morning, he was arrested. As there was no concrete charge against him Bonhoeffer assumed that his time in prison would be short. After a week or so in isolation and in squalid conditions, the authorities transferred him, because of his family connections, to somewhere less harsh. He was allowed to write to his parents and most of what we know about Bonhoeffer's experiences and thoughts during his imprisonment comes from the letters he wrote to family and friends. Of course the letters were censored, and because he wanted to set his parents' minds at rest he said little about the discomforts of prison life. He had his Bible, some books and writing paper. 'Physical wants have to take a back seat for the time being,' he wrote, 'which is something I find a real enrichment of my experience . . . It is quite as good as a Turkish bath for the soul.' He added: 'In the prison courtyard here there is a thrush which sings beautifully . . . One is grateful for little things, and that also is gain.' But he admits to them, 'For all my sympathy with the contemplative life, I am not a born Trappist!' All the same, he is determined to accept the limitations and not give way to feelings of resentment or discontent.

In spite of unexpected delays and disappointments he was determined to be constructive about his imprisonment. He writes: 'Much as I long to be out of here, I do not believe that a single day has been wasted. What will come out of my time here it is too early to say. But something is bound to come out of it.' Bonhoeffer was not merely trying to cheer himself up in order to survive psychologically. He genuinely put his trust in God's ability to control everything and bring good out of any situation. He quotes the psalmist's words, 'My time is in your hand', though he goes on to say that he has also found himself echoing the words of another psalm, 'How long, Lord?'

Bonhoeffer soon won the goodwill and affection of many of the warders and medical orderlies so that they allowed him to write letters to his friends, often on scraps of paper. In writing to them he could be more outspoken. He was frank about the lessons he had been learning. In November 1943 he wrote:

> In the last month or two I have learned as never before how much comfort and help I get from others . . . We often want to do everything ourselves, but that is a mark of false pride . . . When we want to calculate just how much we have learnt ourselves and how much we owe to others, it is not only un-Christian but useless. What we are in ourselves and what we owe to others makes us a complete whole.

In a later letter he confesses that, although he has discovered the easy way of facing adversity is 'to ignore it altogether', he has not yet managed the more difficult way – 'to face up to it and triumph over it'. To some extent, he admits, his cheerfulness is a mask for the horror of what he is going through. He has managed to get used to the physical hardships, but not the psychological strain. He no longer knows whether, deep down, he is the person who is suffering such misery or the man who puts on a show of contentment and cheerfulness for the benefit of others and even for himself. But in a later letter he asserts his firm belief that in Christ God will restore and bring again our past. 'What does "bring again" mean? It means that nothing is lost, everything is taken up again in Christ, though of course it is transfigured in the process, becoming transparent, clear and free from all self-seeking and desire.' He also reaffirms his decision in 1939 to leave the safety of the United States and to return to Germany. He did not know what was going to happen to him, but he wrote to his friend: 'Don't worry if something worse befalls me . . . I must be able to know for certain that I am in the hands of God, and not of men. Then everything can be easy, even the severest privations . . . what matters is that I should face everything in faith.'

As months went by and he was still held in prison he began to realise that the delays might continue – the date of promised release be postponed again and again. Then, on 20 July 1944 the carefully planned plot by the resistance to assassinate Hitler failed. Bonhoeffer was sure that he would be incriminated and believed he might be put to death. His earlier optimism had gone, but he still committed himself to his people and dedicated himself to truth and right.

Bonhoeffer used his imprisonment to ponder deeply in his own field of theology. He began to realise that God did not belong within a framework of religion. Religious people, he thought, used God as a last resort – someone to call to their aid either when they had problems they could not solve or they were too weak to manage alone. For Bonhoeffer, this is keeping God at the border-lines of life, using him as a *deus ex machina*. He foresaw a time when people would push out the boundaries of personal achievement so far that a God who was at the edges would became more and more superfluous. He came to the conclusion that instead of frantically trying to find room for God he would 'like to speak of God not on the borders of life but at its centre, not in weakness but in strength, not, therefore, in man's suffering and death but in his life and prosperity'. In a later letter he asserted, 'Christ takes hold of a man in the centre of his life.'

In the autumn of 1944 Bonhoeffer was moved to much stricter confinement in Prinz Albert Strasse, where he had far less contact with family or friends. Then, one day, in February 1945, he seemed to have disappeared. The Gestapo refused to give his family any information and it was not until some time after the collapse of Germany in the summer of 1945 that the truth about his last months emerged. He had been moved to Buchenwald, then to Schonberg and finally to Flossenburg. He spent his last few weeks with prisoners from all over Europe. In the more relaxed atmo-sphere of the schoolroom at Schonberg, Bonhoeffer was asked to conduct a service on Low Sunday – the Sunday after Easter. Shortly after, two civilians came in and said: 'Prisoner Bonhoeffer, get ready to come with us.' They all knew what these ominous words meant. Bonhoeffer gathered his things together, then wrote his name and address with a blunt pencil at the beginning, middle and end of his volume of Plutarch, which he left behind, in order to leave some trace of his presence there for those who searched later. Then he said to an English officer, Payne Best, also held there: 'This is the end – for me the beginning of life.'

The prisoners journeyed till evening and had then to face a full court martial. But the outcome in every case was a foregone conclusion. It had already been decided who were to be spared and who would die. Next morning, while it was still dark, a convoy set off for Flossenburg and at dawn on Monday 9 April 1945 the condemned men were executed. The camp doctor saw Bonhoeffer at prayer in the preparation cell before his turn came to face death. On the same day, in another place, his brother-in-law was executed too.

Father Frantisek Lizna

Frantisek Lizna was born in Czechoslovakia in 1947 at the time of the Communist regime. I came to hear of him through Keston Institute, the centre in the UK for information about prisoners of conscience in Eastern Europe under Communist rule. That was some years ago but when I tried to track down Father Lizna, hoping I might talk to him now, my efforts were in vain. I believe that he is a Jesuit priest working more freely now in Czechoslovakia.

Frantisek is by no means a typical protester. When he was still a teenager he tore down a Soviet flag to demonstrate his anger at Soviet oppression. As a result he was put in prison for eight months and then, as an ex-prisoner, was forced to serve for two years in the punishment corps of the army. From then on the authorities had their eye on him He was later rearrested and while he was in labour camp he met some of the great religious leaders who had been there since the 1950s, when the monastic orders were dissolved. Lizna was profoundly moved by these men and made up his mind to become a priest too, once he was free. Religious persecution was less harsh for a while and during that time he was out of prison and labour camp and able to complete his training for the Roman Catholic priesthood. He was ordained in 1974, and anticipated with great awe and emotion the time when he would celebrate his first Mass in his home village. But when the longed-for day arrived the authorities revoked his licence and he was forbidden to officiate as a priest again. He accepted the bitter disappointment and the work of a medical orderly which he was forced to do instead. But after a time he was arrested again, sentenced and imprisoned on a charge of sending information about the trials of Christian believers to the West.

The authorities had hoped to hush up this particular trial but foreign reporters crowded outside the court room and a large group of youthful supporters were there too. Lizna's obvious integrity and goodness seemed to expose the tawdriness and falseness of the sham trial. As he left the courtroom after he was sentenced, he held up his handcuffed hands quite naturally in order to give a priestly blessing to the crowd of young people. They broke spontaneously into a triumphant song: 'Christ the Victor has risen, rejoice!'

Father Lizna always behaved with courtesy and consideration to his guards – yet was surprised when they were more restrained and less brutal in their dealings with him than they were with most other prisoners.

I remember reading his letters, written in prison during the 1980s, which somehow managed to reach the West through Keston Institute. Before his imprisonment, a friend had advised Fr Lizna to flee the country but he had replied, 'Why, our prisons are greatly in need of a priest!' A fellow Christian commented, 'Though he is a priest without a parish, a licence and even the right to say Mass, he has become instead a priest for the whole country.'

Somehow Fr Lizna managed to turn the miserable and degrading circumstances of prison life into a celebration of faith. He realised how easy it is in the outside world for the constant busyness and bustle of life to crowd out the spiritual world; but that, he firmly believes, is the true and solid basis of living. So he savoured the quietness and even the bareness of his cell which – he hastened to assure his family – 'is nothing like as gloomy as you imagine'.

One of his letters made a deep impression on me at the time it first reached the West. One April day, Frantisek Lizna wrote about the way in which he was able to see God and be conscious of the spiritual world even through the dust that came into his cell:

A beautiful morning! The sunshine in our cell assures us that God never forgets us. He pours down light on everyone, good and evil alike. How quietly the sun fills the room – quite differently from the way we human beings behave. Its strong delicate rays carefully illumine every grain of dust. We're no longer alone. I'd love to greet every particle of dust – here hated by everyone. I'm grateful that they're here. They show how something normally despised can be transfigured into something beautiful. Look how each grain sparkles! The grace to see God's glory has been given me here in prison.

Then, on 16 June, he ended his letter home: 'I almost forgot that I'm still in Prague. This is when I realise that it's not where but how we live that matters. Let's invoke the Holy Spirit, who can melt all prison bars, for we know that the strongest bars are not made of steel but of hard and cruel hearts.'

13

Hearing a voice

If one of our friends should tell us that they had been hearing voices, we should probably suggest tactfully that it might help to see a psychiatrist. No doubt if Joan of Arc was alive today that would be the reaction of French as well as English, when she referred constantly to 'my voices'. Hearing voices inside the head, when no other person is speaking, may well be a sign of mental illness. And that may be the case even when the voice and the message are believed to have come from God.

But it would be unwise to write off every experience of hearing a voice as caused by mental illness. The problem comes when we try to tell the difference between a psychiatric disorder and a spiritual experience. In the stories that follow, the people involved are emotionally stable, normal people, not in the habit of having out-of-the-body experiences. Added to that, the message they received did not encourage them to kill or attack other people, but was the means of bringing about change in their lives which has lasted and has made them better, more integrated people, with a strength and resolve to lead transformed lives dedicated to God and to doing good.

David Hamilton

When I arrived at Manchester railway station on a January morning, David Hamilton was waiting to meet me and whisk me off to the offices of Teen Challenge. David heads up the Manchester centre of this Christian organisation, whose mission is to bring help of every kind to youngsters who need it – in schools and clubs, but also to those on the streets of the city.

We sat opposite each other in the little basement office while David told me his story. He has a gentle, kind face and unless he had shown me the fiercely patriotic Irish Protestant tattoos on his arms, I would never have guessed that he had been a violent man of action and a terrorist. He told me that he has over four hundred scars on his arms alone, the legacy of street fighting and knifings.

David grew up in Belfast on a large housing estate of some fifteen thousand inhabitants. Although he is a Protestant, he played football happily with his friend Bobby Sands, later to become widely known for his fast to death as an IRA prisoner. But as soon as 'the troubles' in Northern Ireland began, the two religious groups became far more polarised. Bobby and his family moved away. No Catholic family dared to live on a largely Protestant estate nor did any Protestant remain where the majority were Catholic. Street violence would erupt two or three times a week, David told me, and petrol bombs were often thrown. So the rifts between the two groups became wider.

Although the demarcation was religious, the members of each group were not necessarily religious people. David's parents did not go to church. But David entered into the aggression with enthusiasm. In common with nearly all the teenagers on their estate, he joined the paramilitary Ulster Defence Association but soon got into trouble and landed up in Borstal. Once out of Borstal he was arrested not long after for armed robberies, which he had carried out to get money for arms. This time he was sent to Longkesh Prison. Prison officers locked the prisoners in their cells at night and unlocked them in the morning, but during the day they were housed together in a compound without any supervision. They were free to wear their uniform and carry on with their army-style routine. Communication with prisoners in other compounds was officially forbidden but perfectly possible, with notes thrown over the high wire fences. So prison provided an ideal training ground for young terrorists.

By the time David left prison in 1973, he had made up his mind to become a thorough-going terrorist so he joined the more extreme and secretive Ulster Volunteer Force. The local group used to meet weekly to plan their next moves. Before long David was made area commander with a team of his own. The Army would often raid the home where he lived with his three sisters and brother. Later, when he got married he told his wife: 'The UVF will come first.' David left masks and equipment downstairs for his comrades, so that they could come in during the night to collect supplies while his wife and newborn baby son slept upstairs. David realised the danger he was in and supposed that one day he would meet his death, probably at the hands of the IRA. But this was a risk he was well prepared to take. He had sworn on the Bible that he would die for the cause and he was prepared to do so. He lived for the present and the immediate future – the rest could take care of itself.

In 1978 he was rearrested for bank robberies (again to get money for arms), and sent to the Maze Prison to await trial. On the day of the trial his mother was there and heard him sentenced to twelve years' imprisonment – later commuted to eleven. She wept bitterly and told an elderly friend – a woman of eighty-three – 'My David is a hopeless case.' Her friend promised: 'I'm going to pray for him every day, that God will work a miracle and he will come home a different person.'

Two years into his sentence David returned to his cell one night to find a gospel tract had been left there. He laughed and crumpled it into a ball. He was sure that God was interested only in good people and he was well aware that he was not a good man. But suddenly, in the midst of his normal thinking, an alien thought came unbidden into his mind. A voice said: 'It's time to become a Christian.' The thought was so foreign to anything he had ever considered that he tried to dismiss it. Three times he picked up the Gideon Bible provided in each cell and three times he put it down. Once he looked at the fly-leaf and turned up the recommended verse of John 3:16: 'God so loved the world that he gave his one and only Son that whoever believes in him shall not perish but have everlasting life.' It couldn't mean everyone, he decided, and when he told his cell-mate what he was thinking, he confirmed David's fears. 'You couldn't be a Christian even if you wanted to because God wouldn't have you,' he said. David put the Bible back.

But then another unbidden thought came into his head: 'God

has kept you alive.' Again, this thought was so foreign to all his thinking that he knew that it was God speaking directly to him. At first he thought the words made no sense, until he began to think back over his life – not something he was in the habit of doing. He realised how many times he *had* survived against the odds. Once he had been accosted at close range by an IRA man who put a gun to his head threatening to kill him. Somehow he had come out of it wounded but alive. Another time he was inside a café which had been held up by armed men. He began to run towards a door to escape; then, for some unknown reason, he had turned around and made for the door into the kitchen instead, and escaped that way. The police who questioned him afterwards asked what made him change his mind about the escape route he took and he admitted he had no idea. Then they had told him that two or three armed men had been waiting for him on the other side of the door he had avoided on impulse.

Now, the more he went back over the past the more he began to recognise how many times he had escaped death by a hair's breadth. Yes, the voice he had heard was right. He *had* for some reason been given a lease of life far beyond the chances of fate or anything he deserved. It must mean, then, that God *did* care about him. And if God cared about him and had seen to it that he escaped death, then it must mean too that God had a plan for his life. There *must* be an alternative lifestyle to this cycle of terrorism, robbery and imprisonment, that would surely lead to violent death. He made a decision, there and then, to embrace that alternative life – whatever the cost might be. He knelt down and repeated a prayer inviting Jesus Christ to take him and to take charge.

His life, he told me, was literally turned around overnight. No other person, or book, not even the Bible had brought him face to face with the spiritual world. He believes that God spoke to him direct. His life has been completely transformed.

Alec Smith

Being the child of a famous parent can create all kinds of difficulties. Alec Smith insists: 'I don't want to make excuses. I'd have gone off the rails no matter who my father had been . . . and I can't find it in my heart to blame him.' But to anyone who reads his story it seems very clear that his family background had a good bit to do with the turn his life took when he was a teenager.

Alec and his older brother and sister enjoyed an idyllic early childhood in a rambling family farmstead in the lowland hills of Selukwe in what was then called Rhodesia. He was free to explore the scrubland countryside and to watch and investigate the harmless wild life. He was allowed to help by driving the huge ox cart, when they rounded up the cattle for their customary dip against ticks. As a family they would go for walks around the farm with the dogs and enjoy a sundowner on the verandah, watching the spectacular sunsets. Because his father, Ian Smith, was a Member of Parliament, he was away in Salisbury for several months every year, but for the rest of the family life carried on in the same pleasant pattern.

Everything was soon to change. When Alec was seven, he was sent – kicking and screaming – to boarding-school and in 1964, when he was twelve, his father, Ian Smith, became Prime Minister. Nothing was ever to be the same again. The informal, homely farmstead was exchanged for the imposing, glittering residence that he must now think of as 'home'. Thick luxurious carpets covered the floors of every room and Alec calculated that the three enormous lounges in the public reception area could each seat fifty-six people without bringing in extra chairs. Although there was a small part of the house set aside for more informal family use, it felt more like living in an hotel than a normal family home. His parents' official duties meant that he might go for several days without even glimpsing them.

At school he began to be known as 'Ian Smith's son' rather than a person in his own right. He either met with abuse from boys whose parents held different political views or was toadied to by others who wanted to get in with the famous. He began to drink and to enjoy getting drunk along with a crowd of cronies who all hero-worshipped Elvis Presley.

When the swinging sixties eventually reached Africa, Alec joined the hippies with their drugs and flower power. For many of his friends the moral and spiritual standards they had once been taught were thrown out. Relativism and situation ethics had cut the ground from under the feet of moralists, they believed, and, as he put it, 'God went out the window.' Alec himself preferred not to think too hard or to give way to the despair and hopelessness that might have followed. But like many others he turned to drugs, for fun rather than to opt out.

He passed his first exams by swotting up on crib books, and then went home in the vacation to enjoy more drugs sessions with his friends in Salisbury. At university he joined student activists – again for the excitement rather than because of strongly held political views. As their spokesperson he caused a good deal of embarrassment to the government as well as to his own father. By the time he was twenty-one Alec had a reputation for being a political activist and a drop-out. He was sent down from university at the end of his first year and by this time he had broken off relations with his parents.

He was now due for compulsory national service and he hated it. Conditions were brutal. But in spite of harsh restrictions he still managed to get enough drugs to help him survive. Nine months later, immediately he was demobbed from the army, he drove as fast as he could away from the camp, determined to join up with his friends again and to take enough drugs to blot out the memory of those terrible months in the army.

By this time Alec was on LSD and it had become a lifeline. He managed to pay for his expensive habit by drug-pushing, which he justified to himself because he did it only on a small scale and sold only to people who were already addicts. On one occasion he was arrested for smuggling drugs across the border but he was lucky enough to get off with a fine and avoided the harsh imprisonment that might have followed. By now he was out of touch with most of his family but a friend's father got him a job in a photographic business – something that had always interested him. He had to earn enough to pay off his fine and he settled down to the job, though he continued to use drugs himself.

Then, one evening, Alec had an extraordinary experience which seemed utterly unbelievable. He was driving home, high on drugs as usual, when he suddenly heard a voice behind him say: 'Go home and read the New Testament.' He looked quickly into his mirror, but there was no one in the back of the car. But he knew that he *had* heard the voice, so he slowed down, drew in to the kerb, trembling; then stopped the car and turned right round to have a proper look at the back seats. There was no one there. But he was still not satisfied, so he got out and looked all around. There was not a soul to be seen. In the midst of all his confusion and panic he was certain of one thing. He *had* heard that voice and those words *had* been spoken directly to him.

For a couple of days he tried to ignore the words but then he could do so no longer. He had not read the Bible since he was little and did not expect to find a copy anywhere. But when he opened the top drawer in his room, there was a Gideon New Testament. It had been presented to him and to all the other boys at school more than ten years before. He has no idea how it had survived all that time – it had certainly never been used – but now it seemed to be lying waiting for him.

As Alec read, he became aware of a strange thing. Although he was not hallucinating on drugs at the time, he had the extraordinary sensation that the book was alive – pulsing with life, the words shining on the page and leaping off into his mind. He was sure that God had begun to speak to him, and he realised that his life was going to be transformed.

Saint Augustine of Hippo

Augustine was born in 354 in Thagaste, a small-time town in present-day Algeria. His father was a minor government official who worked for Rome and busied himself with bureaucratic affairs. His mother Monica was a devout Christian, who showered intense love and concern on her clever but wayward son. Augustine turned out to be a brilliant pupil at school. He had an emotional, intuitive temperament but was also gifted with a powerful and logical brain. When he was fifteen he had to take a year off school, while his father saved up enough to send him to university. Thagaste was no centre of culture but a small town where teenagers would hang about the street corners or patronise the bars. There was very little to stimulate the mind or encourage culture but Augustine and his cronies made the most of what Thagaste *did* have to offer. Monica was worried out of her mind but there wasn't much that she could do to restrain or influence her self-willed son. He took no notice of his mother's pleas.

When he was seventeen Augustine went up to university in Carthage – a very different place from Thagaste – and was carried away by the glamour and intellectual buzz. Carthage was a great seaport rich in merchandise and intellectual thinking. There was a school of rhetoric down by the quayside and from there ships went to and fro to Rome, trading merchandise and new thinking.

Augustine soon got caught up in the strange half-mythological cult of Manichaeism, which had spread throughout the Roman Empire and even further afield. He also dabbled in astrology. He read widely and enjoyed fierce arguments with his teachers. According to a common custom of the time he set up home with a woman he had no intention of marrying. But Augustine genuinely loved this woman – whose name we don't even know – and he was faithful to her for fourteen years. She bore him a son called Deodatus – 'Gift of God'. It was only years later and because of his mother Monica's insistence that Augustine sent her away.

In time Augustine became a teacher himself but he continued his unquenchable search for wisdom, which had first been inspired by reading Cicero, the Roman orator and writer. Then, when he was twenty-nine, Augustine went to Rome and Monica was distraught. She was afraid he would be completely lost to the Christian faith. But the offer of the professor's chair in rhetoric at Milan was a tremendous career opportunity for such a young man. The imperial court resided in Milan at that time, and Augustine also became court orator as part of the job. He was a young African from an unimportant town yet he had succeeded in arriving at the heart of the Empire, with every prospect of achieving high office and social success. His boyhood friend, Alypius, had also come up through the ranks from his humble start in Thagaste and by then he was a successful lawyer. Yet the two friends knew that they were living shallow and empty lives.

Augustine was still searching for wisdom but he did not believe that religion could satisfy his thirst. All the same, he visited the church in Milan in order to hear Ambrose preach, because he was renowned for oratory. Christian thinkers were then in the vanguard of intellectual investigation. Ambrose was aristocratic, cool and detached and Augustine admired him from afar. He also began to study the Bible in the new way advocated by Ambrose. When Victorinus, who was an eminent academic and literary translator, became a Christian – convinced that he had at last found the truth – Augustine enrolled as a catechumen. This meant that he was formally receiving instruction in the Christian faith. But in spite of the strict moral guidelines that his teachers laid down, Augustine still struggled unsuccessfully against his strong sexual desires. And none of his philosophies seemed able to meet his deep emotional and physical needs.

Then Monica arrived in Milan, determined to arrange a respectable marriage for her son and made him banish his common-law wife of many years. But Augustine took another mistress while he awaited the threatened marriage. It was one day in August that Augustine found the answer to his spiritual search. He had been listening to the story of two young Christians, who had given up their marriage plans in order to serve God wholly. Augustine realised, by contrast, how powerless he was to change his own life. He describes the scene in his *Confessions*. 'There was a garden to our lodging,' he wrote, 'of which, as of the whole house, we had the use, for the master of it, our host, lived not there.' He ran out into the garden, as far from the house as possible. He felt beside himself with anguish and despair. He knew now that it was neither wisdom nor knowledge that he needed. He could not control his own passions and desires and nothing that he had learned or read seemed to help him to do that. His battle was with his will, not his intellect. Unless he genuinely *wanted* to know and experience God, he would remain as much in the dark as he had always been. He could make his body obey his will if he decided to clench his fist or beat his brow. Yet he seemed unable to change his lifestyle or obey the good resolutions he made.

Then, as he was weeping and wrestling with himself he heard a voice. It seemed to be a child's voice. Over and over the voice repeated in a child's sing-song tones, 'Pick up and read. Pick up and read.' At first he thought that the words were part of a children's game, coming perhaps from a nearby house. Then it dawned upon him that the voice was a command from heaven telling him to pick up his Bible and read it. He returned to the spot in the garden where he had laid down his Bible; he decided that he would open it and read the first words his eyes lighted on. And this is what he read: 'We must stop behaving as people do in the dark and be ready to live in the light. So behave properly, as people do in the day. Don't go to wild parties or get drunk or be vulgar or indecent. Don't quarrel or be jealous. Let the Lord Jesus Christ be as near to you as the clothes you wear. Then you won't try to satisfy your selfish desires.' Later, Augustine wrote: 'In an instant, as I came to the end of the sentence, it was as though the light of confidence flooded into my heart and all the darkness of doubt was dispelled.' The spiritual journey of one of the great saints and fathers of the Church had at last begun.

George Fox

George Fox, founder of the Quakers – or Society of Friends – was born in 1624, the eldest child of what one biographer described as 'honest and sufficient parents'. His father was a weaver and a respectable churchwarden in Fenny Drayton in Leicestershire. His mother Mary was proud to be descended from 'the stock of martyrs' and she seems to have been her husband's social superior, an accomplished woman who was a cut above the other villagers. She used to answer George's endless childhood questions and had a strong influence on the boy. People still remembered only too well the times when, in turn, both Roman Catholics and Protestants had been martyred for their faith.

When George was one year old and Charles I became king, churches up and down the country were disgracefully run. There were market stalls in the aisles of St Paul's Cathedral, and local vicars were allowed to keep hens in the chancel of their churches. They used to let their dogs roam in and out of church and cock their legs against the communion table, on which the parishioners flung their cloaks. Archbishop Laud did his best to put an end to such carryings-on and to restore a sense of reverence to the churches; but there were sharp differences between his view that *places* should be kept holy for worship and the Puritans' belief that it was *people*, not places, that mattered. This was the kind of religious climate in which George and his brothers and sisters grew up. (We don't know how many siblings he had because a sexton's wife, some time in the eighteenth century, tore out pages of the baptismal records in order to have covers for her preserves, so no records survive.)

George seems to have been a serious, questioning boy from the start. He was an observant child – shrewd at summing people up even when he was young. When he was eleven he made up his mind that he would always be honest in every way, that he would never say one thing and mean another. He also determined not to be greedy in eating or drinking. His upbringing was strictly puritanical and probably repressive, and as an adolescent George suffered badly from too great a sense of guilt. One of his dreams, which he recounts in his *Journal*, is probably significant. He writes that he saw a woman, dressed in white, who walked with him into a treasure vault. When she held out her hand he stopped her, saying, 'Touch not the treasure.' He became increasingly wretched and unhappy, burdened by the 'whisperings of Satan' and laid low by his fears and uncertainties. He wrote: 'When it was day, I wished for night, and when it was night I wished for day . . . I could not believe that I should ever overcome; my troubles, my sorrows, and my temptations were so great.' He often used to fast and describes how he 'went and sat in hollow trees and lonesome places . . . and in the night walked mournfully about by myself, for I was a man of sorrows'.

Some of his relatives thought he was clearly cut out to be a minister, but others did not agree; perhaps they thought he was a little too much of an individualist. So he was apprenticed to a shoemaker instead. Even then, as a boy, he was known for the way he always kept to what he said. A favourite word of his was 'verily' and those who knew him used to say that 'if George says "verily" there is no altering him'.

One small incident seems to have made a deep impression on his sensitive soul. One day when he went to market for his master, he bumped into his cousin and a friend. Both of them had the reputation of being good, churchgoing young men. They invited George to join them for a drink, but after a while they challenged him to a drinking contest, explaining that the one who gave up first had to foot the bill for everyone else's drinks. George was profoundly shocked and deeply disillusioned. He was looking for a faith that would mean something in practical ways but the kind of Christianity he had met seemed an empty sham.

Soon after that incident he left home to search for a faith he could live by. He was so absorbed in his search that he seems not to have noticed the Civil War which had broken out by this time; he certainly doesn't mention it in his *Journal*. He made his way by easy stages to London, where he began to attend different churches in order to hear the great preachers of his day. But none of them could answer the deep needs of his spirit. His Baptist uncle could not help him either and in 1645, when he was twenty-one, he returned home. His family thought that marriage and the army would do him good but George set off again, this time for Coventry, and spent another year away from home. When he got back he went to see the minister of Fenny Drayton, who encouraged George to talk to him. But when the vicar started quoting what George had been saying to him in his sermons, George's sensitive soul recoiled. He went instead to the vicar of a neighbouring parish who tried to jolly the serious young man along. He suggested that George should try tobacco to calm him down and sing a few psalms to cheer himself up. He also made fun of George to his servants, so that even the milkmaid started giggling whenever he appeared. Dr Craddock of Coventry – another one George consulted – flew into a temper because George trod on his flower-bed by mistake.

George was in despair. He stopped going to church – much to his parents' sorrow – and instead went off alone on a Sunday, taking his Bible with him. Before long he set off on his travels again, this time up to Derbyshire, where he came across a group of Baptists who were as dissatisfied as he was with churchgoing and dead church rituals, without any reality or life. George was particularly struck by a middle-aged housewife called Elisabeth Hooton. (He had very different ideas from his contemporaries about women and had recently taken up the cudgels against a group of men who protested that women had no souls, 'no more than a goose'.) George was influenced by this devout, motherly woman who became a long-standing friend and an early convert and missionary among the Quakers.

By the time he was twenty-three, George Fox had reached the decision that he could not accept any ready-made faith. Nothing that he had seen or heard satisfied the spiritual thirst in his soul. No one seemed able to help him and those who were kindred spirits were as baffled as he was. He was at the end of his tether. Later he wrote: 'When my hopes in them and in all men were gone, so that I had nothing outwardly to help me, nor could tell what to do, then, oh then, I heard a voice which said, "There is one, even Christ Jesus, that can speak to thy condition," and when I heard it, my heart did leap for joy.'

Another experience came as a sequel to this personal encounter with Christ. He was sitting still by the fire in a house where he was staying when he had a sudden stab of doubt, but, he records,

as I sat still under it and let it alone, a living hope arose in me, and a true voice, which said, 'There is a Living God who made all things.' And immediately the doubt and temptation vanished away, and life rose over it all, and my heart was glad, and I praised the Living God . . . Now was I come up in spirit through the flaming sword into the paradise of God. All things were new, and all the creation gave another smell unto me than before, beyond what words can utter.

George had reached the end of his search, but the beginning of his life's work as missionary and apostle of the Quakers.

14

Media encounters

In the Middle Ages, when few people were literate and could not
read the Bible for themselves, the Church used other media to
transmit faith. Stained glass windows told the Bible stories in
pictures, and through the mystery plays the craft guilds acted out
the dramas of Old and New Testaments annually for the people of
their city. The invention of printing and more widespread literacy
in many countries made the Bible and books a means of communicating religious faith. Many of us can think of a particular book
that had a transforming effect on our lives at some crucial stage.
Some would admit that a book first opened their eyes to spiritual
realities. Many of the Christian classics of past centuries – now
largely forgotten – like Bunyan's *Pilgrim's Progress* or William
Law's *Call to a Serious and Devout Life,* profoundly affected
leading preachers and reformers who read them. In fairly recent
times C.S. Lewis's books of Christian apologetics helped readers
to discover that faith is intellectually respectable. But all this seems
rather heavy stuff. Lewis's Narnia books, with their Christian
mythology, are still widely read. Lewis himself was profoundly
influenced in the direction of Christian faith by the writings of the
Victorian poet and writer George Macdonald.

But books no longer hold centre stage as the only medium for
bringing news of a spiritual world. There are probably more people
who glimpse spiritual realities through film, theatre, video and
radio than through books. So I have included stories of people
who have discovered God through some of the different media we
are accustomed to today.

Ignatius Loyola (books)

Inigo de Loyola was born in 1491 – eight years before Martin Luther and one year before the discovery by Europeans of the New World. He was the youngest of his father's thirteen children and lived in the family castle of Loyola, about two miles from the small Basque town of Azpeita. The estate was beautiful – there were orchards and chestnut groves, and streams and deep forests nearby. It was good hunting land too and the family probably kept their own pack of hounds. Inigo was an *hidalgo*, which means that he belonged by birth to an order of nobles, and he was brought up to cherish ideals of knighthood and valour. His brothers all fought for Spain and Inigo – or Ignatius, as he was later called – grew up in an atmosphere of romance and chivalry. The Loyolas were not known for their learning but for enterprise and bravery in arms.

Like others of his class, Ignatius learned the skills of war but he also learned to dance and sing and to write poetry. Young men of his class all hoped to become courtiers and when Ignatius was fifteen or sixteen his father was invited to send one of his sons to join the household of Velasquez, the royal treasurer. He chose to send Ignatius, so for the next nine or ten years he was brought up with Velasquez' children, cherishing a hope of winning the attention of the king. His father was outwardly religious but Ignatius, with his healthy, sturdy good looks and auburn hair, was a normal, high-spirited young man, and a bit on the wild side. A close friend described him at this stage: 'Although he was much attached to the faith, his life was in no way conformed to it nor did he keep himself free from sin. Rather, he was particularly reckless in gambling, in his dealings with women, in quarrelling, and with the sword.' In fact, Ignatius once or twice got himself into trouble as the leader of a gang involved in brawls – probably when they had all had too much to drink. But in terms of the chivalry of the day, he grew up to be the perfect knight, thoroughly equipped for conquest and glory. He read avidly all the tales of romance and chivalry that he could lay his hands on, and their heroes, always courageous, courteous and constant in love, became his role models.

King Ferdinand died in 1516 and his grandson Charles, who

became Holy Roman Emperor, succeeded him at the age of sixteen. He soon dismissed Velasquez from the position of treasurer. A post was found for Ignatius in Navarre, which was a frontier town. So the young knight probably hoped that he would have a good chance of seeing action. France *did* in fact invade and Ignatius bravely defended the garrison against all odds. But in a prolonged exchange of artillery fire he was shot and his leg shattered. The French soldiery soon poured into the town, but they mercifully cared for Ignatius and set his broken leg. Soon after he was carried out on a litter and taken home to Loyola, to the family home where his brother and wife now lived. Ignatius was taken up to the top floor of the castle where he was to stay for nine long months – the time it would take him to recover from his wound.

But soon after he arrived he grew worse and the doctors agreed that the leg must be broken and reset properly. Of course, there was no anaesthetic and the pain must have been excruciating, but with enormous courage and self-control, Ignatius never once cried out, only clenching his fist when the pain was intense. But he grew weaker than ever and his doctors feared the worst. They advised him to make his confession, because if he was no better by midnight he would die. But at midnight he took a turn for the better and began to mend. When the danger was past Ignatius decided that he was not satisfied with his damaged leg. The second operation had left him with a protruding lump. It spoiled the look of his legs and also meant that he would never again be able to wear the high boots that were part of his regalia and a source of pride and joy. So Ignatius determined to have further surgery to saw off the stump. It was desperately painful and so was the traction treatment that followed, in order to prevent one leg ending up shorter than the other. Again, he bore the pain without screaming or crying out, only showing his anguish by his tightly clenched fist. The operation was successful and in due course Ignatius was able to walk again with scarcely a limp.

Meanwhile, a man of action, he had to endure a long and boring convalescence alone in his attic room. As he began to feel better he asked for books, hoping to bury himself again in the stories of chivalry and romance he had once enjoyed. But his pious sister-in-law could only offer him two volumes and very different ones from the romances he had expected. One was *The Life of Christ* and the other *The Lives of the Saints*. Something about the life of Christ appealed to him, because the author presented Christ in terms of knightly ideals. The lives of the saints he found on the whole boring, with the exception of three, the stories of St Francis of Assisi, St Dominic and St Humphrey. But he had to pass the time somehow so he read and reread these two books. In between he sat and fantasised about the splendid exploits he might soon be well enough to achieve in the service of a certain lady. (No one knows whether he had a particular lady in mind or if she too was a product of his imagination).

As time went by Ignatius found himself torn between two very different ways of life. One part of him still longed for knightly glory but another side of him began to admire the life that the saints had chosen in the cause of Christ. After a while, he began to notice that his thoughts and day-dreams had significant after-effects. When he filled his mind with imagined thoughts of worldly glory, he was left feeling dry and agitated; but when he thought about the saints and about Jesus, he felt wonderfully contented.

Then, one night, while he was still hesitating between the two opposing lifestyles, he had a vision of the Virgin Mary. It left him in a state of rapturous happiness for hours afterwards. He felt a loathing for his former way of life with its drunkenness and womanising and he never hankered after it again. Instead he felt more and more drawn towards God. He would talk about God in the most natural way possible, to anyone and everyone who visited him. He seemed able to communicate his feelings simply and easily. He studied the words and life of Jesus with even greater eagerness and began to pray. Like St Francis, whose life he read, he would look out of his window and take great pleasure in the beauty of the sky.

When at last he was fit again, he was offered a prestigious job but he turned it down. He had made up his mind instead to visit Jerusalem, a daring and risky pilgrimage at that time. Before he had gone very far he exchanged clothes with a beggar, hung up his sword and dagger in the monastery where he stayed and insisted on giving the monks his mule.

Ignatius' life took many unexpected twists and turns. He was not able to stay and work in Jerusalem as he had hoped to do, but he and the group of friends who had joined him were content instead to be at the service of the Pope wherever in the world that might be. They did not intend to be an enclosed order, but to go out and about. They wanted no special title, simply calling themselves companions of Jesus, ready to serve him by serving others. Ignatius himself remained in Rome, and later, as the Society of Jesus grew, he reluctantly became its first General. His work was among those who needed help the most – children, prostitutes, the sick. Hard on himself, he was gentle and compassionate on others. His *Spiritual Exercises*, designed and written to help and train his followers, are used today, not only by Jesuits in training but by ordinary people seeking to strengthen their spiritual lives on retreat. Rock-solid and uncompromising where the truth was concerned, Ignatius was never stern or forbidding to the weak. He was remembered in Rome as 'the small Spaniard who limped a little and had such laughing eyes'.

Emmanuel Mate (radio)

Emmanuel is a head teacher in Uganda. The Far Eastern Broadcasting Association or FEBA, as it is generally called, broadcasts from their radio station in Seychelles, in the Indian Ocean, to many different countries – including Uganda. Emmanuel had listened to their broadcast programmes for about twenty years. He had been a schoolboy at the time that he first tuned in, trying to survive amidst the fear and bloodshed of Idi Amin's brutal reign.

These were sad, tragic days for the once flourishing country that Winston Churchill had admiringly called 'the Pearl of Africa'. It was in 1971 that Idi Amin seized power and began a reign of terror, inspired by the mad imagination and acts of a megalomaniac. In 1972 he expelled all Asian businessmen living in the country, although it was their skills and acumen that had created the thriving economy. (Many of those who were expelled came to

Britain where their skills have greatly benefited business and the professions.)

Idi Amin's army pillaged and murdered, persecuting the Christian Church ruthlessly. The much-loved Archbishop of Uganda, Janani Luwum, was murdered, probably by Idi Amin himself, and his death reported to be the result of a car accident. Ordinary, rank-and-file Christians lived in fear of their lives too. Emmanuel and his teenage Christian friends met secretly to pray, in the house of one of their teachers. One day, when Emmanuel was twiddling the knobs on his radio, he heard a broadcast in his own Swahili language; he had stumbled upon a FEBA station which was broadcasting Christian teaching and worship. Once he had found the station, he and his friends were able to listen regularly. At a time when the church could not meet because meetings and services were banned, they gained real encouragement and help by regularly listening to these broadcasts. 'It was like a direct channel to God – it was God talking to us at that moment,' Emmanuel explained to FEBA staff many years later.

Idi Amin's tyrannous regime is a thing of the past but Uganda still has its troubles and FEBA broadcasts are still providing a link with the spiritual world for many Ugandans. Tragically, Uganda has the one of the highest incidences of AIDS in the world and FEBA beams out programmes to provide AIDS sufferers with counsel and information about the disease. The programmes also supply a spiritual dimension for the many who are sick and dying. Emmanuel is married now, with children of his own, but he is still thankful that God is using the medium of radio to make his voice heard in Uganda.

Cyril Kalle (radio)

Cyril lives in Mauritius, which, in fact, is made up of several islands in the Western Indian Ocean, east of Madagascar. Mauritius is a splendid mix of many nationalities. Indians, Africans, Chinese and Europeans mingle, many of them born and brought up on Mauritius although their forebears came from different countries and cultures.

When Cyril Kalle, who comes from Mauritius, visited the FEBA radio station in Seychelles, he told his story to the engineer David Fry. 'I was forty-two and in a very bad way when I first met Jesus Christ,' he began. Cyril explained that he had just come out of hospital after undergoing surgery, and that he was out of work and had a serious alcohol problem. One day, as he was going home, he heard the sound of singing coming from a church. Cyril had memories of hymn-singing when he was young, and he stopped outside the church window to listen as closely as possible to the sound he loved. As he looked in through the window he caught sight of a Bible verse written on the inside wall. It was some words of Jesus: 'Come unto me, all you that labour and are heavy laden, and I will give you rest.' Jesus spoke the words two thousand years ago, but for Cyril they came alive and went straight to the heart of his deepest needs. Without any more thought, he responded to these words of Jesus as if they were spoken to him in person, and asked Jesus to give him the rest he so much needed.

But Cyril realised that he had practical worries that were plaguing him too. Food prices in Mauritius had rocketed following a recent government budget and Cyril had a wife and six children to feed. Rice, milk and bread had all gone up in price and Cyril didn't know where the money to buy them was coming from. But as he stood quietly outside the church he heard the congregation begin to sing another song, based on some more words of Jesus: 'Seek first God's kingdom and his righteousness and all these things will be given to you as well. So do not worry . . .' Cyril decided that he should trust Jesus for the needs of his family too and 'I left that place with peace in my heart and full of joy,' he told David Fry.

Cyril got work as a watchman but it meant that six months later he had to move away from home, and his working hours made it impossible for him to go to church or meet with other Christians. He had his Bible and he also had the daily FEBA broadcasts to give him help and strength. He listened to the broadcasts avidly, writing down all the words that seemed to him to come over the airwaves straight from God.

Cyril recounted one occasion when God spoke to him in a direct way through radio. During the course of his job he had to keep a watch in a rough area, known for violence and drug-taking. 'I remember one night,' he said, 'drug-traffickers were throwing stones on the roof of the building while I was inside, listening to the radio. I felt very afraid, but at that very moment I heard a message from God coming to me through the radio presenter's words. He said, "Don't be afraid, just put your hand in my hand." ' Cyril wrote the words down, then put them into practice, trusting God for the circumstances he was in. 'It's still real,' Cyril said, 'I can hear the voice now! The Lord spoke to my heart and I was not afraid. When I went outside for the next all-round check, there was no one there.'

Premier Radio, London

Not many people living in London go to church these days. Yet the very fact that a church is sometimes called the 'house of God' means that at one time men and women expected to experience God's presence and hear him speak to them through church services. Sometimes a person who is at their wits' end, or in the middle of a crisis of some kind, will go into an empty church, because centuries of prayer and worship of God seem to have made the building itself user-friendly for those looking for the spiritual world.

But now that so many people go to church only for weddings and funerals, there is a need for the church to come outside where people are, so that they can encounter God and learn about him without crossing the church door. London's Premier Radio station was set up specifically for that purpose – it aims to provide a 'church without walls'. The station broadcasts day and night every day of the week and aims to supply those links with the world of the Spirit that a church should give. Among other facilities it provides a helpline for those with problems or matters to discuss; spiritual support for churchgoers who are housebound; and a forum for able communicators from every denomination within the Christian Church.

Premier Radio station has nothing of the whispered solemnity of an ancient church. When I arrived for a visit, I was struck by the cheerful camaraderie and obvious enjoyment that the station staff share. My quest was to discover whether in fact radio is a medium that can make the spiritual world accessible to listeners and I wanted stories to prove it. Here are two that Crystal Callow, the Executive Administrator, had to tell.

A young man phoned Lifeline (the name given to the helpline) from a phone box in the middle of a busy marketplace. He had an extraordinary story to tell. The previous evening he had been so distressed and angry that to relieve his feelings he had hurled his radio set across the room. Hours later, when he had calmed down a bit, he picked it up, afraid that it would have been damaged beyond repair. So he was pleasantly surprised to turn the knob and find that it was still working. But somehow in the fall, the radio had become retuned – the station setting had changed. By sheer accident, it seemed, he was now switched on to Premier Radio. And as he listened, his interest grew. He heard the presenter, Cindy Kent, talking about Jesus. It was good news for the predicament he was in. He went on listening all night, amazed to learn about the Christian news of God's forgiveness, love and peace.

Next morning he found a phone box in town and dialled the Lifeline number. He was certain that luck and coincidence were not enough to explain what had happened the night before. He believed that God had used radio to break into his life and speak to him. Now, over the phone, he was asking how he could become a Christian and discover his own lifeline to God.

At Easter, Premier Radio broadcast a series of programmes called *The Stations of the Cross* describing the experiences of Jesus at his crucifixion. At one point it was explained that although Jesus is usually portrayed by reverent artists as wearing a loincloth, he was probably completely naked when he was nailed to the cross. Among the listeners to that programme was a woman who had been held in a POW camp during World War II. She had been made to strip naked and stand in front of her tormentors, and the feelings of shame and humiliation had never left her. She had now lived for many years with the loss of self-respect and distress she suffered because of that wartime experience. It was a wound that would not heal. When she heard the radio programme, and realised that Jesus, too, suffered the shame of nakedness, it seemed to lift the burden she had carried for so long. *He* had been naked to cover her nakedness, *he* had endured shame to take her shame away. Peace and relief flooded her as she encountered God's involvement with her lot; she was healed once and for all from the pain and distress of the past.

Robert Taylor (Alpha courses)

Many of us live in a society where the best way to find out about something we're interested in is to go on a course. That may be one reason, Mark Elsdon-Dew suggested to me, why thousands of churches have registered to run Alpha courses – many in the UK but others in English-speaking and European countries.

It all began at Holy Trinity Church, Brompton, in London. Mark, who used to be Foreign Editor of the *Sunday Express*, is on the church staff. Alpha began as a course run for church members, to help them get to know more about their faith, but more and more of the church members who attended brought along friends who didn't go to church. So the course became a means of introducing the Christian faith to anyone interested to find out about it. Churches of all the other denominations – Roman Catholic, Methodist, Baptist, Free Church as well as Anglican – have registered to run courses. At least eighty prisons in the UK alone run courses too. Course leaders are provided with the manual and videos to use alongside led discussions, and other volunteers provide a meal that everyone enjoys together.

In the past, Mark explained, people used to go to church to find out what Christianity was all about. Most wouldn't dream of doing that now. But they don't mind attending a course that involves a bit of socialising and a meal as a way of discovering if their friends' belief in a spiritual world is really valid and whether their lifestyle is genuine. Mark has written a book describing the experiences of some of the people who have met God through attending an Alpha course. One of them is Robert Taylor, who lives in my town so I chatted to him on the phone.

Four or five years ago, Robert was living on his own in a London flat when he was asked by two different colleagues to try an Alpha course at Holy Trinity Church, Brompton. Life had been tough for Robert. When he was thirty – about seven years earlier – he had developed cancer. He had gone through all the anguish and trauma of major surgery, chemotherapy and radio-therapy too. It looked at one point as if he was going to die, but he had recovered and the experience had the effect of making him want to get on with his life and enjoy himself as much as possible. When his marriage took a downturn, he walked out, left his wife and two young children, and took the London flat. He had a successful job and a good social life, and was enjoying the advantages of being single. But a friend he'd trained with and known for years was obviously worried about Robert's marriage breakdown and suggested that he ought to go to an Alpha course at Holy Trinity Church. Robert took very little notice until a second person suggested the same thing. This time it was a banking colleague who mentioned Alpha after they had enjoyed a good business lunch. He was persistent so Robert thought he might as well give it a try. Wednesday was a free night anyway, and he might meet a few interesting people as well as having a meal cooked for him.

He was a couple of weeks late in joining the course and he made it clear to his group right at the start that he had no intention of letting the course impinge on his life. 'Look,' he told them, 'I nearly died of cancer when I was thirty. I find life pretty difficult and it's not a great deal of fun as far as I am concerned. Eternal life is the last thing I want, so I really can't see what Christianity has to offer me.' But the rest of the group were nice enough people so he went back the next week. Gradually he grew interested in what was being said about the Christian faith and he began to listen hard. The course involves a weekend away and it was during that time that Robert felt that God was close to him. At one session the leader asked that God's Spirit should come among them and Robert found himself asking God's Spirit to touch *him*. Immediately he experienced a glowing certainty of God's love. He says that even the disco beat seemed to be repeating over and over again, 'Jesus loves you.'

Robert's life changed as a result. He is back now with his wife and family and has a different lifestyle – one which revolves around God. When I phoned him, he was with a group of friends from church who had come to the house to talk together about the Bible and to pray. God's world has met his.

The Jesus Video

Azerbaijan

The Coventry-based Christian children's charity, Global Care, sent a small relief-aid team of eight or ten people to Azerbaijan, soon after it had ceased to be part of the USSR. During the years of Communist rule all religions had been banned, so there was no kind of religious knowledge in the country and no churches or mosques for interested citizens to attend. After working hard all week, the team members used to meet together on a Saturday evening to share a meal and enjoy one another's company. Because they were Christians, they would also spend time praying and singing together. They used to invite their Azerbaijani interpreters, drivers and ancillary workers to come along too and bring their families. The local people enjoyed the evenings and became interested and curious about the singing and praying, so the team decided to send for a video to show to them one evening.

The *Jesus Video*, as it is usually called, and which they used, has an incredible history. By 1998 it was available dubbed in 446 languages (with over two hundred more being prepared) and had been seen in 97 countries by over a billion people. It has been shown in cinemas and on television as well as in halls and churches. It tells the story of Jesus, as found in the Gospels, climaxing in his crucifixion and subsequent resurrection.

The Global Care team showed the video to their usual Saturday evening guests and invited them to bring along other neighbours and friends too. As so often, the video had a dramatic effect on many of those who watched. They were deeply moved by the story of God's coming as a human being and living and dying out of love for the men and women he created. As they identified the kindness and care of the team with the love shown in the video they experienced a spiritual awakening. Many continued to come on Saturday nights, inquiring more about this newly discovered faith, and some decided that they wanted to become Christ's followers too. Soon a new, indigenous church came into being. It followed no set pattern. The new Christians met and shared food and prayer, at last growing too large for the homes they had met in. Soon a young church of some forty to fifty people was flourishing where a short while before no religious faith had been known.

Britain

In the UK a *Jesus Video* project was launched in 1996. The film was offered door-to-door to householders as well as being shown in church buildings. One person who accepted the offer of a video in his home was Graham Thomas. At the time he was struggling to come to terms with his life after being made redundant from his job as finance director of an airline. His marriage was breaking up and he himself was having psychiatric help. After watching the video he was visited by a member of the team who helped him to turn his new spiritual perception into a commitment of faith which, as he puts it, means that a new life has begun for him.

15

Death, near death and bereavement

I read a leader in *The Times* recently entitled 'Celebration of Death'. It described a new approach by a north-eastern firm of undertakers who are offering their customers coffins in colour. The one on display in the window was in the colours of the Middlesbrough football club strip.

The article went on to remind readers that death has not always been characterised by black. Before the Victorians literally imposed their 'black-out' on death, bright colours adorned catafalques and painted tombs made churches and cathedrals glorious. The more I thought about it the more I decided that perhaps death in colour – or at least with some relief from total black – might be a helpful idea. After all, black reminds us of black holes – full of doom and fear of the unknown and terror. It makes us think of emptiness and nothingness, as well as conveying sadness and gloom.

Of course, there is sadness and loss and a feeling that the colour has gone out of life for those who mourn deeply. But for those who have caught a glimpse of the spiritual world that lies around us and awaits us beyond this life, death may not be wholly negative. They believe that for them and for those they love who have died there is the promise of a fuller life, of freedom from pain and evil, and the unutterable bliss of God's presence. So even though we would not all want coffins in football colours we may find colour a more fitting symbol for death than total blackness. As one ten-year-old said, 'I think heaven is red, because red is a happy colour and when you die you are so happy with God.'

Dr Ros Taylor

I had not met the doctor from our my local hospice of St Francis until she came to coffee the other day to talk about her work and answer some of my questions. I wanted to know how people encounter imminent death, and how their relatives and friends face the loss of someone they love.

Ros Taylor is an attractive woman in her forties, smartly and pleasingly dressed, full of life without any overtones of busyness or brashness. I would be happy to have her at my bedside, I decided. She is Jewish as is her psychiatrist husband, and their two sons are being given the opportunity to learn about the faith they have inherited at the nearest liberal synagogue.

Ros has always had an interest in the care of the dying from her student days at Cambridge, when she chose to write her thesis on the social status of dying. Then, when she became a GP she grew increasingly concerned that she had so little time to allot to her patients who were facing death. So she set up a four-bed palliative care unit in the nearby hospital, where terminally ill patients could have the kind of care and time afforded to them that they needed. After hands-on experience there, she took the post of hospice doctor eighteen months ago, in Berkhamsted, a small town some 40 kilometres from London.

She told me that most patients – not surprisingly – do not find it easy to develop an acceptance of death. In fact, most will agree to treatment even when there is only a 1 per cent chance of success. Sometimes their fears may actually be allayed when they come to the hospice and witness the death of another patient. They are able to see for themselves that death can be peaceful and their relatives are reassured as they see that those left behind *do* survive the loss.

We talked about the problem that doctors and nurses themselves often have about confronting the death of their patients, and their unwillingness to admit the defeat that death implies. In some hospitals in the USA, she told me, when a patient dies on the ward, the nurse will wheel the body out still talking to the dead person, so that other patients won't realise what has happened. Surgeons, too, who are trained to save life, feel desperately frustrated when they open up a patient only to find that the cancer is too advanced for them to operate. They can do no more than sew the patient up again but their feelings of failure and distress are such that they may often pass by that person's bed when they do the daily ward round. They do not want to have to talk to them and face up to what seems like their failure to heal; yet by ignoring them they add to the patient's distress by making them feel devalued and passed over as a person. In some situations, Ros Taylor wisely added, a doctor needs to accept his or her own powerlessness.

When Dr Taylor is caring for a patient in the hospice she recognises that pain relief depends on far more than administering the right drugs in the right doses. If a person is at ease in other ways, it becomes far easier to relieve their pain. Any causes of unrest or distress need to be dealt with and that can take time, listening patiently and sensitively to what is not said as well as to the words spoken. 'Terminal agitation' makes it very difficult for the nurses as well as the patient. A patient who is spiritually at ease makes the nurses' and doctors' task easier too.

'When patients are admitted as terminally ill, my task is to help them to move from the doing mode to one of being,' Dr Taylor said. As their life draws near to an end she wants to give them hope and she tries to do so and to help them in three ways: she gives them the medical help they need to keep their symptoms under control; she listens to their story, and – perhaps most important of all I would think – she values them for themselves.

I asked Ros what difference religious faith makes to a patient who is dying. 'Those with a faith seem to fall at one extreme or the other,' she answered. 'They are either the most anguished, as they question the truth of the things they have believed, or else they are the most at peace. Mary Lee, an old lady in her nineties, who was quietly and peacefully awaiting death, told me, "I'm just waiting at the bus stop, for the bus to pick me up." '

Henri Nouwen

I first heard Henri Nouwen on tape. It was a talk he had given at the Greenbelt Festival. I was struck first of all by how little Nouwen said. His words were few; there was no verbose flow of elegant, reasoned phrases, yet what he said seemed to fall like hammer blows on my mind and heart. Every word and thought struck home with certainty and strength. They had the genuine ring of truth. After hearing his voice and trying to absorb the startling but apparently simple things he was saying, I felt that I must read some of the books he had written. The profoundness of his thought expressed in seemingly simple words reminded me of some of Jesus's teaching.

Henri Nouwen was born in Holland in 1932 and became a Roman Catholic priest in the Archdiocese of Utrecht. He had a distinguished university teaching career in the USA, at Notre Dame, Yale and Harvard, and also spent a long time in the solitude of a Trappist monastery. But for the last twelve years or so of his life he was pastor of l'Arche Daybreak in Toronto, a community for people with mental disabilities.

In one of his books – *Beyond the Mirror* – he tells of a near death experience that he had. As always, he speaks simply and with complete honesty. He had been looking after Hsi-Fu, while his usual carers were on retreat. Hsi-Fu, who is blind, unable to speak or walk and with severe physical deformities, lived a five-minute drive from Henri's house. Henri had driven down to him on Monday, Tuesday and Wednesday, to brush his teeth, bath him and help him have his breakfast. But when he looked out of his window on Thursday morning he saw that the road was like a sheet of glass; there was ice everywhere. It was out of the question to use the car, but, keen to fulfil his promised task, Henri decided, against the advice of his colleague, Sue, to set out on foot. He began the half-mile walk, slipping and sliding and even falling once, but determined to carry on at all costs. He tried to beg a lift from car after car that emerged out of the mist but no one would stop for him. So Henri kept doggedly on, even trying to break into a cautious run, in order to reach the Corner House by seven o'clock – the time he had promised to arrive.

Then, suddenly, something hit him – he did not know what. All he knew was that he could feel a sudden searing pain in his back as he fell to the ground, unable even to cry out for help. He remembered wondering if the driver who had hit him had realised what he had done or whether he had driven straight on. But he also remembered afterwards what his emotions were. He knew that somehow, because of what had just happened to him, everything had changed. Sue's warning: 'Henri, it is too much . . .' still rang in his ears. He had been going against the grain, wilfully trying to achieve what he had undertaken to do when everything indicated that he should stop still and calmly acknowledge his own limitations. But now, life had caught up with him and his plans had been forcibly brought to nothing. He was powerless, but strangely enough he did not feel frightened. It was as if a strong hand had arrested him – a strong hand but also a loving hand.

Soon after, the young man who had been driving the van that had hit Henri came running up. It was the van's mirror that had struck him from behind with great force and caused the injury. When it seemed that Henri was not too badly hurt after all, the young man managed to drive him to the hospital, where they diagnosed broken ribs. But it soon became clear that Henri was much more seriously hurt than they had realised at first. He was bleeding internally; time went by but the bleeding would not stop. They knew now that Henri's life was in danger and that it was a matter of urgency to operate and remove the spleen.

For the first time, Henri let himself, as he put it, 'move around in the entrance to death'. He wanted to explore this area that had always seemed so frightening, and make himself familiar with it. But instead of experiencing fear, uncertainty and loss, as he had expected he would, he experienced pure and unconditional love. He did not claim to see a light or a rainbow or even an open door. In fact his chief impression was of *feeling*, not *seeing*. It was as if the Jesus he had known and loved suddenly became very close and warm, clearing away all coldness and fear. He seemed to say, 'Come to me,' and the invitation was to come home – where he belonged and was utterly loved.

Henri still felt in a strange way that he was clinging to this life

187

– and that was not because he would be leaving those he loved. He realised that he was concerned about those relationships that needed putting right. He wanted to make sure that he would die in a way that would be a blessing to others. He knew that where he had borne little grudges or jealousies and where he had remembered and held on to wrongs that others had done to him, he must forgive freely. He also felt concerned about any people who might be out of charity with him. He did not want them to hear of his death and then be full of remorse because they had left it too late to put things right. So when his colleague, Sue, visited him, he asked her to assure all those who had unresolved feelings towards him that he fully and freely forgave them. 'Please tell everyone who has hurt me that I forgive them from my heart,' he said, 'and please ask everyone whom I have hurt to forgive me too.' He recognised that to die well, he must leave no unfinished business.

Once that was done, Henri explained how free he felt. He said it was the way he used to feel when he could unfasten the wide leather belts he once wore as an army chaplain. The belts, which crossed his chest and shoulders as well as circling his waist, were signs of his authority and prestige. When he took them off, he laid aside his power and status. That was the way he wanted to die, laying aside power and any attempt to judge others.

During the operation that followed Henri was very close to death. It was the skill of the surgeon that brought him through and the power of God, which they believed was present too. But he was ready to die. When I heard some years later of his death from a heart attack I wondered how sudden and swift it had been. But he had already made the preparation that was needed and experienced the reality of the spiritual world when, in that earlier crisis, he had looked beyond the mirror and known that Jesus was real and near.

Eve Travers

When I first tried to phone Eve there was no reply. The same thing happened next day, but that time she recovered my number and rang back. Thoughtlessly, I had failed to realise how long it would take her to get to the phone. Eve has suffered for nearly twenty years from myasthenia gravis, a disease I had not heard of before. It is one of the auto-immune diseases, which affects the muscles when the normal signals to the brain are destroyed by the antibodies that are produced. Legs, hands and face refuse to function, so that walking, grasping and even swallowing become nearly impossible.

Eve had been an unusually healthy child. She had a happy childhood, joining the Girl Guides and going to church as a good Christian should, she supposed. She was always so fit that she even remembers praying to catch her brother's chickenpox so that she could have a few days off school.

She married a man in the Merchant Navy when she was still only in her twenties. Then the disease struck. Myasthenia gravis is often linked with the thymus gland which may need to be removed. In Eve's case, she was found to have a large tumour on the thymus, so swift action was required and within a couple of weeks her thymus was removed and chemotherapy began. For some reason the myasthenia refused to respond to medication as it should have done and she was admitted to the acute medical ward of York Hospital. But instead of getting better she grew steadily weaker over the period of a month, until she resembled nothing so much as a rag doll – limp and lifeless and totally without strength.

She remembers the desperate situation she was in one Sunday morning. She could hardly manage to breathe and she knew for certain that something was going to happen; she could not continue like that. Because it was the weekend there were limited staff on duty, but Eve remembers the horror and fear in the eyes of the junior doctor who saw her when she came on her rounds. She rushed away to summon Eve's consultant and Eve was hurriedly wheeled down to the intensive care unit. She can still hear, in memory, the creak of the trolley-wheels and visualise the bold pattern of the wallpaper on the walls as they passed. Every possible drug was administered but nothing had any effect. When her father arrived he was allowed in for a moment to see her, and she remembers saying to him, 'Daddy, I'm going to die.'

Then came the moment when she could no longer breathe and

she felt her whole body go into violent spasm. She gasped to get breath and shook from head to foot. She heard someone cry out, 'She's crashed!' and she was aware of panic and the flurry of activity all about her. For a strange few moments she was aware of her body, still thrashing about – and her soul cut loose. The two seemed to co-exist for a brief moment in parallel. Then, with the freeing of her soul came a moment of profound personal peace and an all-embracing love. It was an experience of rebirth. She had considered herself a Christian all her life, but this was unlike anything she had ever known. For her it marked the entry into a new life in God. People explain near death experiences in all kinds of physiological terms but Eve believes that what happened to her was a genuine, personal experience of the spiritual world because it transformed her life completely. The person she is today is the Eve who was changed by her experience in the intensive care unit that Sunday morning.

What happened next is a blank to Eve. She remembers regaining consciousness to find the consultant sitting beside her saying, 'Eve, don't be afraid.' For many weeks she was on a life-support machine and remained in intensive care, fed by tube. And it was while she was on the ventilator that she learned to draw close to God in prayer, she told me. In complete weakness and dependence, she learned too to trust Christ for everything.

After nine months in hospital she was allowed home, but her ordeals were not over. Further drastic surgery was needed and Eve's life now is a miracle of survival and endurance. Over the phone she sounded cheerful and positive. Although she qualifies for numerous groups set up to give support to sufferers of one disease or another, she does not join them. She wants to avoid concentrating on her disabilities. She is always ready to talk – at the consultant's request – to anyone facing her particular disabilities, but for the rest she puts her limited strength into the life of her local church and work among young people there. Something of the peace and love she experienced in the intensive care unit still sustains her in an outgoing, joyful Christian lifestyle.

Archbishop Janani Luwum

The year was 1977 and the scene an open grave, high up on the Hill of Peace in Kampala, capital of Uganda. Hundreds upon hundreds of African men, women and children crowded around. But there was no coffin to lower into the grave, no body to bury. Archbishop Luwum, their beloved Christian leader, had died a martyr's death, shot point blank in the mouth by the dictator Idi Amin; but his mutilated body was not there.

When Idi Amin became President of Uganda in 1971 he began a seven-year reign of terror that convulsed the whole country. Perhaps the absolute power he enjoyed not only corrupted him but brought on an incipient madness. The army that he commanded was made up of many reckless and ruthless soldiers who went even further than their President in killings and torture.

One night, when the household was asleep, there was a loud, urgent knocking at the gate of the Archbishop of Uganda's red-brick house. Archbishop Luwum got up hastily, although it was 2 a.m., and as he came towards the gate through the thick darkness, he could also hear a man's pitiful cries for help. He knew it was dangerous to open up – that's why the gates were locked at nights – but he could not ignore such urgent pleas for help. He went out and unbarred the gate to let the man in. But he was a decoy, who had been forced by the soldiers to entice the Archbishop to open the gates so that they could gain entry to his house. Immediately Luwum appeared, the soldiers seized him roughly at gunpoint and searched him. They ordered him to hand over the arms cache in his house, and when he protested that he had no such store of weapons, they pushed past him and began to search everywhere, rifling through everything and leaving the house in chaos.

Until this time Janani Luwum had always been on good terms with the President and supported him whenever his conscience would allow, as well as praying for him. But recently the President had put an end to communications with any of the bishops and had refused to listen when the Archbishop spoke out against the increasingly bloody regime and the fate of the many people who were being massacred.

A few weeks after the soldiers' night-time search, Luwum and some of his bishops were summoned to meet the President at the Nile Hotel. Piles of new guns were laid out on the lawns and beside them were the suitcases they were supposed to have been packed in. Janani Luwum was accused of receiving these arms from across the border and supplying them to anti-Amin conspirators and to Milton Obote, the deposed president. President Amin told his advisers that there must be a proper military trial to settle the matter and the bishops were then allowed to leave and go home. But as they were going, some soldiers came up and detained Archbishop Luwum; they told him that the President wanted to speak to him. Two of the bishops suspected he was in danger and chose to wait for Luwum, but the hours passed and whenever they asked the soldiers where their archbishop was, they were told that he was still in conference with Idi Amin.

At last the soldiers forced the bishops at gunpoint to leave the hotel. They went reluctantly. Early next morning the radio news announced that Archbishop Luwum had been arrested pending further investigation. Then, an hour or two later, a further bulletin announced that he had died as the result of a road accident on the journey from the Nile Hotel to the interrogation centre. The bishops went to the hospital to retrieve the body for burial but the hospital staff were clearly frightened and sent them to the mortuary where they were refused entry.

But there were some who *had* seen Luwum's body and they reported that he had been shot in the mouth and chest, almost certainly, from what they had heard, by Idi Amin himself. Information had filtered through that during his interview with Amin, Luwum had refused to confess to a completely false charge of conspiracy in a coup against the President. Luwum began to pray aloud for Idi Amin and in a frenzy of rage the President shot him at point-blank range. The car accident was deliberately arranged in order to cover up the shooting.

A funeral fitting an archbishop had been arranged at the cathedral and the people had flocked to pay their respects to their beloved leader. But, in spite of the bishops' pleading, the authorities refused to hand over Luwum's body. (It was, in fact, buried privately and secretly near his home village.)

The service outside the cathedral continued although there was no body to bury. The huge congregation that had attended morning service and communion inside the cathedral, now gathered in the open air around the empty grave. But there was no atmosphere of gloom. Instead, a triumphant cry rang out from their new leader as he gazed at the open grave: 'He is not here!' he exclaimed triumphantly. 'He is risen!' In response the whole crowd burst out singing, 'Glory, glory Hallelujah!' till the hills echoed to the sound.

The first time those words of resurrection were spoken they had been uttered by angels to the grieving followers of Jesus on the first Easter Day. They too had been looking at an empty tomb. Jesus's body was no longer there, the angels told them, because God had raised him from death to life. Archbishop Luwum's body had not disappeared but been buried secretly and unceremoniously. Yet for the crowds at the empty grave the words rang true for him too – he was *not* dead. Before Jesus died he had told his followers: 'Because I live, you too will live.' They were certain that their Archbishop was alive. Death had meant only the transition from one world to another.

Pat Mood

As soon as I talked to Pat Mood I was at ease. I sensed that she was the sort of person I would feel able to talk to about my deeper feelings – the things I would not normally care to discuss with other people. That's not surprising, because Pat has the skills of a trained professional social worker as well as maturity and experience. She also has that something extra that the best trained professional does not always possess; she is a born listener, naturally gentle, sympathetic and intuitive.

Pat has always worked with children; first with those in care, dealing with young people who had suffered the loss of home, or the break-up of their parents' relationship. After experience with oncology patients she moved to the Douglas Macmillan Hospice in Stoke-on-Trent, where she has worked for the past nineteen years. Her work is still with children, those terminally ill themselves, and more often children facing the death of a parent or close relative. 'There wasn't much written in the early days,' she told me. 'We had to learn very much as we went along and find out for ourselves how best to meet the needs.' Pat runs a bereavement group to help children come to terms with their loss and it is often her task to tell a child when a parent is dying.

I wondered how anyone could cope with such difficult and distressing work. I asked her what she did to work off the stresses and tensions of her job. Did she play squash or go running? She admitted that she had very little leisure time for that kind of relaxation (she has a home, husband and daughters of her own) yet she sounded anything but stressed out. She told me that she believed the secret is to be all of a piece – to have a faith that is thoroughly integrated with what you are doing. It is not part of her task to impose her faith on others, unless they ask her directly about her own beliefs, but her trust in God is absolutely necessary to her as she deals with difficult and delicate tasks. She explained that she is often aware of receiving help and wisdom beyond her own skill and experience. She believes that this comes to her from God. 'So often,' she told me, 'the hardest tasks seem to crop up just when I feel at my weakest and most tired. I may have to break bad news to a child – and I know that it is vitally important to choose just the right words and to give the information at the right moment. I couldn't do it on my own, without God's help.'

Sometimes I expect that a child will want no more to do with me when I have been the bearer of such sad news (she said). But it's amazing how they come up to me afterwards and sometimes they just cling to me. It's as if they are grateful that I have involved them in what is happening and relieved them of the fears that they had because they were kept in the dark. One seven-year-old girl said to me after I had told her about her mother's terminal illness: 'I wondered what was wrong with Mummy, but couldn't ask.' One ten-year-old boy was sent off to go swimming. The family knew that by the time he got back his father would have died. I asked him afterwards how he felt when he got home. He said, 'Everyone was crying, so I thought I'd better smile.'

Sometimes Pat supports the parents and guides them as to how to respond to their child's needs. She may help them sort out how to tell the children themselves about an impending death and she often suggests how they might reframe the funeral so that the child feels involved too. She thinks that the funeral should be planned for as an important family occasion. Often, in an attempt to protect their child, a parent can isolate them.

She told me the stories of two teenage boys. John was fourteen years old and had suffered from a brain tumour for a couple of years. He seemed young for his age because the tumour had slowed his brain down. When the doctor thought he was soon to die, he suggested he should go home. John never asked what was wrong with him but once he got home he began, unexpectedly, to improve. He was able to sit up and he even walked a bit. His mother had told Pat that he was very keen on flying and when Pat talked to him about asking 'Jim to fix it' he gave her a warm hug. A helicopter flight was arranged (I suspect through Pat's planning) which he enjoyed tremendously. Then he deteriorated rapidly and went back to the hospice. No one had talked to him about death or what it would be like, but one day when his grandmother went to see him he asked her outright whether he was going to die. With great courage she told him the truth and he said: 'I've seen through the door. It's all right.' He died two days later.

Ben was nineteen when he was told that no further treatment was possible for the cancer he had suffered from for two years. He wrote a journal which began: 'The impending uncertainty of my future triggered the need to find some answers and take a decision.' Because he was interested in science he decided to study books on cosmology in particular and try to decide if there was a God. Later he wrote that he had concluded that, 'whoever made the stars had thought long and hard'. But it was after he had attended a healing service that he wrote: 'I exchanged a belief in the head for a belief in the gut.'

Pat is frequently amazed at the way in which children face death and its implications. They do not fantasise about the future; they recognise the finality and the need to grieve, but they also have hope. Ten-year-old Anna had experienced the deaths of her two grandparents and an uncle within a short time. (Her grandfather

was a strict Muslim but her father was a nominal Muslim only.)
Anna wrote:

> I think when you die you go to this wonderful place where
> you are happy not sad. My Nanna and Granddad and Uncle
> must be happy there where God is looking after them and
> they do not have pain any more . . . and when you die you
> are so happy with God. I feel there is no reason why you
> should feel afraid about crying. If there was a way to get my
> family who have died back, I would get them back, but there
> is no way back.

Fiona Castle

What is it like to be a famous name, when tragedy strikes? Fiona
Castle says that there are two sides to it. It can add to the pressures
to find reporters jamming up the front garden and collecting
outside the house, waiting for you to arrive home. Handing out
endless cups of coffee and biscuits to a long procession of journalists becomes a matter of course, but it certainly adds to the
exhaustion that grief brings. On the other hand, being a household
name means that sackfuls of letters arrive with kind thoughts and
promises of prayer from complete strangers, which is a wonderful
support and cheer.

Before I talked to Fiona Castle about how she had coped with
Roy's death a few years ago, I read her two books, written with
Jan Greenough, called *Give Us This Day* and *No Flowers . . . Just
Lots of Joy*. The first is about her life with Roy Castle, the well-
known entertainer, trumpeter and presenter of the television
Record Breakers programme. As well as presenting the programme
in his own inimitable way, Roy took part in a number of daring
record-breaking feats himself, getting into the *Guinness Book of
Records*. Roy's infectious enthusiasm and deep happiness and
laughter made him someone the public not only knew but truly
loved. When, with great courage, he went public about the fact
that he had lung cancer, it was a shock and a genuine sadness to
us all, as if Roy was someone we knew at first hand. Since he had

never smoked, consultants decided that the disease had been caused by inhaling smoke in the many places where he had played his trumpet and entertained over the years.

Fiona describes how they faced his illness through the strength of their Christian faith, the prayers of many people and skilled medical help. After painful treatment and therapy it seemed that Roy might have beaten the disease. He never tried to hide what was happening from the public – appearing on television bald rather than wearing a wig. I think he did so partly because of his transparent honesty but also so that others who suffered the same after-effects of chemotherapy might feel comforted.

Tragically, the cancer recurred and this time it was terminal. Again Roy showed enormous courage, and dedication. He was determined to complete a planned rail tour of Britain in order to raise money for Cause for Hope – an ambitious appeal that Roy was sponsoring to establish a lung cancer research centre. At times he was too ill to move from the train, but, with Fiona beside him he always managed to talk and joke with the public who came to cheer him on.

At the end, Roy was at home, receiving constant strong doses of pain-relieving drugs. Fiona nursed him night and day with loving care until he finally slipped away from life. When Roy's agent asked Fiona for some message to give to the reporters, she was able to say: 'No flowers, no fuss, no mourning, just lots of joy.'

Two things made a deep impression on me as I read Fiona's books. The first was her complete honesty, about herself, her marriage, her family and towards the end, about her emotions since Roy's death. She does not pretend to what she does not feel – whether deep sadness or joy. She conscientiously separates out self-pity from genuine grief, allowing herself to feel deep sadness but severely nipping self-pity in the bud. She is honest about Roy too. She will not, as she says, 'canonise' him, just because he is dead, but remembers him as he really was, warts and all. The lugubrious comments and warnings of well-meaning onlookers were taken with a pinch of salt by the family and often helped them to laugh when they might have felt particularly down. She had received dark warnings about how terrible the first Christmas without Roy would be, but the family *did* enjoy the celebration, in spite of how much they had loved Roy and how much they missed him. I think a strong sense of humour, which they all share, helped them to survive many of the worst experiences.

Fiona showed enormous courage as well as honesty. Two weeks after Roy's death she faced an interview on television. She also coped with the ordeal all bereaved people face – that of being ignored or passed in the streets by people too embarrassed to know what to say. She dealt with this by taking the initiative and going up to others herself. She went as usual to the church toddler group she helped with, immediately after Roy's death and talked about him to them to relieve any embarrassment the people there might have felt.

I drew my own conclusions as to how Fiona had managed to keep joy and an upbeat approach to life after the death of a husband she loved so much, but I was glad to be able to talk about it to her in person. Fiona had suffered not only the grief which every happily married woman feels at the death of her husband, but she had to face the press, television coverage of the funeral and interviews. She had to attend public functions in place of Roy or on his behalf – and Fiona is not naturally a public person.

I began by saying that I realised that her Christian faith had given her courage and hope as well as strength. Her books make that abundantly clear. But I asked if her temperament helped too. She seems very at ease with life, relaxed and upbeat by nature. She assured me that was by no means the case. 'I'm a terribly shy little thing,' she admitted, 'and I used to be a terrible worrier. Everything was a worry to me and I was nervous and frightened about everything. I was depressed too and a perfectionist. I was upset unless everything was just right in the house. Jesus has changed me. When I gave my life to him, I began to put his words into practice. He told us not to worry about the future, to take one day at a time and to be assured that our Heavenly Father cares about us and will meet our needs. Living that way has changed me and I believe that God has changed my nature.'

'How far did your professional training help you to carry off situations?' I asked. Fiona had been no mean performer herself before her marriage, trained to dance and beginning to make a name for herself on the stage.

'I was always shy,' she admitted; 'even my agent had sussed me and realised that performing in public was not easy for me. But I so adored dancing – and still do – so I secured good parts and had some good things ahead of me. So I was sad in one way, but I also wanted to get married and have children. After all, I wasn't leaving "the business" entirely – there was still an entertainer in the family!' Then she went on; 'I do believe that my training at boarding-school helped me. The discipline there was terrific, with dance and school lessons to cope with. And no one ever told us we were any good. In a way it sorted out the men from the boys, so to speak. If you wanted to succeed it made you even more determined to stick it. And I did and learned a lot of lessons in self-control on the way.'

A lot is said about the power of positive thinking and Fiona seems to me to be a wonderful example of someone who has learned to turn hard and difficult things, sad things too, into positive good and personal triumphs. But she would have none of that.

She tells in her first book of the problems of marriage to a husband so often away and of the stresses of bringing up four children alone, of her depression and negative feelings. She is convinced that the colour came into her life when she became a Christian. It is her faith in a God who cares and guides for good, that enables her to let God transform even her difficulties and deep grief. Roy's death has been another hard but positive lesson in experiencing God in her life.

16

Nature and ecology

Recently, Dr David Bellamy has been making his voice heard as President of the Conservation Foundation. Like Professor Sir Ghillean Prance, he has worked tirelessly for environmental issues and he too is trying to wake up those with Christian beliefs to recognise their responsibility in the matter.

Centuries ago, Celtic Christianity was closely linked to nature both in appreciation of its beauty and a feeling of oneness with all creation. Ian Finlay (in *Columba*, 1979) wrote: 'The Celtic church grew among people who were not builders, who were not tempted to follow a tradition of containing their gods in temples, but felt closer to them where they felt the wind buffeting their faces, and saw the flash of white wings against the sky, and smelled the sun-warmed bark of trees.' They cared for the creation too. Columba, the sixth-century Irish saint, who established the community at Iona, also built a monastery at Derry. It is said that such was his love for God's creation that he made sure that the monastery was built without a single tree being felled. He wrote that he was more afraid of the sound of an axe in Derry wood than he was of hell itself.

But the Celtic Christians' love of nature was no sentimental maundering. Anyone who has visited Lindisfarne or stayed near the north-eastern coast of England, knows that nature there is cold and raw as well as awe-inspiring and romantic. These men and women who lived close to nature were ready to accept its hardships as well as its beauty.

They were not sentimental about nature, nor did they worship it for itself and raise it to the rank of deity. They accepted that evil as well as good existed in nature as much as it did in people. The commonest legacies of the Celtic Church still visible are the Celtic crosses, which still survive in abundance. For them, the cross of Christ with its message of redemption was central not only for the salvation of fallen sinful humankind but also for the created world. They believed that Nature itself was waiting to be redeemed by Christ and released from the bondage of evil and decay into newness of life.

Catherine Lucas

I talked to Catherine via transatlantic telephone as she sat in her Californian apartment and I in my small study in Hertfordshire, England. As I listened to her warm, friendly voice, I put the face to it – the face I had seen in the photograph alongside her article in *The Times* newspaper. I had been fascinated by what she wrote and impressed by her honesty and the strength of emotion that lay behind the experiences she described. The person I was talking to on the phone was instantly recognisable as the writer of that article, all of a piece with the frank, open person who had been ready to go public about her newly framed approach to life.

Catherine Lucas grew up on the Isle of Wight and was brought up as an atheist by atheist parents. When she grew up she saw no reason to change those views. She read English at London University, then worked as a freelance researcher, rising to be a television producer. In contrast to this hectic and sophisticated lifestyle, she found her recreation and solace in hiking in the countryside – whenever possible near mountains. Her first excursions were in the Oregon mountains, while she was working for a while in the USA. She was eighteen and the beauty of it all overcame her. Such beauty, she felt, must reach out to embrace everything created – herself included. A great joy came over her; as she described: 'My heart broke open and my soul went free.'

When she went home she thought that the experience was over and forgotten. Yet some vestige of that moment of knowing and joy remained and left her with a deep hunger, an emptiness that only the beauty of nature seemed able to fill.

It was some time before she recognised, in a sudden burst of understanding, that the experience was a spiritual one. She was experiencing the presence of God. This realisation came as a shock. It contradicted all the rational teaching she had received and the way of thinking that she had relied on up to this time in her life. 'Civil war broke out,' she says, 'between my head and my heart.' However could the kind of mind-blowing awareness she had experienced have anything to do with God? Surely he was usually pictured as an old man with a white beard up in heaven somewhere in the sky! As her sense that God is real grew stronger, so did her perplexity and the mixed feelings of doubt and certainty that waged war in her mind and heart.

The overwhelming experience of the transcendent that came to her at last took place in quiet Hereford countryside. Here is her story in her own words:

> I was in the countryside on my own and had spent several glorious days walking the hills. One evening I was sitting quietly when suddenly everything around me dissolved. It was like dropping through a trapdoor into darkness and I found myself in what I can only describe as a sea of sparkling energy. I was conscious, but nothing, including my body, had any form or structure. At first I was astonished and then I realised that whereas before I had experienced the presence of God in all things, this *was* God . . . Suddenly, everything made sense. It was like watching the sun sail out from behind a cloud – the light was there all the time, but now I knew its source and everything became more radiant.

Catherine has another way of describing this life-changing event. She says that it was like coming home.

> To find and understand the reality of God is a feeling of coming home in the fullest sense, of finally knowing one's true nature, because everything we experience, from joy, love and acts of genius to pain, grief and destruction – all come from this source. And knowing this has taught me to be grateful for each breath.

Catherine sees this as the beginning not the end of her search for the transcendent. She has gone to the USA for a while, because she wants to write for herself about the new dimension to life that she has discovered. She gave me all the generous help and encouragement she could, allowing me tell her story myself and pointing me in the way of finding others who have chanced unexpectedly upon spiritual treasure as she has done.

Stephen Macdonald

Stephen Macdonald is a Scot, who grew up in the city of Glasgow. But his parents loved the outdoor life so the family took their holiday breaks hill-walking and skiing. Stephen grew up to share his parents' love of the hills and mountains and he also grew up to accept for himself his parents' Christian faith. After leaving school, he spent two years in the Met Office, but then applied for a job at a ski centre.

The Abernethy Trust has four outdoor centres in Scotland, open all the year round and providing a programme of climbing and skiing for people of all ages. School groups often visit the centre, with young people from primary- to secondary-school age. Youth groups come and so do team-building groups sent by large companies. There are adult courses for specific training too. In fact all the year round excited newcomers arrive at the centre at Ardeonaig (pronounced Argonaig), where Stephen has now been promoted to be Deputy Director. He is glad that he is still able to give half his time to leading groups out and about, even though the other half has to be devoted to management and administration. The centre can accommodate forty-six guests at a time and has a staff of sixteen to meet all the needs of the centre. There are instructors, cooks, and housekeepers.

It is also stated clearly in the literature and brochures that the centres run by the Abernethy Trust – of which Ardeonaig is one – are Christian centres and this Christian viewpoint is explained when the welcome talk is given at the beginning of each course. Every evening during the course there is a brief fifteen-minute interlude, called 'Time Out', which takes the form of a presentation of some kind suited to the age of the group. With teenagers there is usually a debate or discussion; for younger children a more low-key presentation, that will not exert any undue Christian pressure. Group leaders are free to let their groups opt out of this brief session, but very few do. But in spite of this informal religious instruction, Stephen made it very clear to me that he would much prefer their visitors to learn something about the Christian faith through the quality of the care the staff give to them and from the unqualified enjoyment they have at the centre.

Stephen is very aware that the beauty and grandeur of the scenery has a profound spiritual impact upon all the newcomers. He is glad of this 'reflected' wonder. 'It's only too possible to become blasé,' he admitted. 'Seeing such beauty every day of your life can make you forget just how wonderful it is. But when I see the awe and amazement on the faces of the visitors, it restores my own sense of the greatness of God.'

Out of many personal experiences of the wonder of the unseen Creator whom he worships, Stephen picked out two. Both occurred when he was overseas on skiing trips. The first time he was in Norway. He was in a remote area – in the middle of nowhere – shacking up in a mountain hut. There were no other human beings to be seen. There was no wind to rustle the trees and no sound of water, because everything was blanketed in snow. When he went out at night and stood alone, there was absolute quiet – quietness of a kind he had never before experienced. Something about the silence spoke to him of the greatness of God. In the silence there was space and time for the world beyond our world to make itself known.

His second memorable experience occurred in Iceland. In geological terms, Iceland is a very young country. It abounds with volcanoes, hot springs and geysers. There is a sense of the earth being still in the process of formation. One day, Stephen and his friend began to climb a mountain with the intent of skiing down the other side. Suddenly, before they reached the snowline, they were enveloped in what they imagined to be cloud. Then, beneath them, they saw a crater at the bottom of which there was a sea of churning, boiling mud. The 'cloud' was not a cloud but the steam from a volcanic crater. Already their sensitivities were heightened, the result of straining every sense to receive any signal of imminent danger. Carefully, gently, they skirted the crater, tentatively testing each foothold, in the search for safe ground around its rim.

'I had never stood anywhere before where the ground was not solid substance,' Stephen said. 'It was as if we were present at the beginning of the world, when everything was being created and order was coming out of chaos. I had an incredible experience of the power of God.'

Very many of the visitors to the Ardeonaig Centre have a sense of the world of the spiritual. 'I don't think that spiritual experiences of that kind necessarily lead any further,' Stephen said; 'but because our centre is a Christian one, I sometimes have the opportunity to point those who experience the spiritual world in the direction of the God whom I know personally through Jesus.'

Professor Sir Ghillean Prance

It was over forty years since I had visited Kew Gardens or, to give the establishment its proper name, the Royal Botanic Gardens, Kew. And when I went back on a cold, British summer day, I was amazed and enchanted. It was no longer the old-fashioned, 'Come-down-to-Kew in lilac time' place that I remembered, but a sparkling, thrilling fantasia of nature, science, poetry and sheer beauty. I knew that whoever had planned and master-minded the transformation must be a person with great joy and love for the world we live in. I walked through the quiet Secluded Garden, set out in small areas to illustrate the five senses – each devoted to plants that smell sweet, look lovely and so on. For every area there was a plaque that bore the verse of a poem to match the sense portrayed. I felt rested, enriched, with all my senses heightened and delighted. But when we went into the large Princess of Wales Conservatory, another sensation awaited us. The house is subdivided into ten areas of different world climates. In the rainforest the giant waterlily flourishes and in the desert section a variety of cactuses bloom and grow in fantastic shapes. But sensation, enjoyment of beauty and multiple experiences of nature are not the only factors determining the management of Kew Gardens, as

I was to discover. Wherever possible, no chemicals are used, but pests are controlled by natural means. Threatened species and even some already extinct in their wild habitat are also preserved here. Kew contains 30,000 different types of living plants as well as millions of preserved specimens, seeds and DNA samples.

The Director of Kew, Professor Sir Ghillean Prance, had agreed to see me and it was with some trepidation that I left the gardens and went into the administrative block for my appointment. I need not have worried. Professor Prance, tall, grey-bearded and slightly stooping, was kindness and courtesy itself. He gently welcomed me and patiently awaited my questions. He may indeed be a great scientist but he is also a humble Christian gentleman, in the best sense of the phrase. Before I left he generously gave me books to help my further enquiries and it was through them that I learned a little more about this world-famous scientist.

Ghillean Prance grew up in a Christian environment but it was as a student at Oxford that he became wholeheartedly devoted to the Christian faith. He is as single-minded about his faith as he is about his plants. He practises no half-measures. He had a passion for plants and animals from his very early years on the Isle of Skye, and he was still a student when he had his first deeply felt experience of God in nature. He took part in an Oxford University expedition to Turkey in 1960 and he describes one memorable plant-gathering walk to the top of the White Mountain:

> We slowly collected our way to the top of the mountain, taking more interest in the plants than the view. Eventually we reached the summit and our reward was what is still one of the most beautiful landscapes I have ever seen in all my travels to many places. To my surprise I broke out in praise of God the Creator in a strange language, my first experience of speaking in tongues. Although I had been studying plants and animals since early childhood, the beauty of this part of God's creation touched me in a special way.

But Sir Ghillean's spiritual 'high' was – and always has been – rooted in practical action. He believes very strongly that Christians should be in the forefront of those who work towards the saving of the planet. He cites the creation story in Genesis, where God gives men and women the task of 'serving' and 'preserving' the earth. More unusually, he quotes the well-known verse, 'God so loved the world that he gave his only begotten Son . . .' to demonstrate that God's love and salvation are intended for the whole 'cosmos', not for men and women only.

Sir Ghillean has spent the equivalent of eleven years in the Amazonian rainforests, his main area of exploration. He recalls the very first day of his first expedition. They came across a huge tree bearing flowering twigs of the genus he had specialised in. But the specimens he needed were at the very top of the tree. The tree was too big to climb and the camp cook was asked to fell the tree so that they could reach some of the specimens. But at first he flatly refused to do so. Only under pressure did he agree and then only after he had had time to appease the god of the tree. As he cut the tree down he chanted a song disclaiming responsibility for this act of destruction. Sir Ghillean learned from the cook's behaviour. He soon devised other ways to collect specimens without felling trees. He also learned much from the local Amerindians who have utilised and lived off the forest without doing it permanent damage. He discovered the interdependence of everything in the forest – plants, trees and animals as the means of survival. Destroying just one link in the chain can have a devastating reaction on the others in the same chain too.

In his book, *The Earth Under Threat*, Sir Ghillean gives fascinating examples of the way in which plants and creatures work together for their mutual preservation. Brazil nuts, the royal water-lily and the calabash all hold within their life-cycles fascinating and almost incredible stories of a complex pattern for survival. Perhaps the most bizarre example is the three-toed sloth, described by the professor as 'a mobile, multi-organism ecosystem'. Its grey fur is covered with green algae which acts as camouflage to protect it from its chief enemy, the harpy eagle. But its fur is also a happy home for beetles, ticks and mites as well as a species of moth. When the sloth comes down from the trees to defecate – about once every three weeks – the moth lays its eggs in the sloth dung. The larvae then have three weeks in which to develop into mature moths, by which time they are ready to link up to their home in the sloth fur when next the host visits the ground.

Sir Ghillean is a man with a mission. In his capacity as Director of Kew he has international influence and clout and he uses it with single-minded determination. Part of his mission statement for Kew states that the role of the Royal Botanic Gardens is

> to ensure better management of the Earth's environment by increasing knowledge and understanding of the plant kingdom . . . through worldwide research into plants and the ecosystem, publication, access to all knowledge so gained for the world's scientific community . . . Wherever possible the Royal Botanic Gardens will endeavour to reduce and reverse the rate of destruction of the world's plant species and their habitats.

Professor Prance is a man of practical sense, adept at organisation and fund-raising, and with great scientific knowledge and expertise. He is also a poet and visionary, a man of faith who has glimpsed the spiritual world that lies behind the beauties of earth and whose mission is rooted in trust and love for God and for God's world.

17

Prayer

It's surprising how many people who don't give God a second thought, pray when they are in a tight spot or if those they love are in danger or facing death. To pray is to break through the barrier between our world and the spiritual world in order to reach God – if it's possible and if he exists. I came across some words of Alan Webster, written when he was Dean of Norwich, in his foreword to a booklet about Dame Julian. They seem to sum up the experience of prayer:

> Prayer is recognising, to use some ancient words, that the Most High has made not one world but two. In our secular world, men and women have never been so technically competent, but the longing for the other world of people of faith, the desire to grasp truth through the imagination, has never been stronger. The other world becomes in prayer a home country, sometimes when we least expect it.

Lilian Baylis

As a young woman of twenty-three, Lilian could have been described as plain, plump and frumpish. One side of her face dropped slightly, and she was highly sensitive about this minor disfigurement, probably caused by Bell's palsy. But these unpromising looks belonged to an amazing and outstanding woman. Already Lilian had acquired a much wider knowledge of the world than most young ladies in the middle classes at that time, and she had a wide range of gifts and abilities too. Added to that, she was extremely practical and very thrifty. She became manager of the Old Vic Theatre in 1898 and was in undisputed control until her death at the age of sixty-three. She gave the Old Vic – and later Sadler's Wells Theatre – their standing and reputation in the world of theatre, opera and ballet.

Lilian was one of nine children (five survived) whose parents had strong theatrical and musical leanings. She was a good musician herself, able to play well on the violin, mandolin, piano and guitar and she literally played her part when the whole family went as a troupe to South Africa, to perform and to give lessons. After some years there Lilian became seriously ill and came home to England to stay with an aunt, Emma Cons. When she was better, her aunt's friends persuaded her to stay and take some of the load from Emma, who carried out a vast programme of good works. She became a strong influence in Lilian's life.

Emma Cons – known affectionately as Emmie – was one of the energetic and eccentric women of the period who did so much to change the lot of the poor and the attitudes of the well-to-do. She was a close friend of Octavia Hill, who pioneered housing reform and founded the National Trust. When they were young, the two friends had planned to be artists but when they saw the desperate needs of so many poor people, they decided to put practical social reform before art. But they fervently believed that to live full and good lives, people need beauty and wholesome entertainment as well as good housing, food and medical care. They were convinced that music would help to improve the lives – *and* the moral behaviour – of the barrow-boys of the day. So when Octavia set up a housing scheme for the poor in Paradise Place, Emma organised brass band concerts for them on Saturday nights. She also planned country outings, strategically routed so as to avoid passing any pubs. They saw enough of the evil effects of alcohol to want it banned at any entertainment they provided. They did not want to abolish the music halls of the day but to improve them. They were determined to provide 'purified entertainment' on strictly teetotal premises.

The Victoria Theatre in Waterloo Road, right in the middle of slums near Waterloo Station, seemed an ideal site for their cherished project. It had been built sixty years before but by this time had a bad reputation. The locals came in their crowds to watch cheap melodrama. The place was unutterably dirty and squalid – and an ideal place to get roaring drunk. Somehow Emma and Lilian managed to raise enough money to buy the freehold lease and began to transform the Vic into a place devoted to 'the benefit and enjoyment of the people for ever'. Emma was determined that it should be a place for innocent entertainment and laughter and *no* alcohol. She had seen too many local women with black eyes – the result of a beating-up by drunken husbands returning from the Vic on a Saturday night. Years later Lilian would tell actors, like Laurence Olivier, 'If it hadn't been for drunken men beating their wives, dear boy, we'd never have got this place and you wouldn't be doing Hamlet.'

With Emma in charge a new regime began for the Vic. In 1888, the *Pall Mall Gazette* was able to report: 'No coarse or unseemly jest or allusion, no word with undesirable double entendre is permitted to be heard on stage.' Emma appointed Lilian to take over as manager of the Vic in 1898, but her aunt was still the power behind the throne until her death in 1912.

For Lilian, the Vic became her whole life. She organised and planned, coaxed and wheedled any who could help the cause and was tireless in her own efforts for its success. She would turn her hand to anything. She interviewed actors, coped unceremoniously with officialdom and red tape, sold programmes, helped make costumes and, according to legend, once even scrubbed the stage. She was certainly in the habit of asking actors who auditioned: 'And would you scrub the stage, dear?'

Until 1914, the Old Vic had no licence to perform plays, but then a special case was made for Shakespeare. Lilian admitted that she knew nothing about Shakespeare at that time, but 'I went to those who knew nearly everything. I have always done that – gone to those who know.' It certainly *was* her method to go to the top – and that often meant going to God about all the decision-making and problems to be solved. Someone commented that 'God was on the staff.'

It is a mark of Lilian's genius and drive – and her faith in God – that the Old Vic succeeded at all. It was not in theatre-land but in a rough district of London and was a most uninviting place.

There was sawdust, not carpet, on the floor, benches covered with oil-cloth instead of comfortable seats, and of course there was no bar serving alcohol. In fact there was a woeful lack of all facilities and rats and mice abounded. But money was very tight. Everything had to be done on a shoestring. Costumes were begged and borrowed, and wigs hired for the night often did not arrive until minutes before curtain up. Props were so tatty and worn that they had to be handled with utmost care. When a coffin was needed a local undertaker obliged. The theatre received no government grant and could not afford improvements. Lilian was in control and refused to spend money on advertising or complimentary tickets for critics. Her argument was: 'Why should we give the bounders free seats and then let them earn their wretched livings by saying scurrilous things about us?' Conditions in the theatre were rough and ready for the audience – and for performers backstage too.

Audiences were not exactly highbrow and there were no full houses at first. But Lilian insisted that she rejoiced more over 'one rough lad who has never heard of Shakespeare than over the attendance of half a dozen Shakespeare students'. And somehow the Old Vic survived. Money came in from the matinee performances of Shakespeare that were provided for schoolchildren – another positive step to help the local population. Surprisingly, the Vic was the only theatre where Shakespeare was being played. Other theatres had given up on serious drama during World War I. Lilian firmly believed that it was God's help that turned the tide. She wanted to 'place on record our conviction that we could not have carried our work through either last season or this season without the aid of prayer'.

For Lilian, the spiritual world – and God himself – seemed incredibly close. She was in constant touch with God and he with her. Along with her high church beliefs and practices went a belief in simple and direct prayers. When finances were desperately low again, because of German air-raids in 1917, a five-hundred-pound grant saved the day. 'A wonderful answer to prayer I call it,' Lilian remarked. Often during those difficult times, she would make a speech from the stage, encouraging the audience to greater efforts at attendance and often asking for their prayers so that the Vic might pull through.

There were – and still are – many legends about Lilian and they include some about her prayers. 'Dear God, please send me good actors – and cheap!' was said to have been one of her wartime prayers. But she occasionally used her access to God for her own ends. When an actor asked for a small rise, Lilian replied that she would need to pray about it and she left the room. When she came back a few minutes later she said: 'Sorry, dear, God says no.'

She also felt able to tell God when she thought he had made a mistake. There was only one lavatory for women backstage, and all the female staff – including the manager – had to queue for it – discreetly. One day, after a particularly long wait, Lilian exclaimed: 'This is simply *ridiculous*. And when I meet my dear Lord I shall tell him so. It's *such* a waste of time for a very busy woman like me. I shall tell him he's really made a very bad arrangement and he'll have to do better.'

The Vic could not run to the expense of understudies, so one day when an actor was ill Lilian phoned urgently to try to get a replacement at short notice. A very surprised person at the other end heard her say: 'God, you've got me into this mess. You've got to get me out of it. You must *help me . . .*'

In reply to the 'I beg your pardon,' Lilian explained, 'I'm so sorry. I quite forgot there was someone else on the line.'

She told the writer Hugh Walpole, 'The great thing is to be quite natural yourself with God as you would with anyone else.'

He replied, 'That's very difficult. To be natural I mean. You feel he sees through you.'

'So long as he helps the Old Vic, dear,' Lilian told him, 'he can see through me as much as he likes.' She believed in being herself, honest and outspoken, whoever she was talking to.

In 1918 Queen Mary was to attend the gala matinee but when she had not arrived in time for curtain up, Lilian refused to wait. 'Queen or no queen we must make a start.' The queen had been held up in a traffic jam and when she did arrive Lilian went to meet her. 'I'm glad you've turned up at last, dear,' she said, 'and I know it's not your fault being late. But we've a got a long programme to get through, so let's get on with things.' While Queen Mary was making for the royal box, Lilian signalled –

with a loud whisper – for the orchestra to strike up the National Anthem.

Her amusing irreverence towards God was only one side of her attitude to him. At least twice in her life she saw a vision of Jesus. Once she was in a church on the Isle of Sheppey, praying for help, when she saw him kneeling at a little table opposite her and they said the Lord's Prayer together. A year later, when she was near the same church, she went in to look for any window with a figure of Christ in it that might have prompted her vision, but there was none. On another occasion she woke one morning to see 'a very wonderful and golden picture of our Lord', between the curtains at her neighbour's bedroom window. There was no picture inside that might have induced the image, although the rational side of Lilian made her examine the room carefully.

Lilian combined spiritual vision with a great deal of down-to-earth practicality. With her indomitable will and cheerful persuasion, she inspired or terrorised others to work almost as hard as she did. She was doggedly determined and through her hard work and her vision she created the Old Vic – and later Sadler's Wells – and provided a stage for some of the great artistes of the time. In spite of the appalling lack of facilities backstage, and Lilian's brusque manner, actors loved to play at the Old Vic. When she died Professor Dent wrote: 'She was undoubtedly a woman of deep fundamental goodness . . . which made her a peculiarly loveable woman, and the only woman who could hold these two entire theatres . . . firmly together, united if for no other cause in personal loyalty to herself.'

St Teresa of Avila

Although she lived almost five hundred years ago, many people find Teresa of Avila surprisingly modern in many ways. She certainly did not conform to the accepted pattern of womanly behaviour of her day, which entailed dutiful obedience, passivity and subjection. Teresa was a born leader, an innovator, an activist, with good looks, charm and a passion for dancing and playing chess. She loved to have friends and shone and sparkled in

company. She also had a deep desire for genuine spiritual understanding and growth. Not many people are pure extrovert or
introvert and Teresa was an outstanding mix of both kinds of
temperament. Although she was extremely practical and a good
administrator, she was also a person who needed solitude as well
as company. She engaged in much deep soul-searching and experienced moments of great spiritual ecstasy.

Sometimes the two sides of her personality came together – or
clashed. She loved cooking and assured the sisters that 'the Lord
walks among the pots and pans' but one day when she was on
duty in the kitchen her nuns found her rapt and ecstatic, with a
cooking pan still clutched in her hand. The sisters were in a twitter
of anxiety, unwilling to disturb her ecstasy but very concerned in
case she spilt the oil from the pan, because it was all the oil they
had left.

Teresa herself sometimes describes her other-worldly experiences in her letters (she was a compulsive letter-writer) but inserts
them alongside practical matters that concerned her too. In fact,
she often felt a little embarrassed by her extraordinary spiritual
ecstasies. Sometimes she would levitate – rising some inches from
the floor – and she tried desperately to prevent this startling event
happening if others were around or if it occurred during a chapel
service.

Teresa was born in 1515, one of a large, well-to-do family,
with more brothers than sisters. Her mother was Don Alonso
Sanchez de Cepeda's second wife and she died when Teresa was
only thirteen. The only choices open to young women at that
time were marriage or the Church. Convents were often sociable
and comfortable places for those whose parents could afford to
give good dowries. Well-to-do girls could take their own maid
and invite friends to stay, sometimes having their own private
sitting-room. After a chequered start and following a serious
illness, Teresa became sure of her vocation and without her
father's permission or knowledge, entered the Carmelite convent
at Avila. But in spite of hopes that her life would now be settled
and under control, she spent the next twenty years coming to
terms with her own complex nature and discovering a way to get
to know God. We know a great deal about her and her spiritual

pilgrimage from her writings and her letters.

After years of introspection, of self-discovery – and discovery of God – the extrovert, active side of her character came to the fore again. She wished to reform the Carmelite Order, which had become lax and unspiritual. She set about establishing a new order of Carmelites, known as discalced, or barefoot Carmelites, who would live in a simpler and more disciplined way. For the next twenty years or so she was constantly on the move, setting up new foundations.

She had a wonderful way of overcoming problems and dealing with difficult people in authority and allowed nothing to stand in her way. Nicknamed 'God's Gadabout' she made endless and difficult journeys., sometimes encountering real dangers. Near the end of her life a midwinter journey was held up by melting snow and floods. Bridges were unusable and the only way for the nuns to get to their destination was to wade through water which was perilously high. Teresa told the sisters that she would go first. If she drowned they were not to try to save her but to turn back. The story is told that after this journey Teresa complained to God about the dangers they had endured. He answered, 'But that is how I treat my friends.'

'Yes, Lord,' Teresa replied, 'that's why you have so few of them!'

Teresa's discovery of the secrets of prayer is relevant today. She struggled for a long time, even giving up prayer altogether for a period when she feared that her methods of praying might transgress the Church's instructions. In the end she made the transforming discovery that prayer is not a ritual or a religious ceremony but the growth of a relationship with God. In her *Life* she writes: 'Mental prayer is for me none other than an intimate relation of friendship, frequently spending time with one whose love for us is beyond doubt.' She found that to imagine Christ within her, and to recall some of the times in his earthly life when he had been lonely or in need, encouraged her to believe that he would be willing to accept her and listen to her prayer. As she imagined herself at Christ's side, she began to experience, only briefly at first, a sense of God's presence and to enjoy what she called 'the prayer of quiet'. This prayer called for no words to be spoken but infused her with a sense of calm and bliss.

Sometimes she experienced a deep and real sense of the presence of God. Once, at prayer, she saw the Lord's hands and later 'the divine face'. Finally she saw the figure of Christ whole. She tried to describe it:

> It is not a radiance which dazzles, but a soft whiteness and an infused radiance which, without wearying the eyes, causes them the greatest delight; nor are they wearied of the brightness which they see in seeing this Divine beauty . . . It is a light which never gives place to night, and being always light, is disturbed by nothing.

Her confessors were sceptical and, happily for posterity, made her write down everything she saw. Teresa had no desk in her cell and wrote kneeling on the floor under a draughty window, never stopping to correct or improve. (She rather regretted time wasted in writing which could have been used spinning or doing work around the house.)

For the instruction of her 'daughters' – the Carmelite nuns – Teresa wrote down some of her explorations in prayer, using metaphors and pictures to help them understand. She compared prayer to the watering of a garden. In the hot dry climate of Castile, plants badly needed water. In the same way, if the soul is to flourish and grow it must be watered by prayer. Teresa described four ways of watering a garden which correspond to four methods of prayer. The first way was to draw water from a well, an exhausting and laborious job. Trying to pray by means of great personal effort and hard work is likewise a tough and difficult discipline. The second method of watering was to set up a system of buckets and water wheels – a method which relieved the gardener of the hard slog. In the same way the method of repeating set prayers and following a ready-made pattern could make the exercise of praying easier.

The third way of providing plants with water was to have a stream wandering through the garden. In terms of prayer this means letting God come in and permeate the life himself. But, as every gardener knew then and knows now, one way of watering is far and away the best – allowing the rain to fall on it. In this way the garden is watered naturally and gently and without any effort on the gardener's part. The same, Teresa concluded, is true of prayer. The best kind of prayer takes place when the soul is passive and all the refreshment and life-giving 'water' comes from God, flowing in blessing, without human effort.

She wrote: 'May the Lord teach me words so that I can speak about this fourth kind of water. Here one does not have to feel, but to enjoy without understanding what is enjoyed ... in this divine union.' Teresa had learned to stop striving to reach the invisible world. God and the world of the spirit had come to her.

Madame Guyon

Madame Guyon was born Jeanne Marie Bouvier de la Mothe in seventeenth-century France. She was a very serious-minded, religious girl and after going to convent school she set her heart on becoming a nun. But her mother thought otherwise, and when her daughter was only sixteen she married her off to Jacques Guyon. He was already middle-aged and an invalid. Worse still for Jeanne Marie, he was still under the thumb of his strong-minded, domineering mother. The young wife reacted to this near impossible situation by retreating more and more into her own religious world. Although she was not literally in a convent, she spent much of her time in spiritual contemplation. After twelve years of marriage her elderly husband died, leaving her free to follow her own brand of religious mysticism. She began to have visions and revelations and travelled around – sometimes in the company of a friar whose teaching she admired – hoping to spread her own way of spirituality.

But in 1688 she was arrested and put in prison by order of the Church. Madame Guyon's spirituality was known as 'quietism' and the Pope had condemned the movement. Because the emphasis was on personal piety, the Church feared that it would lead to an unhealthy individualism. Madame Guyon believed that through her spiritual practices she had succeeded in putting God – instead of herself – at the centre of her life. Madame Maintenon – once the mistress but by then the second wife of Louis XIV of France

– intervened to have her set free. That lady had had a colourful career and may well have remembered her childhood when her own father was in prison. She certainly had great influence with the king. But in 1695 Madame Guyon was thrown into prison again and served part of her sentence in the Bastille. She was released after six years and lived on in freedom till her death in 1717.

This account of her life and her kind of spirituality does not make Madame Guyon sound a very warm or sympathetic figure. It would not seem likely that she could have anything to say nearly three hundred years later to people living in a very different culture. But in the little book she wrote, called, in English, *A Short and Easy Method of Prayer*, Madame Guyon comes across as a very warm and appealing person. She is enthusiastic about a way of prayer that could strike just the right note in our noisy, busy world today. She did not mean her book to be published. She explains that she meant it only for the eyes of those few people who love God and genuinely want to find him. She admits that loving God seems difficult and prayer can be hard work, but her kind of prayer involved nothing more than responding simply to God in love.

She suggests to her readers that they try to focus on God, holding some aspect of his goodness or greatness at the forefront of their mind; then just quietly enjoy God's presence. Don't use many words, she advises, but instead still the heart and mind to enjoy an awareness of God's presence. She believed that God has a magnetic power of goodness which draws the human soul towards him. The more someone turns towards God and away from human self-centredness, the more God will draw that person close to him. It is important to keep silent within and if any distraction occurs, just see that the heart and mind return to God again as the centre of love and desire. Madame Guyon believed that when this kind of prayer is practised it flows over into the whole of life. When the human soul chooses to be passive, God can be active. He will renew their life and restore them to the true image of God which they were intended to bear.

Mme Guyon did not share the modern search for self-fulfilment. Her aim was to please God. 'The soul should have a pure and disinterested love, as it seeks nothing from God, but only to please him, and to do his will . . . Do not turn to prayer hoping to enjoy spiritual delights,' she writes. 'Rather come to prayer totally content to receive nothing or to receive great blessing from God's hand, which ever should be your heavenly Father's will for you at that time.'

Father Sergei Hackel

When I first phoned Father Sergei Hackel, a sense of peace and calm seemed to come across the wires. His perfectly modulated voice is gentle, calm and wonderfully reassuring. I sensed that I was talking to a man of great sensibility and spiritual depth. Yet, as we talked, it became clear that his life is not a leisurely and protected one. When we tried to arrange a time to talk I discovered that he had an extremely busy schedule of lectures to give and meetings to attend. To add to the hassle, his house was undergoing major upheaval so his study was in disarray and many of his precious books were out of the bookcase and stacked on the floor.

Father Sergei was born to Russian émigré parents in Germany. He moved to Holland, and just before Hitler invaded the Low Countries he joined his mother in England and it was here that he went to school and university. He always spoke Russian at home with his mother so he is fluent in Russian and English. He became a Reader in Russian Studies at Sussex University for many years but also, with some reluctance at first, agreed to be ordained as a non-stipendiary priest in the Russian Orthodox Church – he was the first to be ordained in the newly established diocese of Sourozh. For the past ten to fifteen years he has been involved in religious broadcasting to what is now the former Soviet Union. He often visits Russia, for there is still a great need, he told me, for spiritual support and for religious education in the Church there.

On the occasions when I have visited an Orthodox church I have been impressed by the particular atmosphere of quietness and other-worldliness. But I still knew very little about what goes on in Orthodox services and how they differ from Western churches. I specially wanted Father Sergei to explain to me the different understanding of prayer in Orthodox Christianity and what part icons play in worship and in coming close to God. The answers he gave me go beyond those two aspects of worship to point up a whole different emphasis in Orthodox faith.

Worshippers stand in the church service (the few benches provided are for the very elderly or infirm). They often pray with an icon before them. Icons are not intended to reveal the artist's originality and invention. Those who paint icons – perhaps a monk in a monastery – follow certain symbolic representations laid down long ago. There are limited subjects for an icon and ancient icons are followed by the artist who will also work under an overseeing director. The artist uses his own skills and techniques but only within these established parameters.

Father Sergei compared standing before an icon with looking out over a beautiful vista. From that viewpoint the beholder gradually becomes aware of how much is to be seen. An icon is a window into the world of God and the eternal. It opens up and makes accessible the sacred truth depicted in that icon. Like looking at a prism, it enables the worshipper to see the light in its different component parts. An icon obeys different rules from those of classical art. Instead of the familiar perspective – where objects in the foreground are larger and those in the background are smaller – a different perspective applies in the painting of icons. In a classical painting, the objects or landscape world gradually grow smaller and vanish into the distance. In an icon, the artist is aiming to make the viewer aware that he is introducing him to the infinite world where there is no vanishing point. The viewer can be the recipient of all. By an inverse perspective, Father Sergei explained, what is closest to me is also the smallest and least.

'The more you proceed into the icon world, the more of the infinite comes to you.' In an icon of Christ, 'the infinite world is focused in the Christ figure who *recedes* towards us. And we are both less significant and at the same time uplifted.' As we look at the icon, 'we can be silent. The perspective of the world is banished and we are put in touch with the perspectives of the Kingdom.'

I found this very different approach to art and to worship quite mind-shattering. I have had to go back over the words and try to take in their full implication many times since.

I asked Father Sergei next about the Jesus prayer, which is also used now by many people who are not members of the Orthodox Church. The prayer is very simple – one brief sentence, repeated many times. In its fullest version the words repeated are: 'Lord Jesus Christ, Son of God, be merciful to me, a sinner.' Sometimes it is shortened or expanded slightly and often it is repeated in rhythm with breathing in and out or with the worshipper's heart-beat. The prayer can be used in church with others, or by individuals as they take time for prayer. It can be used during the wakeful hours of the night, or during work or travel, to compose, as one bishop said, 'the hands at work, the mind and heart with God'.

The prayer goes back to the early days of Christian faith and was used by the desert fathers – those who went into the desert to seek solitude and separation from the world. It was used by monks in the monasteries, then spread to ordinary homes and general use. The prayer is quite different from the mantras chanted repeatedly in order to induce a relaxed state of self-hypnosis. Its purpose is to help the worshipper concentrate wholeheartedly on the name and presence of Jesus, with all the meaning that name contains about who he is and what he has done. 'Homing in' so to speak, on Jesus in this way, brings a warm and overwhelming sense of his presence. The monks believed that it gave them an experience of the Divine Light, such as the disciples witnessed on the Mount of Transfiguration.

The Jesus prayer helps the one who prays to come into the presence of Jesus but is not meant to encourage flights of imagination. Trying to form pictures of Jesus in the mind can distract, Father Sergei explained, or even become idolatrous. It is the recognition of his presence that matters most.

We live in a secular world where many people value only what can be experienced by the five senses. Orthodox Christianity has much to teach us through its spontaneous, lively sense of the other, spiritual world. The dead are very real to these believers. Icons of saints keep their memory fresh and a corner of the church is often set aside for remembering and praying for the dead. A dish of grain may be placed there as a reminder of the resurrection of the dead at the last day. Like buried grain, they will rise in new and glorious form.

Easter is the greatest of the feast days. After the darkness and solemnity of Good Friday, Easter Day with its news of resurrection bursts joyfully on all the worshippers. The people stand in the dark, outside the church, holding their flickering candles, waiting to hear the joyful words of the minister repeated three times: 'Christ has risen from the dead: by death he has trampled down death: and to those who are in the grave he has given life.' Then the church doors swing open and the people sweep into the church. And throughout the Easter holiday the greeting is repeated: 'Christ is risen!' and the answer comes: 'Risen indeed!'

18

The arts

When George Frederick Handel wrote *Messiah,* his oratorio about
Jesus's life death and resurrection in the words of the Bible, he is
said to have stayed and worked in the house for twenty-four days,
not even stopping to eat. One day, when he was composing the
music for the 'Hallelujah Chorus', his servant came in to find
him sitting with tears streaming down his face. 'I did think I did
see all heaven before me, and the great God himself,' Handel
exclaimed.

Many who have listened to or sung that chorus in the centuries
since have had something of the same experience. Even when a
poem, a piece of music, a painting or sculpture have no specifically
religious theme, they bring us into a dimension far removed from
the practical humdrum of daily routine. I wondered what some of
those who are engaged in the creative arts have discovered about
the spiritual world.

Art

John Houlston

When I saw John Houlston on television he was standing beside a
partly-sculpted plaster head, at his open-air studio beside the tidal
creek at Faversham in Kent. The head was enormous – about four
metres high – and John could reach only to the eyebrows; for the
rest, ladders would be needed. The completed head made in plaster
will weigh about eight tonnes and from it a cast could be taken to

make a head in a modern material such as carbon fibre. The head is of Diana, Princess of Wales, and John has undertaken the work on behalf of the National Aids Trust, of which the Princess was patron. The trustees believed that a popular sculpture by a well-known artist could raise the profile of the trust and make its work among people with HIV and AIDS better known.

The trust was told that the Princess was not sitting for paintings or sculptures, but Diana saw a photo of the head of Archbishop Tutu that John had sculpted. She immediately agreed to let him come to Kensington Palace to make some sketches – as many as he could in the time – from various angles.

Now, much later, John is having to move his workplace from the creek at Faversham. He described his new setting to me enthusiastically. It is on farmland on the North Downs, with a view of the English Channel on a clear day. He has taken over the stable block and he and his helpers have constructed their own building, which John designed. They are still faced with moving all John's precious wood as well as the huge sculpture to its new site. Although it is technically moveable, at this stage John is considering rebuilding it instead.

I visited John and his wife, Rosemary, at their pink-washed cottage in the beautiful Kent town of Faversham. I had talked to him on the phone but I learned so much more about him as a person and an artist by spending time with him. John is a rarity, an utterly honest and true person, and his integrity touches his life as well as his work. He aims to keep his life whole and of a piece, although he constantly wrestles with the big questions of suffering and pain. He is distressed by the blatant contrast between the teachings of Christ and the power structures and privileged life-style of many church leaders.

John and his two sisters were brought up in a genteel, evangelical home – their father was a university lecturer – and John was sent to a minor public school which he loathed. But he always refused to let society or those in authority 'put him through the mincer' as he describes it. With characteristic generosity he suggests that we are all potentially brilliant artists. ('There are no bad cave artists!') But we cease to be artists because it is 'knocked out of us' by those who make us conform and adopt accepted ways of doing things. As a result, only a few *remain* artists. These are the people who refuse to be crushed by society – who won't opt in. They retain the child's ability to look at everything with fresh eyes, as if seeing it new, for the first time.

Although John thoroughly enjoyed the relaxed and tolerant attitude of art school and the company of his unconventional student friends, he is a disciplined artist. He was given a formal and traditional training and he firmly believes that it is necessary to study anatomy and draughtsmanship thoroughly in order to depict the human body beautifully and accurately. He is also fascinated by mathematical graphs and loci. He is excited by the sheer unlimited variety of such shapes, which influence his abstract compositions.

When John had finished at art school he went to London University and read theology. His father wanted him to have a 'proper' job – preferably as a clergyman – but after graduation John went into teaching, at a tough, London comprehensive school, and loved it. (A few days before I visited him, two of his one-time pupils, now in their forties, had been to see him. They had kept in touch.) After a further spell in education, John went back to study sculpture for four years as well as continuing an academic study of philosophy and the history of art.

John also paints and I looked at a beautiful picture he had recently completed of birds in the estuary. He had used a fairly new method of his own, applying water colours to paper that has first been sodden, so that colours merge and soften. The result was a beautiful, warm mingling of pinks, blues and some yellow in the land and sky of the background.

Many of John's sculptures take their inspiration from the living human body, while others are the product of geometrical forms. Possibly his favourite medium is wood from fruit trees. He never works on a tree that has been cut down on purpose, but uses those that fall naturally, including many that fell in the great gale of 1987. I asked him whether he had to experiment when he worked for the first time on a particular type of wood. He agreed that he did have to discover, gently, the way of that wood. The so-called experts who say what can and can't be done with the wood are not always right. John has to go on his own voyage of discovery.

Woods even smell different. 'Until I used olive wood for the first time,' he told me,' 'I didn't know it smelt like mushrooms cooking in olive oil.'

Every individual piece of wood is different too. John talked about the different accidents that befall a tree, through dryness, pruning, the attack of insects or small mammals, the effect of the prevailing wind and so on. Every one of the resulting imperfect-ions produces some unique and beautiful effect – perhaps a knot or a patch of darker wood – something that he can incorporate into the grand design. John did not call them 'imperfections' – that was my word. He saw them not as flaws but as the inevitable results of the chances of life and fortune. He said, with genuine humility, that art is 98 per cent the medium and 2 per cent the artist's skill. 'No human being could create wood, with its beautiful grain. The sculptor's job is humbly to reveal that beauty. He finishes it smoothly to reveal the grain.'

He sees himself as the receptor of spiritual value and truth; his calling is to give it form and make it accessible to others. Over and above the wood and the artist, he recognises that something – or Someone – else is at work when he creates. A spiritual dimen-sion enters into the process, breathing into the work. He believes that sculpture is the most satisfying creative work because it is wholly 'hands-on', thus truly human. Human beings alone use their hands to create beautiful artefacts of their own design and in sculpture the artist is working directly on to the finished work, not via a musical instrument or words on a page.

Not surprisingly, John finds it hard to admire some modern art. He believes that we live in a very sick society and the brutal art that we so often see today reflects that sickness.

Although John is a superb artist he is never precious or esoteric. He certainly does not consider himself superior but takes delight in 'ordinary' people. He quotes a friend who said that God must love ordinary people because he made so many of them. But for him no one is ordinary. He believes that every single person is unique and that all of us have the opportunity to mediate beauty and love to others. 'A teacher, or someone caring for an old person, is probably doing a more important job than I am,' he reflects, 'but then, each of us has to do what we are given to do.'

For John Houlston, this may mean watching the clouds go by, gazing intently at a flower, sculpting at Faversham Creek, painting in his studio or sharing with others the laughter and kindness that make him such a special person as well as a superb artist. 'I believe in the infinite value of every person and thing,' he told me, 'and that infinite value I would call God.'

He recognises the presence of God in the activities and relationships of everyday life. He sees God in the air breathed in by artists, but also in a mother looking after her baby or someone caring for the sick. He believes that art is important in its capacity to cheer and make beautiful, but stopping to talk to a lonely person, giving help to a very sick person or teaching a group of children, are creative ways of giving too. These actions and hundreds of others communicate love, compassion and beauty and so they are all expressions of the presence of God.

What John believes is at one with his art. His artistic values are not elevated above his strong sense of justice and compassion. He once said, in a lecture to a group of artists, that if he saw an old person cold, he would unhesitatingly chop up and burn one of his sculptures to keep him warm. He meant it, but his audience was shocked.

Vincent van Gogh

'A rough dog with wet paws,' is how Vincent van Gogh once described himself. A shy, withdrawn man with fiery red hair and freckles, said by one of his sisters to be a stranger not only to his little brothers and sisters, but 'a stranger to himself'.

Vincent was the oldest surviving child in the family, but when he was born his mother was still grieving for her first-born son who had died not long before. She gave her second son the same two forenames as the dead child. On his weekly visits to church he must have seen the small grave of the first, much mourned Vincent. Perhaps any sense of self-worth or of knowing himself to be loved were sapped at that early age. He certainly saw himself as uncouth and unlovely, especially compared with his younger brother Theo, who, by contrast, he thought, 'brought joy to all'.

Vincent's father was a Dutch Reformed Minister – a Protestant in a largely Roman Catholic farming area of Brabant, not far from the Belgian border. His mother was an outgoing person, a keen botanist. As a boy Vincent kept to his own company. He enjoyed reading and walking; on his solitary walks he followed in his mother's footsteps and collected insects and wild flowers. He was a restless soul, constantly needing change, moving to over twenty different places during his brief life. Yet, paradoxically, he was obsessed with the need for returning to his roots and experiencing a sense of home and belonging.

Vincent had all the vulnerability and sensitivity of the artist, seeing everything with painful clarity. But he did not begin to paint seriously until he was twenty-eight and it was many years before he considered that he was ready to embark on the use of colour. Yet it is perhaps for his colour that we remember him – brilliance and sunlight are burnt into the canvas and burst out to the beholder. The opposite poles of darkness and light fascinated Vincent all his life. Between the two extremes he relished twilight.

Vincent was a realist but not in the sense of reproducing people or places with photographic accuracy. He wanted to represent people as they were in totality, to capture not just the physical likeness but the soul within them. To him, men and women of all kinds were beautiful, in spite of – or perhaps because of – their age, ugliness and deformities. His deep compassion went out to the poor, the over-worked, the ill-treated. His art brought him close to such people, as a fellow human being, not as an artistic observer on a different plane. Most of his paintings are of down-trodden workers – miners, potato pickers – and exhausted human beings.

For a while Vincent trained to be a missionary but his belief in orthodox Christianity and Church crumbled. He still treasured his favourite three books – the Bible, Bunyan's *Pilgrim's Progress* and Thomas à Kempis' *Imitation of Christ.* His belief in Christ remained and never wavered. He wanted to cross the divide between religion and art and he found the bridge he needed in the work of the artist Rembrandt. Rembrandt seemed to him to contain both faith and art. He wrote: 'There is something of Rembrandt in the gospel and something of the gospel in Rembrandt.' But Vincent did not find satisfaction in painting religious scenes. He expressed his religious impulses by using the sun-drenched Mediterranean trees and fields or the starry night skies. He has been described as wanting to portray in the people he drew the same spiritual quality that primitive Christian artists depicted by a halo.

Vincent wanted to do more than draw the down-trodden and exhausted workers he saw around him; he wanted to share and relieve their distresses in every way he could. For a while – during his period as a missionary – he worked among the miners near Mons. He was horrified by the conditions in which they worked and the constant danger they faced. After one serious firedamp explosion, he tended the wounded as they were brought out and tore up his white shirts for bandages. Afterwards, he dressed in sackcloth and went dirty and unshaven, in order to identify with these victims of society. When his landlady asked why he went to such extremes he told her: 'Esther, one should do like the good God; from time to time one should go and live among his own.'

But the authorities at his mission headquarters were puzzled and displeased. In spite of the stories that reached them of Vincent's generosity and care for miners' families, they felt that they must dissociate themselves from this dirty and disreputable man who would bring their mission into disrepute. So Vincent moved restlessly on, always in debt, often rescued from destitution by his brother Theo's gifts of money.

Although he fell in love more than once – with deep passion and desperation – his wooing was never successful. At one time his concern for the desperate and abused led him to provide home and shelter for a sick and worn-out prostitute, whose baby was born while she was with him. He cherished her, trying to restore her sense of self-worth and her capacity for love. He adored the baby and cared for it gently, lovingly placing the cradle near the easel while he painted.

Sometimes he longed for a perfect world where art would be unnecessary, because life itself would be an art. 'Why am I so little an artist that I always regret that the statue and the picture are not alive?' he asked. But for ordinary people like ourselves who look at his pictures, Vincent succeeds in producing that essence of life – the realness of cornfields or sunflowers – made more real for us by his painting and his colours. His chair, his table, his sunflowers are like Plato's ideal realities, expressing the utter 'chairness' of a chair in a unique and satisfying way.

Art became Vincent's religion. He gave up orthodox belief in Christianity or the Church, but he never gave up his vibrant belief in Christ. Like Christ, he saw worth and beauty not as the ordinary beholder does, but in the essential humanity of those who were old, ugly, or worn out with work. For him, Christ was the one who worked in 'living flesh'. He tried, through his art, to reveal the spiritual world, to show the spiritual reality that lay behind the material objects he painted or the broken, ugly forms of his models. He wanted to depict the reality behind the naïve halo of primitive Christian paintings. He suffered from deep melancholy but he believed that he could change even that into gold through the alchemy of art. He loved darkness and often walked in the night; he believed that darkness was the necessary precursor of light, and that death led to resurrection. His periods of insanity and his final suicide seem to be symptoms of a disturbed and deranged mind. But like many artists and poets, Vincent suffered as a result of seeing too well and too clearly. He saw the reality of the spiritual world breaking through all God's creation. At the cost of enormous pain and suffering to himself – and those who loved him – he gave that gift of sight, through his paintings, to us all.

Music

Bernard Salter and Nigel Morris

A splendid sermon, a moving service, a friendly church congregation – an unlikely experience? But that really happened to me when I visited St Peter's Church in Stoke-on-Trent, one of the pottery towns in the Midlands, made famous by Arnold Bennett's novels of the five towns, and world renowned for the beautiful pottery and porcelain made there. The crowning glory of that morning church service was the playing of the organ. Hardly ever have I heard a church organ played with such verve, beauty and sheer glory. I wondered what the organist himself felt about his music and whether, for him, as for me, it was a way in to God. So I talked to Bernard Salter – not himself the regular organist – to learn his story.

Bernard lives in the West Midlands and spends his holidays travelling on canal boats. He plans his trips, he told me, so that when Sundays come he is near the kind of church which makes churchgoing a pleasure. One Sunday the boat broke down and they had to moor at Etruria, an area of Stoke named after the Wedgwood Etruscan ware made there. He and his wife made their way to the nearest church, St Peter's. After the service Bernard chatted with the organist, Nigel, whose playing he had very much enjoyed. Nigel persuaded him to try out the organ, then invited Bernard to call in any time he was on his travels and be the organist for the day. So, from time to time, as on the day I visited St Peter's, Bernard arrives in his canal boat and plays for morning service.

As I had guessed, Bernard believes that music is very important in the worship of God. 'When the music in a church service is not what it should be, then the worship is always disappointing,' he said. Then he went on:

> If you like, I see music as a metaphor for our relationship with God. We are told that we should *listen* to God. By listening to music, we get in touch with our innermost selves and through the emotions the music evokes, God is able to speak to us. So music helps us to listen to God. Music is an enormously potent force to bring us in touch with transcendental reality. It helps us to express our feelings towards God too.

Music, including church organ music, has always been part of Bernard's life. Bernard's father – who is in his nineties and has just come to live next door to them – was church organist at the same church in Wales from the time he began to play, when he was in his teens, to his late eighties, when he had to give up because of failing sight. Bernard remembers when he was a small boy of only four or five, sitting beside his father at the parish organ. His father sent him to the Cathedral School in Chester, where he sang as a choirboy; when he left the choir at thirteen, he began to play the organ, gaining his ARCO (Associate of the Royal College of Organists) at the age of seventeen. With my own painful memories of trying to learn to play an instrument, I asked Bernard: 'How much do the technical skills of playing interfere with your free expression of the music? Having mastered the technique, can you just forget all that side of it?'

'By no means!' Bernard said:

I practised for at least two hours before playing in church that morning you were there. And even at the time, the technique is not forgotten. Playing the organ involves mental work and effort and of course it involves physical hard work too. I like to think that when I play the organ I can offer God my mental, physical and emotional work in playing the organ, as part of my total offering to him in worship. It increases my sense of reward and the benefits I experience – and the congregation gains too, I hope.

Every organ is different, and it's important to know and understand the particular organ you are playing. Of course, every violin is different, too, but a church organ is unique in a way that goes beyond any other instrument. Each one has its spiritual identity, if you like to put it that way – its own personality. Organ builders 'voice' the pipes in their work- shops – that is, they strive to get a pure tone across the whole rank of pipes. Organs are often purpose-built for a church but if an organ is moved from one church to another it must be redesigned for its new home.

Later I talked to Nigel, the regular organist at St Peter's. He too began as a choirboy and longed to play the organ from an early age. He won an organ scholarship at uuniversity and came to play on the organ he had admired in the cathedral as a boy. He helped me understand why organists seem to be a rather special brand of musicians. Nigel said:

We're a solitary lot. When I was at university the other instrumentalists would practise in the building and they would often meet up to play together, while I had to go off to a cold church to practise on my own! The organ is a lone instrument, not played with other instruments although organists tend to know one another and form a little fraternity of their own.

Nigel was twenty years in the police force after finishing at university but, sadly, as a result of an accident at work, he was invalided out. Now he is studying for his MA in music and devoting a lot more time to his organ-playing. I asked him about the organ at St Peter's Church which had sounded so splendid. 'It is actually one of the best parish organs in the country,' Nigel told me, with noticeable pride.

It originally belonged to the Johnson family – famous pottery makers. H. R. Johnson – the boss – played the organ himself. The family owned a huge house called Oulton Abbey and they had the organ built and installed there by a famous firm of organ-builders over a hundred years ago. It was moved and rebuilt when they moved to a new home in Leek. They had a huge music room – like something in a palace. But then World War I came and the Johnsons' son and his friend were both killed. The parents found it too distressing to hear the organ afterwards. It brought back too many painful memories of times together before the war. So they gave the organ to the church in about 1922. It was restored in 1972 but badly needs work done on the bellows now. The cost will be enormous.

'But it's a wonderful organ to play,' he added. 'Even a bad organist can sound good on that instrument.' I still had no doubt that the church is blessed with a good organ *and* a first-rate organist.

Later I talked to Bernard about where he usually plays the organ. He told me that he shares his time between his own home church and one where he deputises for a friend once a month. The organ in that church dates back to the early seventeenth century. At that time two organ-builders were asked to design an organ to suit a London church. They competed in the so-called 'battle of the organs'. The authorities made their choice and the organ not chosen was shipped to Christchurch Cathedral, Dublin, where it remained for about a hundred years. Then an organ-builder bid for it and brought it back to England. He crossed the Irish Sea but when he reached Wolverhampton, in the Midlands, he died. The organ stayed there. His widow bequeathed it to St John's Church. It still has its original case, though the pipework is new.

'You see,' Bernard explained:

Fashions in musical tones change. It's too costly to buy a new organ, so the builders constantly adapt and update the original organ to get the tones required. That's why I think that the church organ is a good metaphor for the Church itself. In one sense it never changes but in another it adapts to meet the needs of the present time.

The organ is a metaphor for the Church in another way, too. There are so many parts to the organ – so many pipes, none of them sounding much on its own, yet combining to make a beautiful sound to the glory of God. The Church is a body of people each very different and some not feeling or seeming of much value on their own. But when they combine together, they can produce harmony and beauty to the glory of God.

Writing

Les Murray

Les Murray has been a favourite poet of mine for some years. I enjoy his poetry for its own sake as well as for its wit, humour and sharp cutting edge. Murray is also delightfully Australian in his laid-back style and use of language. But at first when I tried to track the poet down to speak to him in person I had no success. But I *was* in luck when Les Murray was the guest on a BBC programme (*Desert Island Discs*) and talked a bit about his life. He chatted about his upbringing and gave us insights into some of the factors that have influenced his life and poetry.

Les was brought up in the outback of Australia, an only child. Later he was to learn why. His parents were strict Calvinists, believing that everyone was predestined to be saved or damned. His father was an outdoor man, certainly not interested in reading, but his mother still possessed some treasured school book prizes, which her son eagerly devoured. They were all stories about girls in an English boarding-school – strange reading for an Australian country boy.

When Les was only twelve years old his mother became desperately ill. He probably did not know it at the time, but she had suffered a miscarriage (it was her third) and was haemorrhaging badly. It was absolutely necessary to get her to hospital but the doctor refused to sanction calling an ambulance and medical help arrived too late to save her life. His father never ceased to grieve and mourn her death for the forty-four years he lived on, and he expected Les to continue grieving too.

Les was unhappy at school, bullied by the girls, and it wasn't until his final year that he was introduced to modern poetry. He went up to university but suffered serious depression and at the age of twenty-two he had a complete breakdown. Looking back, he recognises that many of his childhood experiences contributed to it. He felt himself responsible for the death of his mother and the brothers he never had. Her death coloured his attitude to sex too. His mother's miscarriages and her death made him feel at gut level that 'sex causes death'.

His breakdown led to total energy loss. He let himself go completely and drifted around Australia, untidy and unkempt, sleeping rough. He cried a lot and even had phantom heart attacks. When eventually he saw a psychiatrist, he was told that his condition was due to chemical changes in the brain. Drugs seemed to do nothing to help and Les refused analysis.

By now Les had left behind the strict Calvinism of his childhood and joined the Roman Catholic Church. This conversion was a good experience for him – he described it as feeling as if he was coming home. In fact, he said, religious faith and poetry were his two safety ropes during the almost total shipwreck he experienced in his life. Poetry gave him purpose – he *had* to live in order to write poetry. For him, faith and poetry go together. 'Poetry is my work, my field and I think my vocation, the prime channel through which I ever achieve (or am given) any apprehension of ultimate and divine things.'

When eventually Les returned to university it was to find that his own poetry was now on the syllabus. He had achieved status and recognition in an amazingly short time. He is married now, with five children, and is well-known and popular enough to make his living from writing and from the readings he gives. Writing poetry is addictive, he explains, and something like a trance in which body, mind and dreaming mind are integrated. Sometimes a key phrase or a tune may start a poem off; sometimes it starts, he added mysteriously, as a painless headache. When I asked him what that could mean, he told me that he has a sense of pressure in his head before the words of the poem come to him.

Les Murray believes that every human being has a religious dimension. He recognises that some people would define that dimension as the ability to respond to beauty, horror or mystery or to some basic emotional need. But he believes that it is a response to God's Spirit working within us at our deepest level. This spiritual dimension needs to be fed, and to be given the right food. Poetry, he says, is probably one of the few channels of spiritual life we all have in common. Yet 'we have come, over the last few centuries, to think that we live in a prose universe, with prose as the norm of all discourse . . . In fact, prose doesn't answer to our own inner nature.'

Les Murray believes that in order to live a balanced life, human beings need to combine two ingredients – the power to reason and the ability to dream. One without the other is disastrous. Work done without vision becomes mere drudgery and a life lived on the level of vision without reason is equally disastrous. A good poem or a good marriage both require the right mix of reason and vision. *Narrowspeak* is the word Murray has coined for discourse based only on reason – or constructed as though reason were the only human criterion. The fully integrated language of vision combined with reason he calls *wholespeak*. A good poem is *wholespeak*. A person can both live and teach in accordance with *wholespeak*. Murray believes that Jesus's teaching about the kingdom of Heaven is both *wholespeak* and it is also Jesus's poem. But Jesus's own life is his poem too, because it is of a piece with his teaching and perfectly embodies the teaching that he gave. We all have spiritual capacity, Murray says. God's Spirit stirs all our souls at some time and in some way but we may refuse to allow the Spirit to enlighten us.

Les Murray's own poetry is certainly *wholespeak*. His poems possess the ingredients of both vision and reason. They are witty, satisfying to the mind and also to the emotions and, rather in the manner of parables, they always pack a punch.

Murray believes that the many substitutes for religion that exist today deliver what we *want*, not what we need. In contrast:

> The Spirit gives us what we need, and doesn't necessarily heed our petitions. God may not even rescue us from cruel death when we implore him to. He can see both sides of death as we cannot. This is hard to bear – but the alternative is to seek your spiritual supplies from sources which provide, in the end, only what cannot satisfy you, since what humans imagine to be their salvation can't logically be anything greater than the human measure.

When at last I talked to Les Murray over the phone from his Australian home, he was relaxed and kind and friendly as I had imagined. He offered to fax me some of his recent poems and was as good as his word, only hours later. One of them refers to an experience that he had in hospital. Beside the poem that he sent me he has jotted down, in his own handwriting, the circumstances that gave birth to the poem and the change that has been brought about in his own perceptions:

> This came out of a severe illness I had in 1996, a liver abscess which put me into a coma for three weeks. The last thing I remember seeing as I was wheeled to the operating theatre

were fluorescent light panels in the ceiling. I found I could
die, without fuss, and how it feels to let go and not expect to
come back. You don't wholly come back after that. No
melodrama, but this is my earthly afterlife now.

You find you can leave it all

Like a charging man, hit
and settling face down in the ringing,
his cause and panic obsolete,

you find you can leave it all;
your loved people, pain, achievement
dwindling upstream of this raft-fall,

back with the dishes that translated
beasts and croplands into the ongoing
self-portrait your genes had mandated.

Ribbed glass glare-panels flow
over you down urgent corridors,
dismissing midday outside. Slow,

they'd resemble wet spade-widths in a pit;
you've left grief behind you, for others;
your funeral: who'd know you'd re-planned it?

God, at the end of prose,
somehow be our poem —
when forebrainy consciousness goes

wordless selves it'd barely met,
inertias of rhythm, the life habit
continue the battle for you.

If enough of those hold
you may wake up in this world,

ache-boned, tear-sponged, dripped into:

Do you know your name? 'Yes' won't do.
It's Before again, with shadow. No tunnels.
You are a trunk of prickling cells.

It's the evening of some day. But it's also
afterlife from here on, by that consent
you found in you, to going where you went.

Susan Howatch

'Sometimes I can't wait to get started in the morning – writing is an addiction,' Susan Howatch told me. She 'cut her teeth', she says, by writing detective stories and thrillers. They taught her how to plot. In the 1970s she first used her favourite technique of taking a true story from history and updating it to the twentieth century. In 1971 her first international best-seller, *Penmarric*, was launched, later to become a television series. She has never forgotten Iris Murdoch's maxim that 'a writer's first duty is to be readable'. Readable is precisely what Susan Howatch is. Pick up one of her novels, and judging from my own experience as well as that of my friends and countless reviewers, it's impossible to put it down.

When she was young, the author admits that she had two ambitions in life – to become famous and to become rich. Years later – after marriage, life in the USA, the birth of her daughter, the breakdown of her marriage, some years in Ireland and a move back to England – her books had brought her both the international fame and the fortune she had wanted.

It was at this stage that she moved into flats that she had seen advertised, that were right in the cathedral close at Salisbury. It was a tough time for her. The current novel was being troublesome and she had personal anxieties too. The actual day of the move was as exhausting as all house moves are and by evening she was ready to collapse on to the sofa in the study with a stiff whisky. By the time she roused herself to walk through to the kitchen it was quite dark. It was then that she caught sight of the cathedral and saw it as if for the first time. It was floodlit, radiant and astonishingly beautiful. 'I felt,' she said, 'as if I'd been presented with some extraordinary gift, which was over and above all my expectations, and I hardly knew what to do with it. Today I would have said, "Thanks be to God!" but in those days I was not religious and I didn't see God in my life. He was there, I realise that now . . . but I didn't recognise him.'

Susan settled into her new life in the close, and from her flat she looked out constantly on to the cathedral. Her daily walks took her round the close – and so round and round the cathedral too. And always, the cathedral, with its slim, tapering spire, seemed to be pointing in every sense to heaven. Now it seemed to her to be not only splendid and beautiful in its own right but to symbolise so many values that were utterly lacking in her own life. The cathedral had been built by men whose purpose was to create something for God. The beauty of the cathedral had been conceived and executed in order to give glory to God, not to those who had fashioned it. She had written for her own glory and lived her own life to please herself. The cathedral became a presence in her life, almost as if it were a living animal. It drew her, compelled her and became a catalyst for the strange upheavals and reactions taking place within her own life.

She realised that the two goals she had set herself – fame and wealth – had been realised. Yet she was not happy. What could have gone wrong? She began to think about God who seemed to be getting increasingly and dangerously close. Up to this point she had not imagined that God was of any personal concern to her. If she thought of God at all, she imagined him, as she put it, rather like Mount Everest – vast and impressive but a long way away and of no relevance to her. Yet now this God was becoming increasingly real and making inroads into her life. It seemed as if she was being stripped of all that had made up her life until that time. In her own words: 'It seemed that the glittering image I presented to the world had absolutely nothing to do with the person I really was – but who was I, what was I supposed to be doing with myself, and what on earth did it all mean anyway?'

Susan considered her life up to that moment. She had

241

concentrated on pleasing herself, yet she was utterly miserable. Perhaps, then, she needed to turn her life around and try pleasing and serving someone else. Later she told her listeners in a lecture at Salisbury Cathedral:

> I saw that God was not a long way away at all. We were eyeball to eyeball and the pressure he was exerting was so intense that I felt I was going mad. However, I didn't really fancy going mad. I decided it would be much more practical to update my concept of God, acknowledge his presence in my life and his acute relevance to me, and then get off my bottom and begin some sort of new life which reflected not my false glittering image but my true self. (From 'The Birth of the Starbridge Novels' – a lecture given at Salisbury Cathedral in 1994)

Because she is an intellectual – she originally graduated in law – Susan Howatch's search for God began with the mind. She read everything she could lay hands on in every branch of theology. She read church history, biography, the letters of well-known churchmen and, for good measure, studied and sat for an A level in religious studies.

As well as understanding and accepting God with her mind, she gave him her will. Her chief concern now was to know what *God* required of her. She believes strongly that a search for God must involve discovering the truth about ourselves. I must know what the real 'me' is like, not continue to accept the image I present to the world. Then, when I discover the unique person God created me to be, I can set about discovering the unique work God has for me to do.

It was some time before Susan decided that she should continue writing novels. At least, she wrote them – she couldn't help herself – but she withheld publication until she felt sure that was the work God wanted her to do. These novels were different from her earlier ones. She was certainly not going to write religious tracts, or religious dissertations, but novels about people whose lives would explore and experience the religious realities which had become central in her own life. Her sequence of six novels – the

Starbridge novels – do just that and do it superbly. She has lost none of the absorbing readability of her earlier books; she still creates entertaining characters and racy plots. She shows these men and women wrestling with the human emotions of passion and ambition, lust and the desire for power. But she also shows them grappling with failure and repentance, forgiveness and renewal. Without using technical, theological terms, she skilfully communicates the age-long beliefs of Christian faith through the lives and passions of flesh-and-blood people. Each of the six Starbridge novels is about cathedral life and the cathedral close but each is seen through the eyes of one of the characters involved in them all. Each book is complete in itself, but each one fills out the picture, rounding it and showing a different perspective on the whole series of events and the characters who people the stage.

The books are located in a cathedral close that strongly resembles the one the author grew to know so well in Salisbury, and the cathedral itself is a presence in the books as it was in the author's own life. Sometimes the presence of Starbridge Cathedral is brooding; sometimes glorious and triumphant; even, at times, sinister; for, as the author comments, everything has its shadow side and every creation of humankind has something of evil as well as good fashioned in its making. But at its finest it stands, as it has done for centuries, steadfast and immovable, like the God to whose glory it was built.

A Question of Integrity, a later novel, is not one of the Starbridge series, but as readers we are delighted to come across some of the old friends we have come to know so well through the earlier stories. When I visited Susan Howatch in her London flat, I was struck by the appropriateness of the title of this book. She is one of the most openly honest people I have met – someone therefore to whom it is possible to respond with honesty and openness too. She has a personal commitment to integrity, which is neither over-intense nor obsessive. She seems to have learned the precious secret – rarely found – of being herself before God and her fellows, without the need for cover-up or of uncomfortable self-display. She lives out the integrity she writes about so brilliantly.

19

Solitude and quiet

I am fortunate to live near Old Jordans, which is linked to the earliest history of the Society of Friends. Once a medieval farm, it was taken over in 1639 by William Russell, one of the early Quakers, and meetings of worship were held there in the early days of the movement. George Fox himself and William Penn (who was later to found Pennsylvania) worshipped at Jordans. At that time Dissenters were persecuted, and the Jordan Meeting was often broken up by order of local Justices and the worshippers hauled off to prison. But in 1688 the Declaration of Indulgence gave Quakers the right to build their own meeting-house, separate from the farm. It still remains, along with a wooden building called the Mayflower Barn, said to be built from the timbers of the *Mayflower*, the ship which took the Pilgrim Fathers to America.

There is a great sense of peace and tranquillity everywhere at Jordans, but my favourite place of quiet is the graveyard outside the meeting-house. Here William Penn, his two wives and ten of his sixteen children are buried. A little further away, small gravestones to mark the graves of other Friends are arranged in semicircles in the green grass among the trees. The early Quakers may have known noise and disruption from an intolerant world, but the peace and quietness which marks their spirituality still enriches the place where their bodies lie.

Most of us crave quiet in a busy, noisy world but complain that it is impossible to find. Places like Jordans still offer quiet and times of retreat to visitors; yet it is not only finding a suitable location that will create an atmosphere of quietness and solitude. Centuries ago, a wise man called Syncletica wrote: 'There are many who live in the mountain but behave as if they were in the town and they are wasting their time. It is possible to be solitary in one's mind while living in a crowd and it is possible for one who is solitary to live in the crowd of his own thoughts.'

Brother Ramon

Our car bumped along a narrow pitted track for about a mile or more; either side were fields of grass and wild flowers, or cultivated crops. The rough path seemed to go on for ever, but then ahead of us we glimpsed the firm outlines of the monastery of Glasshampton, upright and orderly in the midst of the rolling Worcestershire countryside. It seemed like a haven of peace and purpose surrounded by overgrown nature all around. We arrived, scrunched up the gravel path to the door and rang the monastery bell. After a suitable wait (for a different kind of time observance probably obtains here) a brother came to meet us, mobile phone to his ear. So we were not caught in a time warp. I had come to visit the hermit, whose small hut had been built in the monastery grounds. As he sees only five or six people a month – and sometimes takes a month clear of visitors altogether – I knew I had been very fortunate to be invited to visit him. So while my husband rested in the monastery gardens (where roses, buddleia and hebe bloomed large and lovely) I was taken past a neat and thriving vegetable garden, down a grassy slope, through an arch to Brother Ramon's hut, where the brother who led the way clanged a large and noisy bell. There was an icon on a stand under the trees opposite the hut and a Celtic cross stood at the door of a second hut, which I later discovered was the chapel. Brother Ramon came hurrying out to greet me.

What do *you* expect a hermit to look like? Thin, austere, with piercing, solemn eyes? The man who came towards me was well-built, with grey hair and beard; he was warm, welcoming, and very clearly accustomed to smiles and laughter. He was decidedly talkative and so am I – so from the moment we sat down we both began to talk. He had placed me in a shabby but very comfortable armchair, while he sat in an upright one, with his back to the desk where his elderly typewriter stood. The hut is 3 metres by 2 metres, so space is at a premium. There was a bed along one side of the hut and at the back shelves were stacked with tins of beans and other ingredients used for vegetarian meals. Not an inch of space was wasted.

Our conversation kept taking off in new and interesting directions as we found fresh topics to share and discuss, but I had really come to ask Brother Ramon about his chosen life as a hermit and to discover how he experienced God in solitude. I tried to ask the questions most people would put. Wasn't he just escaping – opting out of *real* life? How could he reconcile his faith with a life lived away from the world, when there were so many wrongs in the world to be righted and so many people who needed help? Wasn't it rather self-indulgent to be a hermit, cut off from the rat race?

So Brother Ramon began to tell me his story, and to give me plenty of answers to the questions I'd asked. 'Always,' he explained, 'I have felt split down the middle. One part of me longed to go out into the world and evangelise – to tell others the good news, the gospel. But the other half of me pined for solitude and prayer.'

For many years Brother Ramon preached, taught and fully pursued his vocation to communicate the gospel, as a parish priest and then as a university chaplain. But in 1975, while he was a parish priest, he attended a symposium of about thirty hermits of all kinds. It made such a deep impression on him that he felt the need to try the solitary life himself and asked permission of his provincial minister to do so. He was given leave in order to try out this vocation for two separate periods of six months each.

'The first time,' he said, 'in 1982, was a time of joy and glory. The second was quite different. It was dark, not light, and I felt not only darkness in my own soul but the power of satanic attack.'

After these trial periods, he became Guardian of Glasshampton Monastery, home of an Anglican order of Franciscan friars. But after a while he knew that God was calling him back to a permanent life of solitude. 'God was saying very clearly, "Be silent, or I will silence you." The words came not as a threat but as a very real warning.' For years, he had fulfilled one side of his nature in serving God by preaching, teaching, writing and communicating the Christian message to others. Now he was to begin fulfilling the other side – the side that hankered after solitude and prayer.

When I was preaching, meeting others, sharing the sacraments and the Bible, I had an awareness and enjoyment of God, but in solitude it is very different. Alone, I experience a confrontation of love. It is difficult to describe the intensity of the love I experience and my awe in the presence of God. I tremble, and I weep and I laugh, both with joy and with sorrow. I can only explain it by comparing it with the meetings between two lovers. They long to be alone together – to be close, to feel love, and not just to use words to communicate their love. I don't have to use words or speak to God in my times with him. I am not using my brain to *think* – I am just resting in his love. Solitude increases my love for God and my awe of him too.

'Might some people think this selfish? How is it helping others?' I asked.

'When a man and woman love, the result is another life,' he answered.

Similarly, solitude with God begets compassion, joy, hope. By being alone with God I enter into the web of compassion. I am taken into the whole world's sorrow by God, and it is he who breathes into me compassion, so that I can lift up before him the needs of others. Through being alone with God I can experience his power given to me.

'Is solitude lonely?' I asked.

'Being alone – aloneness – can lead to loneliness or to solitude,' he answered.

Without God, being alone does lead to loneliness and alienation. With God it overflows into richness and power. It may sound like a paradox, but I have a greater sense of humour – I am more truly human – since I have spent time alone with God. Of course some days seem pedestrian, and there is a boredom barrier to be crossed, but on other days I am on the mountain top. I may be digging in my vegetable garden when I hear God calling me to be still with him. Then I put down my spade and go to prayer. We need to pray with our mind but also in our heart. In earlier times, my prayers would almost be sermons! Now I'm content to feel God's presence and be silent.

My time was nearly up – not that we had run out of things to say, but my husband had by now waited some time in the monastery garden and we had a long drive home. But before I went Brother Ramon took me into his second hut, which is the chapel. He took off his shoes, then gently led me to a bench beside one wall. The hut was carpeted and there was a warmth and gentleness that had been lacking in the living hut. But I was not aware so much of altar, candles and furnishings; I experienced instead an overall sense of holiness. There was such quietness, such peace, such love, that I did not know whether I wanted to laugh or cry. My own thoughts seemed to dissolve and give place to a deep sense of the presence of God. Brother Ramon prayed for me and my family, gave thanks to God for our time together; then, with his hand on my shoulder, he blessed me. Then together we said the words of the Grace.

Before I left he told me quietly of other things resulting from his solitude which overflow to help others. He no longer thinks and plans how to answer those who come to him with their troubles. He feels that the answer is 'given' – it reaches their needs and their hearts without any planning on his part. He says that he finds now that he can understand what people say, their body language even, and what they really mean and feel. He told me too that sometimes he knows whether a sick person is going to be healed or is going to die. He pointed out to me a card bearing a man's name, propped up in front of one of the icons. 'That man will soon die,' he told me. 'My task is to pray with him through the stages of dying. To pray that he may be spared pain and may have a good death. I can take him to the threshold where he will be received by God.'

Brother Ramon brought me laughter, happiness and a sense of God's peace. He made me feel I could be myself without pretence or cover-up. The love and joy he receives from God overflowed to bless me. Perhaps we need more hermits to bring us in touch with God in our rushing, superficial world.

Carlo Carretto

'You must "make some desert" in your life.' That was the advice of Carlo Carretto to everyone who wanted to learn to know God and experience the spiritual world. He explained that for him the desert was a real one – the Sahara – but for most people the desert will have to be a space, an emptiness and solitude, created in the midst of a humdrum busy life.

It was in 1954 when Carlo Carretto was forty-four that he heard God's call to a contemplative life. Previously he had been a powerful figure in the Italian Catholic Action Movement, but he renounced the power, the politics and the prestige to become one of the Little Brothers, the name of the religious community founded fifty years before by Charles de Foucauld. De Foucauld had been an army officer who had loved the good things in life, but had come to faith and practised asceticism first as a Trappist monk. Then, some fifty years before Carlo's time, he came back to the Sahara where he had once lived and served, to establish a community and to live as poorly and powerlessly as the lowliest of the local people.

In his *Letters from the Desert*, Carlo Carretto tells of some of the lessons he himself learned during his time in the Sahara.

The lesson of love

It was nearly midday and Carlo was driving his jeep through the burning white sand, tense and alert to avoid the deep ruts made by the wheels of huge oil trucks – aware too that his engine was boiling in the intense heat. He watched the horizon, scanning the landscape for a sight of the huge granite rocks that thrust up from the sand, hoping to find one that would afford him shade from the merciless rays of the Saharan sun that were beating down. At last he found what he had been searching for, a 10-metre high slab with a sufficient patch of slanted shade for him to rest in. He decided to spare a little of the lukewarm water in his supply to pour over his head, then stretched out on his mat for a siesta, using for a pillow one of the two blankets always carried as a traveller's necessary equipment. He looked at the other blanket, lying alongside, and felt a stab of remorse.

The night before, Carlo had passed through a village of black ex-slaves where, as usual, the villagers had all come out to greet him. Among them he saw Kada, an old man, who was shaking with cold. Not everyone realises how cold the Sahara can be at nights, when the sun has gone down. For a moment Carlo thought of giving the old man one of his two blankets. But he knew that he, too, would be cold at nights and almost without making a deliberate decision, he left the blanket where it was and went on his way. Now, as he drifted into sleep, he was feeling ashamed that a Little Brother could show so little charity and think so much of his own comfort. And when he slept he dreamed. He dreamed that the rock beneath which he sheltered began to move, then fell on him with a shuddering shock. Yet, although he felt the judder and grating of bones, he knew that he was alive and was conscious that no bones were broken. But he could not move a muscle.

When he opened his eyes he saw Kada, shivering before him. He gladly made to give him the unused blanket but though it was near him, it was just out of reach and the boulder pinned him down so that he could not move an inch to pick it up. He realised the torment of knowing too late that he could not do what he had refused to do when the opportunity had offered. He wondered how long he would remain under the rock and the answer seemed to come: 'Until you are capable of an act of perfect love.'

When Carlo woke up he was unsure whether he had had a dream or a vision. He only knew that it changed his life. He recognised how far he was from imitating the self-giving love of Jesus. 'What's the use of giving up everything and coming here to the desert and the heat, if only to resist love?'

The stars in space

Carlo learned from the desert at night-time as well as at noon. The cool and calm of the night provided wonderful relief from the remorseless heat of the day. The dry, burning wind that blows in daytime changes to a gentle breeze; coolness and freshness restore the weary workers. That was the time when Carlo would walk away from the camp to the solitariness of the dunes in order to pray. There he would gaze up at the sky – a vast expanse illuminated by scattered points of brightness. There are no man-made lights or buildings, and no limits to the horizon's expanse.

His first reaction to this sight of the desert sky at night was to send off for books on astronomy so that he could learn the names and positions of the stars that he saw. Before long he found that he was able to find his way through the desert far more easily by night than by day, guided by the position of the stars. But he relished the rest, the security that the night sky of stars seemed to offer far more than their usefulness. At night-time in the desert he felt at home, safe. He seemed to himself to be a point lost in infinite space, yet protected by the night and the gentle light of the stars. He felt no fear of the darkness; he was the point in space, but the stars were witnesses to God's faithfulness and truth and the darkness seemed to represent faith. He realised that the full light of God's presence would be too bright, too searing for human beholding. Instead, the pinpoints of the stars' light were sufficient to pierce the darkness of his faith and assure him of the reality of God's presence. Faith – the need to trust God in the darkness – is not a trick on the part of a God who hides himself from humankind. It is a necessary way of shielding men and women from an encounter that, in this life, would be too great for them to bear.

Carlo Carretto would have liked to stay in the desert, encountering and worshipping God in the solitude. But, like his earthly leader, Charles de Foucauld, he believed that the life of love must be lived with other men and women, in acts of self-giving in the ordinary encounters of every day. The time in the desert is necessary, not as an end in itself, but as a means of renewing and making a person strong to live a life of 'contemplation in the streets'.

Quiet gardens

Years ago it used to be popular to have a plaque or sundial in the garden inscribed with the verse that ends: 'You are nearer God's heart in a garden than anywhere else on earth.' Sentimental, but it's true that many of us experience a sense of peace and spiritual well-being in a beautiful garden. We enjoy the results of the gardener's creative skills and maybe the hand of the Creator too. We feel deeply satisfied by the order and beauty and rightness of it all. Many full-time gardeners seem to have a temperament that matches their gardens. They are often characterised by gentle humour and a relaxed approach to life. Perhaps that is one reason why gardening programmes make such popular viewing and listening.

Some months ago I read a short article in the paper about a scheme called Quiet Gardens Trust which had been set up by a vicar in Amersham and the owner of a beautiful house and garden in Stoke Poges. Remembering how Jesus often went away to a beautiful place – a mountain top or a lakeside – to pray and feel close to God his Father, the Rev. Philip Roderick wondered if it would be feasible to try to provide beautiful places where others could relax and know God's presence too. Perhaps some who owned suitable gardens would be willing to open them up for visitors to come and find opportunity for quiet and meditation, so badly needed in our busy world. Even though the visitors might have gardens of their own, Philip Roderick recognises that many people are unable to find rest and quiet in their own garden. They are too busy worrying about the fact that the grass needs cutting and a hundred and one other jobs are waiting to be done to sit down and relax. Perhaps it would be easier to find peace and quiet in someone else's garden.

I was interested to hear more and so I rang the trust's number and since I don't live far away I was invited to go across and join them for one of their arranged meetings. These are held on some

Thursdays when a speaker is invited to lead a time of contemplation, silent meditation and prayer. At Stoke Poges the Quiet Garden
is open on some Fridays too, when people can come and devise
their own time of quiet, joining if they wish in three led periods of
contemplative prayer at 10 a.m., 12 noon and 1.45 p.m. Sometimes
a simple communion service takes place. Anyone is welcome to
the Quiet Garden but, as Philip Roderick explains: 'Quiet Gardens
are open to anyone of any or no religion, but the teaching is in the
Christian tradition.' The patrons include well-known members of
every branch of Christian faith and include Professor Sir Ghillean
Prance, whose story is also told in this book.

The subject on the morning we attended was 'In Praise of God'
and brief thought-provoking talks alternated with times of silence
for personal prayer and meditation. Even the coffee break was
silent (what a relief, for a change, not to have to exchange
pleasantries with other strangers!).

During the times of quiet, visitors can walk in the garden, but,
sadly, it had begun to rain heavily and I could only look out
longingly at the garden, still beautiful on a dank November day.
The wall surrounding the large open expanse of grass, trees and
flower-beds had the date 1691 built into it in darker bricks.

Afterwards, when the rain had nearly stopped, I went into the
office to meet the regular staff who are kept increasingly busy as
the trust expands and spreads. Many people in the UK have now
joined and many lend their gardens to provide a place of quiet and
retreat for those living near to them. The trust has also spread to
many other countries, including Canada, New Zealand and South
Africa. Christine Claydon lives in Israel and felt that a quiet garden
in Jerusalem would meet a real need. With help from a keen
English gardener, a South African, a Cherokee Indian and a
German, a rubbish tip was transformed within three months to a
garden with trees, raised flower-beds and stone seats. Jerusalem is
quiet from sunset on Friday to sunset on Saturday, when Shabat
(the Sabbath) is observed. So this is the time when the Shabat
Prayer Garden in Jerusalem offers peace and rest for those who
come to enjoy its beauty.

Sometimes, from necessity, the 'garden' is only a metaphor for
a place of quiet, where people can get away from the relentless

pressure of work and activity and take time out. The silence and peace afford time to listen to God.

This is true in a shantytown near Nairobi. A few months ago, its vicar, the Rev. Franklyn Otwoma, visited Stoke Poges and told them about his own, rather different 'Quiet Garden'. He works in a town called Korogocho, where the slipshod buildings are made of tin, wood, mud and plastic and most people earn only a pittance from casual work. Most of the young people are unemployed and drugs, illicit brewing, prostitution and crime of every sort are rife. Franklyn and his friends have set up a mission in order to meet the needs of the townsfolk. They provide food, literacy classes and vocational training. A simple building in the main street has to serve as their Quiet Garden. People from many different churches in Korogocho come on a Saturday afternoon for prayer, meditation and, as he words it, 'resting in Christ'. There may be no green grass, trees or secluded flower-beds, but Franklyn believes that this time of quiet and renewal enables the helpers to continue with their heavy work of mission and help in that destitute town.

It is possible to find quietness and peace in a building at the centre of the traffic and turmoil of a busy city. It is also possible to take our anxiety and hectic thoughts into the tranquillity of the loveliest garden. The peace, after all, has to come from God's Spirit within.

20

Work

Work – the word conjures up a different picture for different readers. Some people look on work as a necessary evil and day-dream about the things they'll be free to do once they reach the enviable stage of retirement. Others – myself included – genuinely *like* working and feel slightly ill at ease being on holiday. Many, sadly, who are unemployed or made redundant through no fault of their own, would give their eye-teeth to have a job to go to.

In the biblical account of the scheme of things, man and woman were given work to do when the world was still perfect. Working against the odds, not work itself, was the result of the human fall from grace. Agriculture became a battle against weeds, stony ground and inhospitable weather. Work was 'by the sweat of the brow'. But Judaeo-Christian belief is that work itself is a creative activity shared by humankind with their Creator. When Jesus was on earth he said: 'My Father (i.e. God) is always working and I must work too.'

Some people look on their daily work as more than a necessity and more even than an enjoyable activity. They insist that work for them is part of their intercourse with the spiritual world. That is not because they are ministers of religion or live in a religious community, but because they look upon their daily work as a kind of sacrament – a working out in practice of their inward spiritual life. The monks of old used to say '*Orare est laborare*' – to pray is to work. But the saying was also used in reverse: '*Laborare est orare*'. It seems that for some people even humdrum daily work can be a spiritual enterprise.

Mark Greene

I sat opposite Mark Greene in his office at the London Bible College. Although he is vice-principal of the college, I did not have that queasy feeling brought on by a session in the head-master's study. Mark is lively, unassuming, humorous and concerned with the interests of his visitor rather than his own status. He spends half his time lecturing to the students on communications and creative writing and he writes himself, excellent poetry as well as prose.

I had been reading his book, *Thank God it's Monday,* and wanted to know how he came to see everyday work in a light that would surprise and even bemuse most ordinary people. For him, the everyday, common or garden job can and should be a spiritual experience. But first I wanted to hear his story – where he came from and what has made him the kind of person he is.

Mark's grandfather was born in 1892 – conceived, so the story goes, on his Jewish parents' voyage to Britain as émigrés from Russia. Good, orthodox Jews, they must have been grieved when their son, Mark's father, married out of the Jewish faith. Mark's mother took lessons in Judaism and although she did not convert, she promised that their children would be brought up in the Jewish faith. So every Friday night the family spent together, sharing the celebration Sabbath meal. Mark went to Jewish instruction classes and the family attended the reformed synagogue. After public school, Mark spent a year in Israel, working on a kibbutz, where he learned some Hebrew – the ancient Jewish language, literally brought back to life in Israel during the last fifty years. He went up to Cambridge planning to study modern languages, but after the first year he settled instead for Hebrew studies.

Before he came down from university, Mark had converted to Christianity – not through the many Christians he had met who were willing to argue theology with him, but through a new, tentative Christian, who appealed to him at a deeper level than the purely rational. Mark admits that he liked to give the impression, at first, that his conversion had been at an intellectual level – that he had been convinced of the logical claims of the Christian faith. That somehow seemed more respectable. But he knows that something took place that was deeper within him than rational conviction. Beyond the intellect and the emotions, Mark found a God who answered to something in his inmost being and satisfied his whole person.

As a dynamic, creative and brilliant young man, he went into advertising and was soon in New York, working in a creative and strategic capacity in one of the largest advertising agencies in the world. Many religious people would – and do – keep their spiritual world and their everyday world in separate compartments. After all, how you choose to meet your own spiritual needs and what you do with your Sundays are very much a personal matter, aren't they? After the first year or two at work Mark began to think differently. He believes that 'the workplace is God's place, and his place is just as much there as in the church prayer-meeting'. And he is willing to argue his case theologically. The word for work in Hebrew is the same word that is used for worship. It is often translated as 'service'. But in Mark's view, we can worship God when we are busy about our daily work, whether on the shop floor, office, hospital, schoolroom or home.

Jesus told us that God works – in the evolving universe – and Jesus, God's Son, worked for thirty years as a small-time builder and joiner. Human beings are made for work – whether paid or unpaid and whatever status it may carry. Work becomes worship when it is deliberately offered to God, and, as a result, carried out wholeheartedly, with honesty, justice and with genuine care and consideration for those in the same workplace.

After a theology degree at London Bible College, Mark intended returning to the so-called secular marketplace. But when he was offered a lectureship at the college he stayed on, later to become its vice-principal. He refuses to recognise some jobs as more obviously 'spiritual' than others. Every kind of work can become a spiritual experience, offered in worship to God. Mark has also discovered that God is at work – at work.

Mother Teresa

People probably know more about Mother Teresa than they do about the Pope or the Archbishop of Canterbury. A few people criticised her aims and her methods but most agreed that she put into practice what Christianity is supposed to be all about. When she died, thousands waited to pay their respects to this amazing small woman. For many people, she represents the nearest thing to a saint that they expect to see during their lifetime.

Mother Teresa was born into an Albanian peasant family in Yugoslavia. It was a very happy home, and love for her family seems to have been the only thing that could have stood in the way of her calling to be a nun. She became aware of her vocation when she was still only a schoolgirl and followed it to enter a teaching order and to travel to India, to the Loreto convent school in Calcutta. One day, some years later, she found herself on convent business in some of the poorest streets of that city. It was then that she had what she used to say was her 'call within a call'. Suddenly her strict convent life seemed easy and comfortable compared to the life of the utterly destitute, the poorest of the poor who barely scratched a living but somehow subsisted on the streets of the city. She knew with certainty that she must leave the pleasant gardens and cool surroundings of the school, and say goodbye to the healthy, successful young pupils and congenial staff at Loreto.

But it was not possible for her to get up and go on the basis of her personal convictions. She had to wait two years before she could be released from the vows she had taken and allowed back into the world, to live now not by the rules of any existing order, but by far stricter vows of her own making. For a start, she found a lodging in the meanest, dirtiest part of the city and gathered around her some of the children who had been abandoned on the streets. There she began her work, amid the dirt, disease, and desperate need. But Mother Teresa believed that there is something that men and women, children and even babies, need even more than food and shelter. They need to know that they are wanted. And if this is true for the thousands of well-fed, healthy and comfortably housed inhabitants of our cities, how much more is it vital for the outcasts, the sick, the dying, without home or family to love and nurture them.

Mother Teresa loved them all and in her eyes they were all of equal value – because that's how they were to God. None was excluded from her all-embracing love. She explained how it was that she had the motive and the resources to give love freely whatever the state of the person she was caring for. Mother Teresa looked at each patient she tended as if he or she were Jesus himself. Jesus, her Lord, was no longer on earth, but he was present in the person of his sick and dying ones, his homeless and abandoned ones; as she cared for *them* she was caring for *him*. Jesus had told his disciples that whatever they did to the least of one of his 'brothers' or 'sisters' they did to him. Her work was a sacrament; there was a spiritual reality behind the material care. Two worlds met as Mother Teresa lavished her love on Jesus seen in the people that others might count insignificant and worthless.

Every day Mother Teresa repeated a prayer that reminded her of the spiritual reality behind her acts of love and devotion to the diseased and dying:

> Dearest Lord, may I see you today and every day in the person of your sick, and while nursing them, minister unto you. Though you hide yourself behind the unattractive guise of the irritable, the exacting, the unreasonable, may I still recognise you and say: 'Jesus, my patient, how sweet it is to serve you.'

James Turnbull

I have never had to appear in a coroner's court but I can imagine what an ordeal it must be, especially as it usually follows recent and tragic bereavement. In England, any death that occurs in unexplained or suspicious circumstances must be reported to Her Majesty's Coroner's office. James Turnbull, now semi-retired, was Coroner of Bradford, a large northern city. Out of the five thousand or so unexplained deaths reported every year in the Bradford area, some five hundred will have to be investigated at a coroner's inquest. The coroner's job is to answer the question, 'Why did the deceased die?' And finding the answer can mean going back a long way in order to arrive at the truth.

When I talked to James Turnbull he was up to his eyes in papers, preparing for an inquest that was likely to last several weeks. It concerned a seaman from his area, who with three colleagues had been drowned, far away on foreign seas, when a typhoon struck and the oil barge they were on sank. The simple answer to the question, 'Why did he die?' is that he drowned. But behind that accident are many other factors that require investigation. Was the barge seaworthy? Should there have been decompression equipment on board? What is known about the nature of typhoons in that area? The coroner must decide how many of these possible questions to explore and try to answer. He has control of the investigation and makes his own parameters for every case. It is for him to decide how far back the questioning will go and whether it is reasonable to pay expensive assessors to provide him with the specialist knowledge that he may need in order to conduct certain aspects of the inquest.

Some coroners err on the side of being restrictive – limiting the inquiry strictly – others are determined to get to the bottom of the accident as far as is possible, however complex and long-drawn-out it may be. A good coroner tries to find the right balance. Within the law he must decide how far to extend the inquiries, making limits which he believes are reasonable and feasible, but not going beyond such boundaries. He is answerable only to Queen and State, and is conscious that he has a duty to be thorough but also to limit expense and investigate further only those aspects that will be fruitful in the case. An expert adviser – an assessor – can cost £1,000 a day and if the inquest lasts four or five weeks that soon adds greatly to the burden of cost. But these days the public are often anxious to press for more investigation than the coroner has made and even to appeal against the coroner's inquiry. They are naturally concerned to discover who is to blame for the death of a relative and expect the coroner to be able to answer their questions. Sometimes he is unable to do so, much as he would like to. Many will have read of appeals made by relatives of those killed in the Hillsborough football stadium disaster and their demands for the coroner's inquiries to be extended.

Coroners are chosen by Queen and State and in the past the post was often kept in the same family or allotted to members of the same legal practice. Once appointed the coroner is free to choose the deputy coroner, and nowadays will choose someone who seems suited to the work, or a man or woman who has shown interest in taking the post. Coroners are either doctors or lawyers – more often solicitors or barristers. There *are* now some training courses for coroners, but apart from a good knowledge of the law, much of what needs to be known is best learned on the job. The coroner must liaise with pathologists, police, forensic experts and so on, and the variety of specialist lore involved will be enormous and very varied. One case may require a visit to a factory and some knowledge of manufacturing techniques or machinery, while another will involve a coal mine or a sport. James Turnbull relishes this constant widening of his horizons and the chance to get to know about other people's work and interests.

So how does James Turnbull's Christian faith come into operation in his constant brushes with death – often death of a tragic or brutal kind? I knew one answer to that question before I asked it. His gentleness and compassion and obvious sensitivity – all of which came across so clearly to me – must have brought balm to hundreds and thousands of grieving, frightened people who have stood in his court over the years. He trained as a solicitor but when he was newly qualified a colleague, representing the opposing side, refused a reasonable request he had made to see some documents on compassionate grounds. 'You are a lawyer, not a parson,' his opposite number reminded him, with the ruthless approach of a prosecutor.

Naturally, dealing with death is part of his daily work and to some extent he must remain detached to do his job well. But he admitted that where a child is concerned, it does bring tears to his eyes. It would be wrong for him to impose his own beliefs on those who are grieving in the court, but he has found that, faced with tragedy and death, many with no religious faith look for and find a spiritual dimension. He knows that his inquiry can in fact help them. 'Now that we know the facts, we can grieve,' they often tell him. Sometimes, very rarely, he may add a few words to help them to find a spiritual dimension. He quoted the case of a young boy who had collapsed and died when playing football. No kind of heart weakness had previously been suspected. 'I might say to the parents,' he told me, ' "I know you want to ask 'Why?' and I can't answer. I know you want to ask, 'Why has it happened to us?' and I can't answer that either. But people with a faith in God sometimes find it helps to realise that in this life we are living in a dark patch. There may be no answer to our questions now, but we will know." '

I asked if he ever saw the family involved in an inquest other than when they were all appearing in the court. He told me that he had to be very careful about having anyone into his office as it is illegal to hold a private inquest and the press might well learn about it, draw the wrong conclusions and bring accusations. 'But, just occasionally,' he told me, 'I have asked one member of the family to come to my office. That is when I know something which has not been mentioned in the inquest because it was not relevant, but which could bring comfort to the family.'

Ten years ago James Turnbull, Coroner, was ordained the Rev. James Turnbull in the Church of England. He had planned to retire from being a coroner but his bishop encouraged him to remain in his secular post. The bishop was certain that his influence as a coroner was just as spiritually valuable to those who came into his court as his work as a vicar would be to those who came into the church.

James Turnbull continued to combine his coroner's post with non-stipendiary work as a clergyman. He remembers with some wry amusement the comment made at the first funeral that he conducted. The undertaker said, 'Aren't you Mr Turnbull the Coroner?' He admitted that he was. 'Then you've cornered the market!' the undertaker replied.

Susanna Wesley

Susanna was the youngest daughter of Dr Annesley, an outstanding Puritan preacher and scholar in seventeenth-century England. His first wife died at the birth of their first child but his second wife bore him a further twenty-four children. (Someone asked a friend how many children Dr Annesley had and he answered, 'Either two dozen or a quarter of a hundred – I can't remember which.') From the age of five Annesley read twenty chapters of the Bible every day and he continued doing so for the rest of his life. It's not surprising that his children grew up with pious patterns of life too. Susanna told one of her sons that it had been her habit, from the time she was a young girl, never to spend longer in play or leisure during a day than she spent in spiritual practices. Her father laid down the principle: 'Make an examination of your conscience at least three times a day' and no doubt Susanna did as he said; she certainly kept a spiritual journal in which she recorded her daily meditations and resolves in the light of her Bible reading.

Dr Annesley was a nonconformist or Dissenter at a time when it took courage and strong principles to be so. After Charles II was restored to the throne in 1662, all Christian ministers were required to adhere to the Church of England and to follow its practices. But about two thousand ministers steadfastly refused to do so on grounds of conscience and for the next ten years, before the law was relaxed, they were thrown out of university, their livings taken from them and their families evicted from their parsonages. They were also forbidden to preach on pain of fines or imprisonment often in foul conditions. Some were banished from the country. Dr Annesley escaped the worst of these punishments but he suffered for his principles.

Susanna herself was a person of a very determined and independent turn of mind. When she was nearly thirteen she decided to look for herself at both sides in the dispute between the Church of England and the Dissenters. She examined all the evidence carefully – even writing a treatise on the subject – and came to the conclusion that, unlike her family, *she* was in favour of the Church of England. So at the tender age of thirteen she left her father's church and joined the Church of England, causing considerable grief to her parents.

It wasn't long after this that she met Samuel Wesley, who was a friend of the bridegroom at her sister Elizabeth's wedding. His father was also a dissenting minister who had tragically died when he was still young as a result of repeated imprisonments for his belief. Dissenting friends rallied round and put Samuel through one of their theological colleges so that he could be a dissenting minister too, but Samuel, like Susanna, had begun to think things out for himself. He too decided to turn his back on dissenting circles and become an Anglican. Friendship blossomed between the two young people and when he was twenty-six and Susanna nineteen they were married.

Poor Susanna, with her clear thinking and independent opinions, did not quite realise what kind of life lay ahead of her. She was to endure constant childbearing (nineteen children in nineteen years) and to be dogged by her husband's constant debts. She was often ill, had to cope with wretched housing and defer to a husband who believed it was his Christian duty to be master of his household – and of his wife. In one of his many poems he wrote about Susanna: 'She studied my convenience day and night' and also affirmed:

> Yet still I bore an undisputed sway
> Nor was't her task, but pleasure to obey.

Samuel was only acting as most husbands would have done at that time and it would be wrong to see their married life as wholly unhappy. Samuel probably had more sense of humour than the serious-minded Susanna and he did have a lighter and kinder side to his nature too. But he was proud and hot-tempered and both partners were strong-minded, so it is not surprising that their marriage was not all plain sailing. Susanna commented dryly in a letter to one of her sons: 'Tis an unhappiness almost peculiar to our family, that your father and I seldom think alike.'

After the comfort of her home life as a girl she must have hated the scrimping and scraping and the constant debts that dogged their married life. Nine of their nineteen children died in infancy and Susanna was often in poor health. But she made a virtue of necessity and determined that her children would be her life work. She would find her spiritual satisfaction in planning and creating a home in which her children could be nurtured and educated in the best possible way.

A turning point in her life came after a serious rift between husband and wife. When William and Mary were jointly offered the British throne in 1688, many people were unwilling to accept William of Orange, and would own allegiance only to Mary, who as daughter of James II was surely rightful queen. Some clergy among these 'non-jurors' as they were called, were expelled from their livings. One evening, during prayers, Samuel noticed that Susanna failed to say 'Amen' to his prayer for King William. When he taxed her with it she told him that she could not do so when she did not believe that the Prince of Orange was rightfully king. Samuel then swore solemnly that he would not live with her until she acknowledged William as king. He left home and stayed away for six months. When he returned for a couple of days, and found that Susanna refused to retract, he rode away threatening never to see her again. (The fact that William was dead by this time did nothing to weaken his resolve!)

He was barely out of sight when news was brought to him that the rectory was on fire. He hurried back, relieved to find that his 'wife, children and books' were all safe. This time he stayed. The need to rebuild the house provided the justification for breaking his rash vow.

From this time on, Susanna kept even more closely to house and children and made this work her entire life. She commented herself that 'there are few, if any, that would entirely devote above twenty years of the prime of life in hopes to save the souls of their children'. But that is exactly what she did. She drew up rules for their guidance from the time they were very small. They were taught from a year old to 'cry softly' and to fear the rod, 'by which means,' she explained, 'they escaped abundance of correction . . . and that most odious noise of the crying of children was rarely heard in the house.'

She also made it a rule that provided a child confessed to a wrongdoing, he or she would not be punished for it. She believed that honesty and openness mattered more than any childish misdoing; but she felt deeply grieved when their hot-tempered father would often lash out in heavy punishment and did not abide by her rule. Susanna also set up a school for her children where 'no such thing as playing or loud talking was allowed but everyone was kept close to business for the six hours of school'.

In 1709 another crisis – and a second, worse fire – proved a further turning-point in Susanna's life. It was night-time and everyone was in bed when little Hetty woke to find a piece of burning roof had fallen on her bed. She shouted for her father. The household was aroused and the children shepherded out of the burning house. Susanna herself was eight months pregnant; when she thought that everyone was safely out in the street, she discovered that 5-year-old John – little Jacky – was still inside, trapped, crying, in the nursery. Samuel tried to re-enter the house in vain. But John had the sense to cross the room to the window and from there he was hauled to safety by someone with a ladder – just before the roof fell in. Susanna felt sure that God had some purpose in saving this 'brand plucked from the burning' and determined to take especial care over John's upbringing. She prayed:

> I would . . . humbly offer thee myself and all that thou hast given me, and I would resolve (O give me grace to do it) that the residue of my life shall be all devoted to thy service; and I do intend to be more particularly careful of the soul of this child that thou hast so mercifully provided for, than ever I have been . . . Lord, give me grace to do it sincerely, and prudently, and bless my attempts with success.

The damage to the rectory was so severe that the family had to be dispersed to various places for nearly a year while Samuel saw to the rebuilding of the house – which left him further in debt again. When at last all the children returned Susanna was horrified to see how much they had run wild. She bent her mind and will to bringing them back to right behaviour and manners. She decided to set aside time for a private talk with each child once a week and allocated a different time in the week for every member of the family. She also wrote some theological treatises for their instruction.

As far as we see it, Susanna Wesley's life seems strangely lacking in spiritual excitement. Hers was a religion of work and duty. She wrote: 'This life is a probation, wherein eternal happiness or misery are proposed to our choice; the one as a reward of a virtuous, the other as a consequence of a vicious life.' We may not be attracted today by such a pattern of constant discipline, and a studied routine of work aimed at nurturing others' souls. But her conscientious and painstaking care over the spiritual needs of her children reaped an incredible harvest later on through the preaching of John Wesley and the inspired hymns of his brother Charles. Years later too, Susanna herself enjoyed a spiritual experience of joy and liberation.

She was an old woman of seventy and a widow, living with her son John at his meeting-house in London. Susanna described her experience one Sunday, at a communion service conducted by her son-in-law, Westley Hall. She wrote: 'While my son Hall was pronouncing these words in delivering the cup to me, "The blood of our Lord Jesus Christ which was given for thee," these words struck through my heart, and I knew that God, for Christ's sake had forgiven me all my sins.' After years of duty, followed by some sadness and depression, she seems to have experienced a flash of spiritual insight. Duty was lighted up by joy and love, freedom and forgiveness. When she was dying she made the request, 'Children, as soon as I am released, sing a psalm of praise to God.' And they gladly did.

Envoi

As I send this book on its way, I think with affection of those who people it. Some, long since dead, still seem to live, but within the completed circle of their lives. There is a framed and finished feeling to their encounters with the spiritual world. Others, who have been torn from the present, confess that they are only just embarking on their journey into spiritual awareness. There may not be an aura of completion about them, but there is the freshness of the immediate that has its own particular attraction and excitement as we read their stories.

I think too about the ones who got away – men and women who were too busy or too much in the public eye to tell me their story, as well as those who probably put my letter at the bottom of a pile, where it still lies undisturbed.

To all these men and women I offer my heartfelt thanks. You have given me an exciting and exhilarating run for my money. You have reawakened me to the realities of the spiritual world and to truth about God, who not only says, 'Seek and you will find, knock and it will be opened to you', but who frequently comes knocking at our door too, whether we are expecting him or not.

Acknowledgments

I am grateful for the help I gained from the following publications – written by or about the men and women in this book – and also the societies and organisations associated with some of those whose stories are told.

1 Visions

Peter Ackroyd, *Blake* (Sinclair-Stevenson)

Bradley P. Holt, *A Brief History of Christian Spirituality* (Lion Publishing, 1993, 1997)

Sister Wendy of the Community of All Hallows, *Julian of Norwich* (Carmelite Monastery, Quiddenham, Norfolk)

London City Mission (Paul James-Griffiths)

2 Dreams

Catherine Bramwell-Booth, *Letters* (Mary Batchelor, ed., Lion Publishing, 1986)

Patricia St John, *Patricia St John Tells her Own Story* (OM STL, 1993)

Christians in Sport (Kriss Akabusi)

The Salvation Army (Catherine Bramwell-Booth)

3 Appearings

Bill Kirkpatrick, *Aids – Sharing the Pain* (DLT, 1988, 1993)
Bill Kirkpatrick, *Going Forth* (DLT, 1997)
Bill Kirkpatrick, ed., *Cry Love, Cry Hope* (DLT, 1994)
Fred Lemon, *Breakout*

Centrepoint; Streetwise Youth; Cara (Care and Resource centre for persons affected and infected with HIV); St Cuthbert's Drop-in Centre (for those in bed-and-breakfast places in the Earl's Court area of London) (Father Bill Kirkpatrick)

4 Moments of crisis

Records of M. Beaufort, *The Practice of the Presence of God* (Spire Books, Jove Publications for Fleming H. Revell Co., USA, 1958)
Robert Bowman, ed., *An Account of the Mutiny of HMS Bounty* (Sutton, 1989)
Ross Dunn, an article on Jaime Jaramillo in *The Times* (December, 1997). Ross Dunn and *The Times* kindly gave me permission to base my story on his article.
Gillian Orchard, *Once and Future Foundress* (Vario Press, 1997)
Other private papers written by Sister Gillian Orchard and kindly lent to me by her

Ross Dunn directed me to Children of the Andes, where Marilese Turnbull, then Director of the London-based charity, kindly furnished me with additional information and material.

5 The Bible

Ian M. Ball, *Children of the Bounty* (Victor Gollancz, 1974)
Martin Luther, *Table Talk* (Fount, 1995)
R. B. Nicholson, *The Pitcairners* (Angus & Robertson, 1965)

Robert Backhouse, ed., *The Life and Letters of Martin Luther* (Hodder & Stoughton, 1993)

Avrahm Yarmolinsky, *Dostoevsky – His Life and Art* (Arco Publishing, 1957)

Bible Societies (The British and Foreign Bible Society)
United Bible Societies (Paul James-Griffiths)

6 Angels

Global Care (Ron Newby)

7 Moments of knowing

Dag Hammarskjöld, *Markings* (Faber & Faber, 1988)
C.S. Lewis, *Surprised by Joy* (Geoffrey Bles, 1955)
Elfrida Vipont, *George Fox and the Valiant Sixty* (Hamish Hamilton, 1975)
John Wesley, *Journal* (Moody Press, Chicago, no date given)

8 Suffering and tragedy

Stuart and Brenda Blanch, eds, *Learning of God (Amy Carmichael)* (SPCK Triangle, 1985)
Frances Young, *Face to Face* (T. & T. Clark, 1998)

The Dohnavur Fellowship

9 Love

Wolfgang Bader, ed., trans. Alan Neame, *St Francis at Prayer* (DLT, 1988)

Lavinia Byrne, *The Life and Wisdom of Francis of Assisi* (Hodder & Stoughton, 1998)

Thora Hird, *Scene and Hird* (Fount, 1995)

Thora Hird, *Is it Thora?* (Fount, 1996)

Festo Kivengere, *Revolutionary Love* (CLC and Kingsway, 1983)

African Enterprise (Festo Kivengere)

Ichthus Fellowship (Raj Kumari)

10 Miracles

John Gunstone, ed., *Meeting John Wimber* (Monarch, 1996)

Malcolm Muggeridge, S*omething Beautiful for God* (Collins, 1971)

Malcolm Muggeridge, *Chronicles of Wasted Time* (Collins, 1973)

Corrie Ten Boom with John and Elizabeth Sherrill, *The Hiding Place* (Hodder & Stoughton, 1971)

11 Science

Ernest Mortimer, *Blaise Pascal – the Life and Work of a Realist* (Methuen,1959)

Angela Tilby, *Science and the Soul* (SPCK, 1992)

Fraser Watts, ed., *Science Meets Faith* (SPCK, 1998)

12 Prison

Dietrich Bonhoeffer, *Letters and Papers from Prison* (Fontana, 1970)

Alexander Tomsky Papers published by Keston Institute, circulated to members, 1982

Terry Waite, *Taken on Trust* (Hodder & Stoughton, 1993)

Philip Walters and Jane Balengarth, eds, *Light Through the Curtain* (Lion Publishing and Keston College, 1985)

Keston Institute (Father Frantisek Lizna)

13 Hearing a voice

David Hamilton, *A Cause Worth Living For* (Highland Books, 1997)

Alec Smith with Rebecca Saintonge, *Now I Call Him Brother* (Marshalls, 1984)

Introduction by Murray Watts, *Praying with Saint Augustine* (SPCK Triangle, 1987)

Prison Fellowship (David Hamilton)
Teen Challenge (David Hamilton)

14 Media encounters

Philip Caraman, *Ignatius Loyola* (Collins, 1990)

Mark Elsdon-Dew, *The God Who Changes Lives* (Holy Trinity Brompton Publication)

Alpha courses (Robert Taylor)
Far Eastern Broadcasting Association – FEBA – (Emmanuel Mate and Cyril Kalle)
Jesus video (Graham Thomas)
Premier Radio

15 Death, near death and bereavement

Fiona Castle with Jan Greenhough, *Give Us This Day* (Kingsway,1993)

Fiona Castle, *No Flowers ... Just Lots of Joy* (Kingsway, 1996)

Diana Dewar, *All for Christ* (OUP, 1980)

Henri Nouwen, *Life of the Beloved* (Hodder & Stoughton, 1992)

Henri Nouwen, *Our Greatest Gift* (Hodder & Stoughton, 1994)

Henri Nouwen, *Beyond the Mirror* (Collins Fount, 1990)

The Hospice Movement (Ros Taylor and Pat Mood)

L'Arche Communities (Henri Nouwen)

16 Nature and ecology

Clive Longmead, *A Passion for Flowers* (Biography of Ghillean Prance) (Lion, 1995)

Ghillean Prance, *The Earth Under Threat* (Wild Goose Publications, 1996)

Abernethy Trust Centres (Stephen Macdonald)

Royal Botanic Gardens Kew (Ghillean Prance)

Catherine Lucas told me her own story, but our contact resulted from an article I read which she wrote in *The Times*, 24 December 1997, on which this account is partly based.

17 Prayer

Shirley du Boulay, *Teresa of Avila* (Hodder & Stoughton, 1991)

Lavinia Byrne, *The Life and Wisdom of Teresa of Avila* (Hodder & Stoughton, 1998)

Stephen Clissold, *St Teresa of Avila* (Sheldon Press, 1979)

Richard Findlater, *The Lady of the Old Vic* (Allen Lane, 1975)

Lev Gillet, *On the Invocation of the Name of Jesus* (Templegate Publishers, 1985)

Madame Guyon, ed. Halcyon Backhouse, *A Short and Easy Method of Prayer* (Hodder & Stoughton, 1990)

Sergei Hackel, *The Orthodox Church* (St Stephen's Press, 1994)

Elaine Storkey, Introduction to *Praying with Saint Teresa* (SPCK Triangle, 1988)

Kallistos Ware, *The Power of the Name* (SLG Press 1986, 1997)

18 The arts

Philip Callow, *Van Gogh – A Life* (Alison & Busby, 1990)

Susan Howatch, Lecture given in January 1994 in Salisbury Cathedral. (Transcript printed by R.J.L. Smith and Associates for the Dean and Chapter of Salisbury Cathedral)

Susan Howatch, The Starbridge Novels (HarperCollins): *Glittering Images* (1987); *Glamorous Powers* (1988); *Ultimate Prizes* (1989); *Scandalous Risks* (1991); *Mystical Paths* (1992); *Absolute Truths* (1995)

Susan Howatch, *A Question of Integrity* (Little, Brown and Co., 1997)

Les Murray, *Embodiment and Incarnation: Notes on Preparing an Anthology of Australian Verse* from *The 1986 Aquinas Lecture* (Aquinas Library, Brisbane, reprinted by the Eremos Institute, Sydney, 1987)

19 Solitude and quiet

Carlo Carretto, *Letters from the Desert* (DLT, 1991)
Brother Ramon, *Franciscan Spirituality* (SPCK, 1994)
Brother Ramon, *The Heart of Prayer* (Marshall Pickering, 1995)

The Quiet Gardens Trust

20 Work

Arnold A. Dallimore, *Susanna Wesley* (Baker Book House, 1993)
Mark Greene, *Thank God it's Monday* (Scripture Union, 1997)
John A. Newton, *Susanna Wesley and the Puritan Tradition in Methodism* (Epworth, 1968)

Sisters of Charity (Mother Teresa)